YOUR MARRIAGE – *Making it wo*

W9-DGN-178

WITH

Wheth
newly
here is

Choo
lifetime
like con
roles an
about al

And i
advice. F
you rate'
think thr
decide ho
use. The
anecdotes
are talking

They of
build on, a
lasting mar

Peg and Le
They have
and Canada
three sons.
and that of
which hits h

This book is dedicated
to our children

Dirk and Laurie
Greg and Kari-Joy
Jeff and Kyra

for whom we desire
the best marriages possible

*With thanks to all our friends
who contributed ideas, shared experiences,
sharpened our thinking, and prayed for
wisdom*

YOUR MARRIAGE

MAKING IT WORK
A Self-Help Guide

PEG AND LEE RANKIN

A LION PAPERBACK
Tring · Batavia · Sydney

Copyright © 1986 Peg and Lee Rankin

Published by
Lion Publishing Corporation
1705 Hubbard Avenue, Batavia, Illinois 60510, USA
ISBN 0 7459 1007 6
Lion Publishing plc
Icknield Way, Tring, Herts, England
ISBN 0 7459 1007 6
Albatross Books Pty Ltd
PO Box 320, Sutherland, NSW 2232, Australia
ISBN 0 86760 827 7

First edition 1986

Library of Congress Cataloging-in-Publication Data
Rankin, Peg.
  Your marriage–making it work.
  (A Lion paperback)
  1. Marriage. 2. Communication in marriage.
  3. Interpersonal relations. I. Rankin, Lee. II. Title.
  HQ734.R24 1986   646.7'8   86–154
  ISBN 0 7459 1007 6 (pbk.)

British Library Cataloguing in Publication Data
Rankin, Peg
  Your marriage – making it work: a self-
  help guide.
  1. Marriage
  I. Title II. Rankin, Lee
  306.8'1   HQ728
  ISBN 0 7459 1007 6

Printed and bound in Great Britain by
Cox & Wyman Ltd, Reading

CONTENTS

143322

G

"If it doesn't work out, we can always call it quits."
"I'll stay with you – promise – as long as we're still in love."
"Let's try it for awhile to see if we're suited for each other."
"I just don't care about you anymore. Sorry."

Marriage is under attack. More and more couples are living together without the ties of a contract. And in the case of many couples who *do* enter into contract there is lack of commitment on the part of both partners, role confusion as to who should do what, realistic fears concerning each other's sexual fidelity, career demands that rob couples of precious time together, and a mind-set that reasons, "Sharing bed and board is what it is all about, we don't have to share our *lives*." In a few years, sometimes even months, these marriages fail and the divorce statistics continue to climb.

Nobody wins when a marriage breaks up. Nobody. Not the one initiating the divorce. Not the one on the receiving end. And certainly not the children. Under a tremendous weight of guilt, everybody becomes a loser. And our whole society suffers from the disintegration of yet another home.

These trends might cause us to ask, "Is marriage still a valid relationship?" We believe so, because marriage is not simply a good idea in human terms: it is God-ordained for our benefit. Therefore, it will *never* become invalid. Again and again we hear the familiar words at the beginning of the wedding service: "Dearly beloved, we are gathered together here and in the sight of God, and in the face of this company, to join together this man and this woman in holy matrimony, which is an honorable estate instituted of God...," yet so often we fail to dwell on its significance.

Whether we acknowledge it or not, marriage *does* come from God. And he has principles for making it work. In fact, if a relationship has deteriorated badly enough, God's principles may be the only thing that can save it.

Stop for a moment to take an inventory of your marriage. How would you describe it? Harmonious? Workable? Tense? Impossible?

Now ask yourself an even more important question: Do I want it to change? If so, am I willing to be the major instrument to implement that change?

You will probably find yourself approaching this book with your own special needs in mind.

Perhaps you are single, just beginning to contemplate the important step of marriage. How can you prepare yourself?

Perhaps you are engaged, frightened by the realization that what you merely contemplated is fast becoming a reality. How can you avoid the pitfalls that have trapped many of your friends?

Perhaps you are already married but tensions are straining your relationship. How can you lessen those tensions?

Perhaps you are divorced and want to do better the second time around.

Or perhaps you have a happy home but you are realistic enough to admit that there is always room for improvement. What can you do to make a good relationship better?

In this book we give some basic principles that have worked not only for us (we have been growing in our own relationship for over twenty-eight years) but also for many couples who have taken our "Marriage As God Meant It To Be" Seminars. We only *give* the principles, however, what you *do* with them is up to you.

PRINCIPLES TO BUILD ON

1. Choose your life's partner well.
2. Take your vows seriously.
3. Keep what takes place in your bedroom private.
4. Avoid morally compromising situations.
5. Be the first to say, "I'm sorry."
6. Talk things out, talk them over, talk them through.
7. Establish clear, agreed roles and keep them flexible.
8. Work at developing a successful partnership.
9. Render small kindnesses daily.
10. Commit yourself 100% to making your marriage work.

There you have ten principles upon which to build your marriage. We can point to couples we know, including ourselves, who are together today as a direct result of having these principles presented to them. These same couples will be together tomorrow as the principles continue to be practiced. It is our hope that as you put these principles into practice in your own life, you too will be "together tomorrow" – happily.

1

How Do You Choose?

In this amazing world of people interacting with other people there comes a certain time when a phenomenon called "dating" occurs. It is that time in life when you test your compatibility with different individuals, at first in groups and then with just the two of you alone.

Dating is an activity that can be almost frightening if you don't know the rules. To make the most of this time in your life, determine from the beginning to be yourself and then wait and see who is attracted to the real you. Be careful not to "put on airs," wear a mask, or try to appear more sophisticated than you really are. Be natural. Be real. Let your personality show. Not only will you have more fun but you will also pave the way for wholesome relationships to develop.

Because people to whom dating is a new experience are usually young and full of life, sharing an evening with someone of like interests can be a real highlight. Avoid ulterior motives. Try going out just for fun – at least at first. Test your wings in a world in which you will soon fly. Learn to react effectively to this strange species of humanity called the opposite sex. And enjoy yourself.

Besides being a time of fun, dating can also be a time of testing, of weighing a decision that could affect the rest of your life, of looking beyond the physical for that which is permanent and enduring, of establishing patterns of romance that will brighten a future marriage. So don't take the dating phase of your life too lightly. It can turn into serious business very quickly.

One day, perhaps without any conscious effort on your part, you may begin to realize that something beyond mere friendship is developing between the two of you. When that happens, keep in mind that there are many questions to be asked and many situations to be evaluated. And the dating phase of your life is the time to attend to them.

Have I met a potential life-partner?
What are his/her values?
Can we adapt to each other's lifestyles?
If we marry, how faithful will he/she be?
Would he/she love me no matter what?
How willing am I to make up for his/her deficiencies?
Am I willing to cover his/her shortcomings?

GETTING TO KNOW EACH OTHER

During the dating phase it is important to spend as much time together as possible. Don't rush things. Remember that relationships recklessly put together may not last.

Realize, however, it is not the length of courtship that matters so much as the length of time spent talking things over. Therefore, choose your activities well. Watching a movie or attending a football game may be fun things to do, but they do not lend themselves to good communications. In fact, couples whose dating consists only of attending spectator sports often discover that they have married strangers. Then the challenge of discovery really begins. It is a challenge that should have begun *before* the vows were exchanged, not after.

During the time of dating you want to get to know your prospective partner so well that after the marriage ceremony there are few surprises. Observe him or her not only in well controlled situations but also in times of stress, pressure, and exasperation. Evaluate the reactions. Are they controlled or does the temper flare up unexpectedly? If so, can you handle the outbursts? Is your potential partner totally selfish, or do you detect consideration for *your* feelings too?

People sometimes choose partners who end up verbally or physically abusing them. Then they come to us complaining, "I never knew he was like that" or "She totally changed after we were married." A courtship laced with a few stressful situations might have served as a needed warning.

Let's face it, most dates are idyllic. You know – the canoe trip on the lake with the orange moon reflecting its perfect image over the calm waters. Both canoers are sporting stylish clothes, weighing every word they say, and intent on having an enjoyable evening.

Unfortunately, this is not "life." In "life," the moon may be up indeed, but so are you – quieting a screaming baby. In "life" the waters are rarely calm. In fact, there's a storm in somebody's experience almost every day. Couples rarely dress up in their finest – with the exception of a Saturday wedding or a Sunday church service – if that! More than likely you will be faced with hair rollers, blue jeans, and a shirt the baby just puked all over. And as far as watching what you say is concerned, forget it. People tend to say the first thing that comes into their minds – then spend the evening trying to undo the damage it caused.

When you date, talk about things that could become threats to your marriage later on, things such as separate careers, personal habits, the number of children desired, attitudes toward sex, handling of finances, church affiliation, and entertainment preferences. Establishing such a relationship takes time. But it is some of the best time you will ever spend in your life. Because you are not really "spending" it. You are investing it – investing it in a lasting relationship.

IS THIS THE REAL THING?

As you get to know each other, try to determine exactly what kind of relationship is developing between you. Is it real love or is it one of love's deceiving substitutes? Substitutes for love are numerous. We'll examine two of them: passion and physical "likes."

What about passion?

First test whether you are mistaking passion for love. Is the attraction you have for each other primarily or exclusively sexual? Now let us say at this point that there certainly should be a strong sexual attraction in a relationship that is to be physically consummated. But your relationship should not be *primarily* sexual. If the goal of each date is to "go a little further" in arousing each other's passions, then your relationship is bound for trouble, maybe even infidelity later on, for you will be driven to find more and more exciting ways to fulfill your sexual desires. Since passion is essentially self-centered, it can be detected by asking yourself these questions: Am I dating to *give* or dating to *get*? How about my prospective partner? Is he/she dating me for what he/she can get out of me or for what he/she can contribute to making me a better person?

God made us sexual beings, but when he gave us the gift of sexual expression, he intended it to be used in a particular way. We are not to experiment with it, to offer it at the wrong time, or allow ourselves to be tempted to compromise our moral standards. Sexual expression is to be enjoyed within the context of marriage, for only then can it be both given and received in the safety and security of a legal commitment without physical, emotional, or spiritual harm coming to either individual.

God wants the best for the body he has given you. The fact that you can practice restraint and understand why you are doing so is one of the things that sets you apart from animals. But you are more than just a body. When you give your body to another person your whole self – mind, spirit, personality – goes along with it. So don't be misled by those who would entice you with, "Come on and sleep with me. No one will ever know." What a lie! You will know. Your partner will know. And God will know. There is more to life than feeling and perhaps forgetting. There is knowing – and always, always remembering.

Although practicing sexual restraint during the pre-marital state may seem like denying yourself one of life's greatest thrills, in the long run it will be best for you. For on your wedding day you will be able to present yourself to your chosen partner whole and complete. There will be no disease, no haunting memories of past encounters, and no guilt – only the anticipation of a very exciting union.

The physical part of your relationship will develop as you date – and well it should. Just make sure you keep it under control. A very subtle shift in thinking can occur in kids who have no intention of getting into trouble. For example, as your relationship progresses, she may say to herself, "If a guy of his calibre is going this far, then it must be all right. I'll let him go as far as he wants." At the same time he is saying, "If a girl of her character is letting me go this far, it must be all right. So I'll go as far as she lets me." Such reasoning breeds disaster. Soon what started out to be a relationship with high ideals has degenerated to the point where it is beyond reclamation. Be aware of the dangers of blindly trusting the other person.

Don't ruin a good relationship by wanting too much too soon. Keep your passions under control until the time when it is right to unleash them. That freedom will not be yours until the moment your marriage vows are publicly exchanged. Having committed yourselves to each other in your hearts is simply not enough. There must be a full commitment before witnesses. Then the physical benefit of marriage can follow.

Such an order of events is established by God in Genesis, the very first book of the Bible. There two happenings are described: the first a "leaving" and the second a "cleaving." The leaving was a very public affair during which both the man and the woman picked up their personal belongings and departed from their parents' homes. This leaving was their declaration to form a partnership in marriage. It was then – and only then – that they were instructed to cleave to each other, forming "one flesh" (a phrase which refers to sexual union). In other words, sexual union is to follow a public declaration of intentions. Such an order is for the couple's benefit. It lifts the act of sexual intercourse from the degrading back-seat-of-a-car encounter to the place of honor it deserves within the heart of the marriage relationship.

"I like you"

After you have tested your relationship for the passion factor, make a test to detect physical "likes." Before you do this, however, we want to make it clear that two people who intend to get married should genuinely like each other. Do you?

Men, do you like the way she dresses? Are you attracted by the way she moves? Do you enjoy the way she talks, the speech intonations and expressions that are uniquely hers? Do you admire the way she conducts herself in public? Great! You should be attracted to her, thrill to her, admire her, "like" her. But your marriage cannot be founded solely on these "likes."

Women, ask yourselves the same kinds of questions. Do you like the way he looks – clean-shaven, or bearded? Are you attracted by his smile? Is he polite, courteous, and kind to you? Do you enjoy his physical appearance? Again we say "Good!" But not everybody whom you "like" will necessarily make a good partner in marriage.

You see, "likes" don't last. Marriage is meant to – long after the youthful good looks are gone. When she can no longer swing her hips and he has no more muscles to flex, the marriage is meant to endure. When she gets fat and he has become bald, the marriage is meant to endure. It is meant to endure breast surgery, cataract operations, and the frustration of physical impotence. It is even meant to endure midlife crisis.

Midlife crisis is that time in life when you begin to lose everything you ever thought you had – at least that is our definition of the phenomenon. Whereas today he's sporting curly hair, impressive biceps, and lots of vim and vigor, wait! Twenty-five years from now he'll have no hair, flabby biceps, and a body collapsed in an easy chair behind an open newspaper. And her perfect hour-glass figure will have given way to sags and bulges. So look beyond the physical. What is the person like *inside*?

Never make your choice expecting your partner to change. If any change occurs, it is often for the worse. So "likes" are simply not a good foundation for choosing a marriage partner.

Real love?

What you need is real love, and it stems from the will, not simply from the passions or from the emotions. Once you set your affection on whom you are going to love, then your passions and emotions follow. If they *precede* love, love may never come at all.

Love involves *giving* rather than receiving. According to the Bible, in a favorite chapter often used at wedding services, love is "very patient and kind, never jealous or envious, never boastful or proud, never haughty or selfish or rude. Love does not demand its own way. It is not irritable or touchy. It does not hold grudges and will hardly even notice when others do it wrong. It is never glad about injustice, but rejoices whenever truth wins out. If you love someone (with this kind of love) you will be loyal to him (or her) no matter what the cost. You will always believe in him (or her), always expect the best of him (or her), and always stand your ground in defending him (or her)" (from 1 Corinthians chapter 13 in *The Living Bible* version). Honestly now, are you nourishing this kind of love with your prospective partner?

THE MERGER

Suppose you answer yes to that question. Does that mean the two of you will make excellent marriage partners? Not necessarily. For marriage partners must do more than "love" each other. They must work at developing a oneness. When marriages break up because of "incompatibility," a message is sent to all who care to read it: "You are witnessing the death of the marriage of two people whose desire to make that marriage work died long before the marriage itself."

When two people come together in a marriage relationship, they come with different lifestyles, different family traditions, different personalities, different personal habits, and different goals and preferences. The fact that *any* marriages make it is really quite a miracle. We venture to say that none of them make it without work, for a good marriage doesn't just happen.

Night people team up with day people, breakfast eaters with non-breakfast eaters, cabinet door shutters with non-cabinet door shutters, toothpaste tube squeezers with toothpaste tube rollers, structured people with free spirits, introverts with extroverts, and social beings with loners.

Problems begin immediately. Do we get up at dawn to watch the sunrise or do we recover from the day before by sleeping in? Do we sit down to bacon and eggs or do we grab a bun on the run? Do we plan the day's activities or do we just sort of play it by ear? Shall we invite that couple to go with us or should we go alone? You can have terrible fights on your honeymoon over really nothing at all. And the honeymoon is only the beginning.

What seems like normal behavior to one can be quite abnormal to the other, requiring tremendous adjustment to the other's unorthodox habits. If you discover a habit that is driving you crazy *now*, evaluate your future together very carefully. For example, while you may be able to tolerate your fiancée chewing gum for an evening, ask yourself if you can tolerate it for thirty-five or forty years. Or when your boyfriend sucks his teeth all the way to the football stadium, say to yourself, "Can I stand this the rest of my life?" Remember, it is the *straw* that breaks the camel's back, not the big burden.

If you decide to continue your relationship, be prepared to make accommodations. If the cabinet door opener does the opening, then the cabinet door shutter must do the shutting – no big deal. Day people have to learn to stay up a little later and night people see sunrises once in a while. Social beings set aside time for being alone and loners learn to socialize. Gum chewers either give up chewing or non-chewers take on the habit. The one who has to listen to the teeth sucker, however, either turns off the hearing aid or thinks, "How cute." Whatever adjustment you have to make, be prepared to work at it.

Closely linked to the merger of habits is the merger of personalities. When two people unite in mariage they bring to each other not only their strengths but their weaknesses as well. If the union works properly, each partner should gain support in the area of his or her greatest need and each partner should experience the joy of giving, that the other might be strengthened and made to feel secure.

Ask: Does my prospective partner complement my personality? Is he/she strong where I am weak? When I am with him/her, am I a better person? Does our relationship bring out the best in me? Do the two of us make a good team? Are we on the same wavelength about the important things? Can I respect him/her when I hear what he/she says?

Most of us are acquainted with people who bring out the worst in us. For that reason we can't stand to be around them. They are constantly bickering, fighting, arguing, tearing each other down, and embarrassing each other in front of others. How terrible to live like that! Don't let it happen to you. Look now for the right complement to your personality. There is someone somewhere who will bring out the best in you.

Once you find the right person, start working on the merger of your personalities. How is this merger supposed to work? Well, let's say a man with tremendous initiative but very little humility begins to date a woman with plenty of humility but little initiative. His initiative brings out her hidden talent and her humility tempers his aggressiveness. Gradually they learn to blend their strengths and weaknesses, filling the void in each other's personality. Not only does each one personally benefit from the union but the union benefits as well. The team now possesses both initiative *and* humility. And each member of the team is discovering that together they can be more effective than each one alone could. Smart couple! They are going to have an effective marriage.

Are you learning how to unite *your* personalities for each other's benefit? Why don't you take a few minutes during the dating phase to assess the approaching merger that will be uniquely yours? Share with your intended some of the strengths that you feel he/she is contributing to your relationship – strengths that you personally need. Then talk over some of the ways that you can help develop the full potential of your union. This exchange should get you thinking on the right track before, rather than after, your vows are exchanged.

ROLES AND RESPONSIBILITIES

Still another consideration involves roles in the home. A fuzzy definition of roles and responsibilities has broken up too many marriages. You don't have to become one of the casualties. Determine what your potential partner is thinking along these lines and do it *now*, during the dating phase, while there is still time to break off the relationship if danger signals flash.

Women, you should quiz yourselves in the following manner: Will this man take on responsibility in our home? Will he be flexible enough to let me become my own person? Do I respect him and can I trust him fully? Is he able to love and to lead? If he is weak, can I help him grow? If he is too strong, can I mellow him a bit? Can I live with him the way he is now – if he never mellows at all? Can I give him my love – without reservation? Will he make a good father for our children? Is he likely to become a workaholic?

Men, you likewise need to ask several questions: Will I be proud to introduce this woman as my wife? Is she someone for whom I am willing to sacrifice? Can I work with her in real partnership? Does she show any signs of wanting to dominate our relationship? What kind of homemaker will she be? Will she make a good and loving mother for our children? Do we see eye to eye about the place of her own career? Would it be pursued at the expense of our family? How would she react if I tried to stop her?

TALKING ABOUT SPIRITUAL THINGS...

After you have the issues of habits, personalities, and role concepts settled, ask yourself the most important question of all. What kind of foundation are we building? Are we agreed on the really fundamental aspects of life? Are our attitudes toward God compatible? How about toward Jesus Christ? the Bible? church? Does he/she regularly attend a place of worship? Is that place of worship different from mine? If so, where will we worship?

For the Christian, the Bible offers good advice which every reader should consider. It tells believers not to marry non-believers and people of different religious persuasions not to become "unequally yoked." There are enough problems that occur in marriage without adding those you *know* are potentially divisive.

Religious differences can cause tremendous tensions in a marriage. Problems *there* are problems at the core of the marriage. Compromises are hard to reach and often quite impossible. Furthermore, the underlying tensions surface at the most bizarre times: "I know why you never pick up your stupid socks. It's because you're a Catholic (or Baptist, or Jew), that's why!" Or, "If your parents hadn't dragged you to so many meetings in that fundamental (or liberal, or charismatic) church, they would have had time to teach you housekeeping techniques." Such underlying resentments, which can be masked quite successfully during the dating phase, often erupt with volcanic force when the guard is let down in marriage.

It is our advice that you choose a partner with similar religious interests. If one of you is spiritually minded and the other couldn't care less about religion, there can be nothing but heartache ahead. Come to grips right now with the fact that the religious one rarely changes the non-religious one. It is usually the other way around. Do not be deceived by a sudden burst of interest in attending worship services during the dating phase. People will do almost anything to please the one they love – *before* marriage, that is:

Those who hold the Christian faith should have a head start in marriage because they are acquainted with the biblical principles that make a marriage work. Some of these principles are:

1. Love your partner as you love yourself.
2. Forgive and you will be forgiven.
3. True love involves sacrifice and self-giving.
4. In giving you receive.
5. The closer you draw to God, the closer you will draw to each other.

God makes available to all who seek and follow him a power greater than themselves. This power – God's power – not only helps them fulfill these principles – a feat which would be quite impossible otherwise – but also helps sustain them when the going gets rough. It is our observation that when two people have committed their lives to God through a personal relationship with Jesus Christ, which is a "vertical" commitment, they understand more fully what commitment on a horizontal plane means. So weigh the spiritual interests of the man or woman you love very carefully. You will *not* be sorry.

KEEPING YOUR ROMANCE ALIVE

Once you have made your choice, determine to stick by it. One way to ensure that you will be together "tomorrow" is to vow to keep your romance of today alive. The things that are so exciting about the dating phase of your relationship are the same things that will make the marriage phase exciting.

The first consideration is physical attractiveness. Dress up for the one you love. If he likes jeans, then wear them. But if he prefers pretty dresses, wear *them*. If he likes your hair long, or short, try to please him. Whatever pleases your partner, do – within reasonable limits, that is, without sacrificing your own individuality.

Watch your figure too. Don't let it go to "pot." That can easily happen after pregnancy. Although you may never regain the shape you once had, you can trim up your new shape with proper exercise, diet, color coordination, and clothes that are right for you. You want your husband to continue to be proud of you.

Men, similar advice goes to you. Wear clothes to fit the occasion. Choose colors your wife likes to see you in. Pay attention to your "pot" too. A few jogs around the block do wonders when you can pinch much more than an inch. If the hair is becoming a little thin, she won't mind – as long as it is neat and clean. Lose a little here and gain a little there – but pay attention to your appearance.

Perhaps the most important key to attractiveness is attitude. Don't let a day go by without determining to make what you are as attractive as possible – both for your own sake and for the sake of your partner. Eat sensibly, exercise, dress appropriately, and be positive about life. You want your partner to be proud of you.

Besides appearances, fun is very important to keeping a marriage alive. Be exciting to live with. Don't ever become totally predictable. React unexpectedly once in awhile. Let the adventure in you show.

Feel free to laugh, for humor heals a multitude of wounds. Laugh at yourself and the absurdity of the situations in which you find yourself. Laugh with your partner – at some of the silly things that happen when you are together. These are the times you'll remember when much of the past is forgotten. They are treasures in a sea of cares.

Do spur-of-the-moment things together. When passing a sign that says "Antiques," stop, if you enjoy that kind of thing. Go in and browse – together. Accept that last minute invitation to attend a game or a function with friends. Take your partner with you on a business trip. Go out for ice cream, coffee, or hamburgers – just any time you feel like it. Make an oasis in your desert of routine.

Also plan some "biggies" together. Make the most of your anniversaries. If the budget will stretch, go out to dinner and a show. Plan a weekend getaway or even a week or two if you can afford it. We know couples who "date" once a week. They say it has done wonders for their marriage. You don't have to spend a lot of money. Just get away from it all and enjoy each other's company.

But most of all plan romantic evenings at home. Put the kids to bed early. Feed the dog. Play background music on the stereo very softly. Light a few candles in strategic places. Dress up. Rule out hair rollers, beard stubble, and garlic breath. Then make a special evening happen. After all, if you don't, who will? It's *your* marriage.

The dating phase is one of the most exciting periods in any couple's life. Make the very most of yours. Have fun. Stay in control. Do a lot of talking. Personally do some evaluating. Then decide. When you are sure you have selected your life's partner, begin the job of merging your lifestyles, habits, and personalities. As you enjoy each other's company, take note of what makes your courtship exciting. Then vow to continue to do it throughout your married life. Keep that romance alive!

HOW DO YOU RATE?

1. At the present time the purpose of my dating is: ☐ *for fun;* ☐ *to find a marriage partner;* ☐ *both of the above.*
2. The feelings I experience when I'm with my date can best be described as: ☐ *attraction;* ☐ *interest;* ☐ *unrest;* ☐ *a liking;* ☐ *passion;* ☐ *true love.*
3. If we got married we would probably adjust to each other's backgrounds and personalities: ☐ *quickly;* ☐ *in time;* ☐ *never.*

4. With regard to compatibility I would rate our relationship in the following ways:

   TEMPERAMENT: ☐ *very compatible;* ☐ *acceptable;* ☐ *needs work.*

   INTERESTS: ☐ *very compatible;* ☐ *acceptable;* ☐ *needs work.*

   ENTERTAINMENT PREFERENCES: ☐ *very compatible;* ☐ *acceptable;* ☐ *needs work.*

   ATTITUDES TOWARDS SEX: ☐ *very compatible;* ☐ *acceptable;* ☐ *needs work.*

   ATTITUDES TOWARD FAMILY PLANNING: ☐ *very compatible;* ☐ *acceptable;* ☐ *needs work.*

   ATTITUDES TOWARD MONEY: ☐ *very compatible;* ☐ *acceptable;* ☐ *needs work.*

   ATTITUDES TOWARD ROLES AND RESPONSIBILITIES: ☐ *very compatible;* ☐ *acceptable;* ☐ *needs work.*

5. I intend to keep my marriage alive by: ☐ *giving compliments;* ☐ *continuing to "date";* ☐ *preparing special evenings at home;* ☐ *paying attention to my appearance;* ☐ *doing spur-of-the-moment things* ☐ *going away for a weekend now and then;* ☐ *other.*

2

Getting Down to Business – Living Out Your Vows

You have made your choice of a marriage partner and now you are about to take your vows. That prospect can be a frightening one. These vows will bond you together "for better for worse, for richer for poorer, in sickness and in health, to love and to cherish till death do us part."

The vows are the most critical part of the marriage ceremony. They serve not only as the gateway that leads from the dating phase into the marriage relationship itself, but also as a pledge committing you to the permanence of the marriage. Therefore, we need to take a good hard look at their nature.

THE MARRIAGE VOWS

As we examine the vows, we discover at least five important characteristics: the vows are voluntary, public, unconditional, serious and binding. Hopefully, by the time you "old marrieds" finish reading this chapter, you will want to locate a copy of the marriage ceremony you participated in (if you have one), looking again at what you promised. Perhaps those of you who have not yet exchanged vows but are planning to do so shortly will look hard at what you will be promising and how "total" your commitment is expected to be.

A voluntary decision

To start with, the decision to exchange vows is a voluntary one. You do not have to make it. Remaining single is an equally viable option. There is a certain freedom in the single life that a married person does not have. You have only yourself to worry about: only yourself to feed, clothe, and house; only yourself to make plans around. In some ways life can be more simple for the one who decides to go it alone.

You do have a choice. Even if you are dating seriously, you *still* have a choice. Nobody is going to drag you down the aisle or force you to say something you have no intention of saying. Just as in the courtship period when you were free to date or not to date, to spend time together or not to spend time together, to make sacrifices or not to make sacrifices, now you are free to marry or not to marry. If, however, you *do* decide to marry, remember that you are pledging yourself to live by the terms of the marriage contract, as they are set out in the marriage vows.

A public proclamation

A second characteristic of the exchange of vows is its public proclamation. Before witnesses you will turn to your intended and say, "I will love you, comfort you, honor and keep you, in sickness and in health, and, forsaking all others, keep myself only unto you as long as we both shall live." By publicly repeating your vows to each other, you are saying that this commitment is one you aren't afraid to admit to the world. This is one promise that you won't turn back on.

Saying vows publicly makes them special. When you invite relatives from all over the country to attend your marriage ceremony, you are saying, "This is a special day for me; please come and share it with me." And they do! When you ask friends to drop their daily activities to witness your exchange of vows, maybe even to participate in the ceremony, you are saying, "A special occasion is about to happen and I want you to be part of it." They are usually happy to do so. If your budget allows, you may go "all out" and celebrate with flowers, catered food and expensive clothes. Or, you may just pick a bouquet of wild flowers and wear a borrowed dress. In either case, this is your special day. It *should* be special, for you are getting married. The public nature of the event distinguishes it as a very important affair.

An unconditional promise

A third characteristic of the exchange of vows is its unconditional nature. What you are really promising is that nothing but death will separate you from your husband or wife. You do not say, "I will stick by you until things get rough" or "I'll be your companion until I get bored with our relationship" or "I'll care for you as long as you are not a burden" or "I'll be faithful to you as long as you meet my needs." You do not say any such silly things.

But maybe you should! If you have no intention of keeping the traditional marriage vows, be honest enough to admit it. Say what you mean. If you mean, "I will stick by you until somebody better comes along," say it. If you mean, "I promise to forsake all others and keep myself for you as long as our love shall last," then say it. Whatever you mean, say it. You may have to administer smelling salts to some fainting relatives, but better to begin your marriage with a specific declaration that is honest than a sweeping one that is dishonest.

If you decide to repeat the traditional vows as they are written, in essence you will be saying something like this:

"I take you, my beloved, to be my wedded husband/wife (I have weighed the situation very carefully and I know what I am doing)

– to have and to hold from this day forward (I am planning to stick by you no matter what)

– for richer for poorer (whether we get promoted or passed over, get transferred or laid off, make it big or lose everything we have – we're in it together, sharing our lot)

– in sickness and in health (I don't know what the future

holds, but if you face a mastectomy or prostate surgery, contract Alzheimers or Parkinson's disease, you can count on my going through it with you)

– to love and to cherish (I will make an effort to enrich your life with the warmth of my words and my deeds)

– till death do us part" (I'll let God take care of his business and I'll take care of mine).

Now that is unconditional commitment!

A serious purpose

Such commitment involves the utmost seriousness of purpose. You cannot take vows like this lightly. In fact, just thinking about them may cost you a few restless nights. At the beginning of the marriage ceremony, you will be reminded that your vows "are not by any to be entered into inadvisedly or lightly, but reverently, discreetly, advisedly, soberly, and in the fear of God."

It is safe to assume that "the fear of God" means that God would rather have you break off your engagement at the last minute than take your vows with the notion that "If things don't work out, I can always get out of my pledge." In the Old Testament book of Ecclesiastes, the Bible says, "It is far better not to say you'll do something than to say you will and then not do it" (from chapter 5, in *The Living Bible*). The minister adds these words of Jesus, from Matthew's Gospel, "What therefore God has joined together, let no man put asunder." The use of the word "man" includes you. You yourself must never dissolve a union made by God. It's serious business, this exchanging of vows.

Perhaps one of the reasons marriage is often not taken as seriously as it should be is the flippant attitude modern society has developed towards relationships in general. If something doesn't please us, we just assume we have a right to change it. This attitude becomes action as soon as we are in a position to make decisions. "If I don't like my college, I'll change colleges. If I don't like my field of study, I'll change fields. If I don't like my roommate, I'll change roommates.

If I don't like my job, I'll change jobs. If I don't like my husband/wife, I'll change him/her."

Wait a minute! You can't do that with your life-partner! You may change colleges, studies, roommates, jobs, towns, churches, political parties, and clothes, but you may not change your husband or wife. Why? Because of the vow. In none of these other situations have you publicly pledged yourself to faithfulness but in *this* case you have. Now keep the pledge you have made.

A binding pledge

As well as being serious, your vows are also binding. They obligate you for the rest of your life. "Till death do us part" is the pledge that is made. Notice, you do not say, "Till divorce do us part" or "Till adultery do us part" or "Till incompatibility do us part," but "Till death do us part." If you are contemplating any termination date other than the one specified, it would be better to change the wording of your vows than to recite them hypocritically. At least by doing so you can tell everybody what your true intentions are. Some will admire your honesty and some may even admire your vows. But few will expect your marriage to last.

If you want to have a lasting marriage do not tamper with the traditional marriage vows. Recite them exactly as they are written in *The Book of Common Prayer* or in some other equally sound publication. And while you are reciting them, pledge in your heart to live them. In other words, say what you mean and mean what you say. By so doing you will be declaring to everyone present, including yourself, that, in this particular marriage at least, divorce is not an option. Divorce can *never* be an option in a marriage that hopes to last.

DIVORCE IS NOT AN OPTION.

If you make divorce an option, then it will *be* an option. It will lurk in your subconscious, always beckoning, an open door through which you have an invitation to pass. In every argument, every crisis, every period of boredom, it will be there, offering an alternative to the frustrations that you are presently experiencing. "Come out, things are easier here," it will promise. "The adventure of new beginnings lies through this open door."

"The adventure of new beginnings" indeed! Don't listen to lies like that. Granted, there may be a façade of adventure surrounding divorce, but not the kind of adventure you may think. It's the adventure of confronting in court, before witnesses, the one who has shared the most intimate part of your life; the adventure of suddenly being alone, with nobody to help share your problems – financial problems, home maintenance problems, housekeeping problems, child-rearing problems, car problems, health problems, personal problems, all kinds of problems; the adventure of watching your children cope with guilt and divided loyalties, inch by painful inch. Adventure indeed!

If you *really* want adventure, stick by your partner. Don't let divorce even enter into your thinking and certainly not your vocabulary. If divorce is *not* an option to you, your love will have a better chance to grow. Then, when the crises come – and they *will* come – the only alternatives to be considered will be ones that foster unity, endurance, and success, rather than division, resignation, and failure. Talk things over, work things out. Perhaps try something you've never tried before. Be creative and vulnerable for the sake of love. That's *real* adventure. That's coming to grips with what marriage is all about.

PRACTICING WHAT YOU'VE PROMISED

Your vows will be tested daily. When you are dealing with *two* lives, not just one, you face double the problems. Working those problems out is what makes being married to the right person exciting. Here are some hints on how to work through your problems.

Consider your problems as opportunities. When you come to an impasse in your thinking, don't give up; find a new route around it – together. When you're faced with a mountain of problems, don't lie down and pray to expire; climb over it, side by side, hand in hand – together. When uncertainty threatens to overwhelm you, build a protective shelter, then climb into it and snuggle up – together. Whatever happens, determine to face it and conquer it, but make sure you do it together.

The problems that face married couples are opportunities for growth, both for the individual and for the marriage itself. By trying to live with someone who may at times be difficult to love, you develop a deeper appreciation of what love is all about. When plunged into unexpected turmoil, you are forced to create for yourself a consistent place of refuge. When faced with teeth-grinding frustrations day after day, you learn the value of patience. By working through painful experiences, you not only watch perseverance grow, but you also find yourself gaining a much greater appreciation of the problems that others are having to face. It is when doubts are threatening to envelop you that faith becomes a reality. You have begun to grow as a person.

Personal growth, however, does not necessarily ensure growth in your marriage. That takes a conscious effort. The first thing to realize is how quickly a marriage can die with just a little poison. Apply it daily in the right spot, in the right way, and you can watch your marriage wither before your eyes. A derogatory word, a supercilious look, a cold shoulder, a rotten attitude – any one of these will do the trick. Pile them up together – and disaster!

The choice is yours. Kill your marriage or help it grow. You can grow a good marriage quite successfully with some old-fashioned, tender loving care. But you must work at it with the diligence of a dedicated gardener. Nourish your marriage regularly with the encouragement of well-deserved praise; water it daily with refreshing, unexpected kindnesses; give it room to extend its roots into deepening trust; and warm it with the sunshine of a loving touch or hug. When you get up each morning, remind yourself that you promised "to love, to comfort, to honor, and to keep" your partner

"in sickness and in health as long as you both shall live."
Then act on that promise.

Crises will do one of two things to your marriage: they
will either make it or they will break it. The choice is up
to you and your partner. If you choose to live out your vows
on a daily basis, both of you will witness the miracle of a
marriage in the making, rather than in the breaking. We use
the word "miracle" for, without God's help, establishing a
lasting relationship in today's society is almost impossible.

Consider the pressures that face all of us: juggling separate
careers, making business deadlines and quotas, being forced
to spend time away from home, struggling to get ahead or
to keep the position you now have from being filled by
somebody else, meeting monthly payments on the house
or car, trying to keep yourself and your family healthy,
stretching the budget, getting enough sleep to keep going –
not to mention meeting the needs of your partner, your kids,
your friends, your neighbors, your church or synagogue,
your community, your world...Help! How can we do it?

WE ALL NEED HELP

We can't. We need assistance. And our need is where God
can come in. He majors in what to us are the minors – in
loving the unlovely, in enduring all kinds of offenses, in going
the extra mile, in turning disasters into blessings. If we
can somehow tap into God's limitless resources, we too will
be given power to do what at the time of our distress may
seem like an absolute impossibility – the power to enjoy a
triumphant married life.

God's power, however, is like a great river that has been
blocked by our stubborn refusal to admit that we need his
divine intervention. Until this blockage is removed, we
cannot tap God's power to meet our daily needs. We have
to come to him and ask for help. We have to acknowledge
our failure to live by his standards, and ask his forgiveness.
Not until then can we tap into his infinite resources. But
when we do make the tap, we discover a marvelous truth:

we cannot contain the blessings that the reservoir of God's power and love holds. We find our own lives flooded with the power to forgive, to bring healing to broken relationships and to mend broken hearts. But we must take that first important step of admitting our inadequacy and asking for help.

A PERSONAL EXPERIENCE

That's what we did ourselves. With one set of in-laws against us, our marriage was in trouble from the beginning. Even though we moved several hundred miles away from them, we couldn't move away from their constant harassment. Their continual attacks on our values and our characters started to undermine our relationship with each other. After all, it's pretty difficult to enjoy each other's company when you're constantly wondering if you chose the right partner.

We survived that first year of marriage for one important reason: divorce was not an option to us. We had vowed to stay together "till death do us part" and we intended to honor that vow. We were forced to work through the problem, not give up on it. We knew that. But we had no idea where to begin.

At this point, we were invited to attend a weekly neighborhood gathering where biblical principles were presented and discussed. We had never been part of such a gathering before and approached that first meeting with our guards up high. But the fellowship was warm and the material presented was fascinating. We quickly and enthusiastically became regular attenders.

In that close neighborhood gathering, with people from different religious backgrounds, we met God for ourselves. As we began to study the Bible on our own, we discovered that it contained – together with much else – some great principles for making marriages work. As we began to practice some of these principles, we found the tensions between us beginning to subside. We could turn to God with our frustrations and anger. We could tap into him as a source of peace and understanding that we'd never had before. We were making a new start in our relationship.

VOWS ARE TWO-WAY

What happens when one partner breaks his or her vows and the other remains faithful? Can you still have an effective marriage? Unfortunately, no, not until trust is restored between the two of you. Up to this point we have talked about you, the vow taker, and *your* obligations to the marriage vows. But we need also to talk about what your partner is experiencing while you are pledging your faithfulness. The exchange of vows is a two-way communication, even though only one person at a time is doing the talking.

As he/she listens to your words of commitment, your partner is also making a silent pledge – to accept at face value all you have said and to stake his or her life on the fact that you will live up to your vows. At the moment of verbal expression a bond of trust is formed between the speaker and the listener. It involves the whole person: intellect, emotions, will, and spirit. In essence your partner is saying to you, "With my mind I comprehend what you're saying. With my emotions I want to believe you. With my will I choose to trust you. But my spirit is vulnerable, please understand that. I am giving you all that I am, even those parts of me that I've hidden from others. So handle me gently, please. Everything I have is riding on this commitment."

A broken marriage is rarely the fault of only one partner. Usually both have slighted their vows. However, when one partner breaks a particular vow, the other person is stabbed in a very tender spot. Trust is violated, vulnerability is taken advantage of, and the sacredness of the marriage ceremony itself is desecrated. That very slender thread of believing, hoping, expecting, counting on, has been broken by the selfishness of one partner.

Although things can be patched up, it is not possible to restore the marriage to its former effectiveness unless both partners *want* that marriage restored. Anything less is only a partial healing.

A PATTERN TO FOLLOW

A good place to begin the restoration process is to go back to the concept that marriage is instituted by God and, therefore, has a pattern in the kind of love that God bestows upon us. He too makes vows – vows to love us no matter how unfaithful we are, vows never to leave us or forsake us, vows to cover our shortcomings with his all-encompassing love. And he is not afraid to make these vows public. In fact, he has written them in a book which is so comforting to its readers that thousands buy it year after year, causing it to maintain its position at the top of the best seller list. This book, the Bible, produces readers who have trusted their lives to its marvelous promises.

If anyone should want to prove God unfaithful, all he would have to do is locate someone somewhere willing to testify that God failed to live up to one of his promises. But, as far as we know, no such person exists, for God is always true to his vows.

What a pattern to strive to emulate in marriage: to be as faithful to our vows as God is to his, to strive to love our partner with his kind of love. It is a noble resolution to be sure, but resolutions are only the beginning. They must be worked out in the daily routine of life. And they must be worked out together.

The result, however, will be well worth the effort. You will find yourself enjoying a relationship that is absolutely liberating. At last you will be free to love without restraint and to be loved that way in return. You will be free to give as well as to receive, free to fail and try again, even free to fall short of your own ideals, knowing that in the other half of your relationship there is a partner who will understand and cover for your shortcomings. You can't ask for a better relationship than that.

HOW DO YOU RATE?

1. When I recited my marriage vows, they were taken:
   □ *voluntarily;*   □ *publicly;*   □ *unconditionally;*
   □ *seriously;* □ *bindingly.*
2. As I was pledging my faithfulness I felt: □ *elated;*
   □ *optimistic;* □ *serious;* □ *scared;* □ *self-sacrificing;*
   □ *unsure of myself;* □ *hypocritical;* □ *other.*
3. In our marriage, divorce is: □ *not an option;* □ *sometimes thought of as an option;* □ *often discussed;* □ *a very real possibility.*
4. When crises come to our marriage, they: □ *draw us closer together;* □ *drive us farther apart;* □ *do a little bit of both, depending on the crisis.*
5. To prevent division between us in future crises I need to:
   □ *be more open with my partner;* □ *rely less upon my own resources;* □ *seek outside help;* □ *turn to God;*
   □ *all of the above.*

3

Learning to Communicate

Good communication is an absolute *must* for couples who intend to stay together. But communication involves more than just an exchange of words. It is also an exchange of looks, of touch and of feelings. And it takes work to develop, especially for those who are non-communicative by nature.

THE BARRIERS ARE UP

Unfortunately in our modern society there are many hindrances to good communication. Have you ever tried to carry on a conversation over the riotous cheers of a televised football game or the chatter of a radio program? Or have you ever had your remarks bounce back at you from the raised front page of the daily paper? If so, you have experienced the frustrations of trying to break through three of the barriers we have allowed twentieth-century technology to erect in our homes.

In addition to the clamor of the media, there are the outbursts of children, expressing their needs and demands, interrupting any quiet time you might have been able to snatch. Added to that is the tyranny of the frantic pace at which we live, requiring us to eat on the run, sleep on the run, and even socialize on the run.

With all these ready-made barriers, who needs personal

grudges – the kind that lead to "the silent treatment"? Nobody does.

People assume, "My partner knows how I feel. There is no need to communicate." But your partner most probably does *not* know how you feel. He/she can only guess, and that guess is often wrong.

TEARING THE BARRIERS DOWN

Some communication barriers are easy to overcome; some are not. Reading the evening paper can wait until the day's events have been shared. Watching television can be regulated. The flip of a switch can ensure relative silence, and husbands and wives can learn how to talk again. The same is true of the radio. Unfortunately there is background music almost everywhere today and many people are so used to it that they actually feel uncomfortable without it. If this is true for you, perhaps you could begin every day with just a few minutes of silence. Before long, you may find yourself treasuring these quiet moments so much that noise becomes an intrusion.

The noise that children make cannot be turned off so readily. Nor would you want it to be. When they grow up and leave home the silence they leave behind can be awesome. So enjoy their chatter while you have it. But don't let that chatter interrupt communication between the two of you. Set aside time for talking after they are in bed or, if they are older, while they are doing their homework or pursuing their own activities. If your dinner hour is bedlam, either decide to subdue that bedlam, or learn to shout above the din. But whatever you do, keep talking. See that those lines of communication remain open.

Personal grudges that develop into a cold war between the two of you are a harder problem to deal with. We are all aware of how communication can break down over the slightest incident. It is not the breakdown itself that is the real issue, but how the breakdown is handled.

The cold war syndrome

Let's create a hypothetical situation in which the husband has done something to incur the wrath of his wife. (The situation could just as easily be reversed with the wife, instead of the husband, being the cause of provocation.) Instead of voicing her displeasure immediately, the wife decides to harbor her hurt for awhile. During the process of mulling over her list of gripes, she vows to get even. All day long she plans her strategy, but absolutely nothing is said. By the time bedtime rolls around, she is ready for action – or inaction, whichever the case may be.

She retires with her husband, just as usual. But this is where the semblance of normality stops. How can she possibly respond to the overtures of the ogre who is lying in bed beside her? She decides she can't. So she turns her face to the wall and fumes. She is managing to communicate her displeasure quite effectively, yet not a word is spoken.

Her husband reaches out in love but finds he can't break through the barrier of ice. Tenderly he tries again, but "Don't touch me" signals continue to ward him off. Finally, after several more unsuccessful attempts to establish communication by touch, the frustrated husband blurts out, "What's the matter with you?"

"Nothing," the martyred wife replies. "Nothing." Then she stiffens again.

In this case the husband should continue to reach out until his wife responds. And the wife *must* respond if she wants harmony to be restored. Until she does, there will continue to be a barrier.

Reading this you may be saying, "Nobody is going to make *me* respond." But surely you are prepared to sacrifice a few moments of pride for the sake of your marriage. Don't let your emotions rule you. Rule them! Refuse to clam up. Let your partner know what is troubling you and how you *feel* about what is troubling you.

When an unfortunate incident threatens to destroy your marriage, try to keep it in its proper perspective. After all, it is only one event in many years of a relationship. Remember too how precious your fellowship was before the incident occurred – if indeed it *was* precious. Go back to your beginnings and get the bigger picture.

If a wrongdoing needs to be confessed, get up the courage to confess it. Although you will be humbled in the process, you will also be cleansed. Confession of personal wrongdoing is therapeutic, both to the individual and to the partnership. It helps bring relief to the tensions that are building between you and paves the way for subsequent communication.

If you can't verbalize your confession, perhaps you can write it. A letter can be read again and again, even years after being written. So if you want a lasting communication or if you express yourself more effectively through the written word, by all means write a note.

If communication has reached a deadlock, come up with a creative alternative. Perhaps a mediator could help. Just make sure you choose your mediator carefully and give him/her precise instructions as to how he/she is to be used. Partners who won't listen to each other will sometimes listen to a mutually trusted party. It is at least worth a try if conditions in your marriage are desperate.

No letter, though, regardless of how well written it is, nor any mediator, regardless of how effective he/she is, can communicate as effectively as you can on the scene and in person. Face-to-face communication utilizes facial expression, touch, and voice inflection – both through the person himself as well as through the words.

Christians believe that God realized this. They believe that for the infinite God to communicate his nature to the finite creatures he had created, a drastic step had to be taken. God actually had to *become* man. Then man would understand more what God is like. Christians believe God did that in the person of Jesus Christ. They believe that Jesus Christ was the ultimate communication of God to man, that without his appearance in the flesh, man would continue to "misread" him.

Place yourself far back in time, to the beginning of things, if you will. Imagine yourself examining the intricacies of your own body and the complex details of the world around you, then coming to the conclusion that somebody somewhere must have made all of this that you see. Who is he? What is he like? Nature speaks to you, your conscience speaks to you, and every once in awhile you even sense that God speaks to you. But you don't really know him. His messages seem to you to resemble a giant rubber stamp in the sky – the kind of stamp you would use to print your address on an envelope. Although all of God's attributes are included on the face of that stamp, they are incomprehensible from your point of view. They appear to be written backwards.

One day, however, the stamp comes down in the image of a carpenter from Nazareth named Jesus. The Bible calls him "the exact likeness of God's own being." No wonder. At last humankind can see what God is like. His compassion shows in an arm outstretched to children, his empathy in the tears shed at the tomb of a dead friend, his justice in the overturning of the moneychangers' tables, his sacrificial love in his arms outstretched in death. At last God is understandable, God is approachable, God is real. He has communicated effectively to man.

Whether or not you accept the Christian viewpoint that Jesus Christ is God enfleshed, you can acknowledge the principle presented. The most effective communication in heaven or on earth is person-to-person confrontation. That is why communication experts, rating methods according to their effectiveness, come up with the following order:

1. letter, least effective
2. phone call, more effective (at least you add the urgency of your voice)
3. personal confrontation, most effective (in addition to your voice you add total body involvement – looks, gestures, touch, or anything else you want to throw in)

Remember this order as you learn to communicate with your partner.

LET'S BE HONEST

Sharing your feelings with your partner makes you vulnerable. But the possible gain to your marriage is worth the risk. If a problem arises, talk it through. If there is a decision to be made, talk it over. If there are differences of opinion, talk them out. It is easier to communicate in times of crisis if the routine lines of communication are already open.

Fears

Sharing your feelings involves many things. One is being able to express your fears about the future. Maybe your job is shaky and you need somebody to unload on. Or perhaps the doctor's wording of your latest health report made you nervous. Or there is a possibility that your child won't move up with his class and you're concerned about his reaction – and yours! Because you are part of that intimate relationship called marriage you have a privilege many single people do not share. You have a built-in listening ear. Take advantage of it.

Frustrations

Sharing your feelings also involves letting out your frustrations, whatever they may be at the moment. Perhaps your occupation is driving you nuts, either at home or in the business world. If you continue to harbor these frustrations they could destroy you. But if you let them out, your partner can help you handle them. The physical body is equipped with a marvelous device, the mouth, through which all the junk that is building up inside may be escorted out. There is another device, the listening ear, through which a sensitive partner can remove all that rubbish. So communicate – share your frustrations with each other and enjoy sweet release.

Aspirations

In addition to sharing your fears and your frustrations, share your aspirations. Where do you want to be five years from now? What blocks stand in your way? Can those blocks be removed? If not, can you be content with things as they are? Let your partner in on your secret desires – if not all of them (for privacy is a valuable commodity), at least enough to give you both a goal to work towards – together.

If you can't express your reactions to your partner, who can you express them to? He/she should be your confidant, your encourager, and your most trusted friend. If this is not the case, start talking. Good communication builds good relationships.

UP FRONT WITH EMOTIONAL DIFFERENCES

Men seem to have more difficulty than women in honestly and openly expressing their feelings. Perhaps the reason is past conditioning. Too many of us were brought up to think that it is not "macho" for a man to let his feelings show. From early childhood young boys are often admonished, "Don't cry; that's baby stuff." Why have we equated emotional strength with pent-up emotions when in fact *real* emotional strength is the ability to let those emotions *out* in the right way and at the right time?

Women may lean too far in the other direction by being *too* emotional. The slightest provocation may evoke buckets of tears, a weapon of sentimentality some women learn to use to their advantage.

Perhaps this is one reason why God made us "male and female" – to balance each other's emotional make-up. There is no better place to work at doing this than in the marriage relationship. After all, it is the most intimate of all interpersonal relationships. And communication through words can cement it beautifully, but those words must be chosen carefully, then spoken in the right way, at the right time, with the right emphasis.

LOOKS CAN SPEAK

Words, however, are not the only means of communication available to us. Looks can communicate too. A shifted glance suggests, "I've had enough of that, thank you!" A penetrating gaze, "What do you really mean by that?" A cold-as-steel glare, "I'll get even with you later." A raised eyebrow, "You don't really expect me to *believe* that!" A nod of the head, "It's time to leave the party." And a warm inviting look, "Come closer, I want to feel your touch." Since one look can replace many words, we need to learn to use looks to solidify, rather than to fragment, our marriage.

TALKING BY TOUCH

Touching is an intimate means of communication. Why then in marriage, which is the most intimate of all relationships, are so many of us reluctant to do more of it? Think of how much you can "say" through a simple touch. An arm around the shoulder indicates, "I'm with you all the way." A snuggle shoulder to shoulder declares, "I love you and am glad you're by my side." A finger run up the spine says, "I'm playful. Let's have fun." A gentle caress can be an invitation to physical intimacy. And clasped hands tell observers, "We're going through life together, side by side."

By the way, who says a couple married for twenty-five years can't hold hands as they take a walk around the block? That simple act speaks much more deeply of real love than the spectacle of teenagers hanging all over each other. Let's vow to do more touching, more hugging, and more caressing in our marriage. All are excellent ways of communicating feelings.

COMMUNION – THE EXTRA STEP

Communication is definitely important in building solid marriages. But it is only the beginning of what *can* be yours in the realm of effective interchange. There is a step beyond communication that should be the goal of every married couple. That step is communion.

Communion is different from communication in that it is an exchange of spirits or of "heart vibrations," if you will. It is a sense of quiet oneness. When partners are united in real communion, they are comfortable with silence. For example, they can ride in a car for hours at a time with scarcely a word said between them. And maybe when they do speak, they express the same thought in the same way. Has this ever happened to you? If so, you know about communion.

Another way to test whether you are experiencing communion is to ask yourself, "Do I know without asking my partner how he/she will react?" In other words, are you so tuned in to your partner's desires that you don't have to ask if it's okay to have friends over for coffee? You already know that it's okay because through regular communication you have reached the point where you are tuned in to your partner's wishes and feelings almost as closely as your own.

Communion is a step up from communication. It also differs from mere union, even though "union" is part of the word "communion." If you tie the tails of two cats together and fling them over a clothesline, you will have a union, but you certainly will not have communion. The cats will screech at each other, claw at each other, bite each other, and struggle to be free. They may be united in flesh, but they are certainly not united in spirit. Unfortunately, these cats are symbolic of far too many marriages. Couples today share the same house, share the same food, and share the same bed, but they don't share each other's lives. At the slightest provocation they screech, claw, and bite. Communion of spirit is therefore impossible to attain.

How then do two people reach that level of exchange where communication has developed into true communion? There are two ways. One is through prayer, which leads to a communion of spirit, and the other is through sexual union, which leads to a communion of body and spirit.

PRAYER AS A GUIDE TO COMMUNION

We will consider prayer first. Most people do not realize that prayer is really a two-way communication: listening first and then responding. When we have learned how to listen for God to speak to us, then we are most apt to know how to

respond to him. The same is true in our marriage relationship. Good listening produces good communication.

Listening is almost a forgotten art today. Few people know
how to listen to what another person may *really* be trying
to say. And almost nobody listens to God. There are so many
noises in our contemporary world that if God *is* trying to
communicate, we have a hard time getting the message. We
are subjected to the jangle of telephones and alarms, the blast
of horns, and the shrieks of sirens. Even our "quiet" places
have been invaded by the rumble of jet planes, air condi-
tioners, and tourists.

Can God's voice get through all this? We believe so, for
he speaks in many different ways: in the beauty of the sunset
and the intricate details of the flowers, through the change
of the seasons and the control of the tides, through the
twinkle of the stars and the rising of the sun. The message
is always the same: "The hand that controls all this is divine."
But do we hear the message?

God speaks in another way too – through the Bible. "The
whole Bible was given to us by inspiration from God and
is useful to teach us what is true and to make us realize what
is wrong in our lives; it straightens us out and helps us to
do what is right. It is God's way of making us well prepared
at every point, fully equipped to do good to everyone."

God's message through this medium is often missed too
– but not because of noise. This one is missed because of
personal neglect. We either don't make time to stop and read
the Bible or we don't feel it's that important. When we do
read it, though, it's amazing how penetrating we find it to
be. Sometimes what we read will be a comfort and sometimes
it will be a reprimand. Often it will be like a healing salve
but occasionally it will be like a sword. Sometimes we will
not understand what God is saying and other times we will
understand all too well. We will receive practical help in
solving our everyday problems and a bigger perspective on
what life is all about. Perhaps the biggest advantage, though,
is personal peace. When we read it, we are learning to listen
for God.

One who listens properly is one who knows how to respond. If you venture outside on a crisp dark night and catch the timeless message of the stars, it is quite natural to exclaim, "Oh God, how great you are!" Or when you read a passage from the Bible and discover that it meets the need of your heart, you can't help responding, "Thank you, Lord." In both cases your response has been limited to only one sentence, but that one sentence is prayer.

Soon your one sentence responses will turn into paragraphs. You may find yourself saying something like this: "I love you, God. Your natural wonders fill me with awe. You have made a beautiful world. And I thank you that I am part of it. I thank you for life and breath and the capacity to enjoy the beauty around me. Thank you for a life-partner who loves me and whom I am learning to love in return. And while I am on the subject of my marriage, could you give me the wisdom to solve this problem that is creating a barrier between us? Thank you too for friends who enrich me and care enough to confront me. Now help me to live this day with clarity of purpose. I want to be a reflection of your self-giving love." If you have expressed any such sentiments to God at any time in your life, you have prayed. Remember, though, prayer is not just a thought *about* God. It is a verbal response *to* God, either silent or aloud. And it comes as a result of what you have either "heard" in the world around you or read in the Bible.

A similar result occurs in marriage. When you take time to listen, you know how to respond. On those special occasions when you make the effort to close your windows to the deafening sounds of the city or to switch off the box that produces a constant barrage of meaningless chatter, you are ready to "hear" the unspoken messages your partner may be trying to send you. Is it a sigh or a catch in the breath? Whatever it is, you hear it because you have been listening. And you recognize its subtle cry for help. In a response that is as natural as breathing, you venture, "Having a hard day? Me too. Let's talk about it. Maybe we can pray about it too."

While simply talking about the problem will foster good

communication, it is praying about it that will develop real communion. We firmly believe that strong interpersonal relationships ("horizontal" relationships) are helped by a strong "vertical" relationship – to God. If each individual partner by himself or herself has a strong vertical relationship to God, that will help. But if the couple together has a strong vertical relationship, that will be very strengthening to the marriage. What we are talking about (at least in part) is praying together as husband and wife.

Praying together may be embarrassing the first time you try it. You may have prayed alone before, but now you are about to pray in front of your partner. Can you do it? You take your partner's hand, bow your head, close your eyes, and wait. There is silence – a very uncomfortable silence. One of you is expected to break it. Dear God, let it be my partner. But the silence continues. It must be you. So in an uncertain voice you begin, "God, I thank you for..."

How strange your voice sounds when you use it to talk to God. But before you have time to worry about the strangeness, you hear your partner's voice joining yours. You have broken the sound barrier! And you have done it together. Now you are ready to experience the excitement of a whole new dimension of sharing. And it will come about because you have concentrated on the vertical as well as the horizontal. You have included God in the interchange of your thoughts.

COMMUNION THROUGH SEXUAL UNION

As rewarding as prayer is, however, it is not the deepest level of communion possible between husband and wife. That honor is reserved for the act of sexual union.

Sexual union is one of the first acts of love most married couples share. If they have abstained during the dating phase of their relationship, this expression of love is both long-awaited and anxiously anticipated.

"Don't you think we should leave now for the church? Did the soloist stick an extra verse in that song? Is it really necessary for the photographer to take so many shots? How long this receiving line is. Is it time for the cake cutting yet? Why do the guests keep lingering?..."

At long last the couple is alone, finally free to express their love in their own privacy. It is, and always has been, an important moment.

In the Hebrew tradition the marriage ceremony was not considered complete until sexual union had taken place. In fact, the wedding guests actually waited until evidence was given that the bride and groom had become "one flesh." Can you imagine anything more embarrassing? The couple was considered married in name only until the time of consummation, when their marriage was made actual, physically as well as legally. There are remnants of this emphasis still with us. Lack of physical consummation is a legal reason for the annulment of any marriage.

Although for some the adventure of the wedding night may be a comedy of errors, for others it is sheer bliss, an experience no words can describe. Those who have waited until their wedding day for this special relationship agree on one important truth: the blending of bodies for the first time is an experience beyond the physical. It is a spiritual happening of the highest order. Whereas sexual union outside of marriage is often dirty, guilt-ridden, and selfish, in the context of marriage this same act becomes pure, sacred, and spiritually exhilerating.

It is important to retain this awareness of the sanctity of sex in the marriage relationship. That does not mean you are not supposed to enjoy it. You are – but with proper respect for your partner's body, mind, and spirit. Modern free-thinking may try to convince you that the body can be divorced from the rest of the person and given in sex without having any adverse effect on the mind or on the spirit. But that is not true. When your partner gives his/her body to you, the whole person goes with it.

In your enthusiasm to learn all you can, refrain from turning to sources that degrade or cheapen sex. Be careful what type of literature you read. Although a good understanding of the physiology of the human body is helpful, you do not need texts filled with explicit diagrams to show you "how to do it." You also do not need to be instructed from pornographic movies.

Our sexuality is God-given and intended to be enjoyed according to his instructions. Properly channeled and delicately expressed, sexual passions become one of the greatest gifts God ever gave to humans. On the other hand, when they are allowed to run free of restraint they become a curse to the body and an even greater curse to the spirit.

It might be wise at this point to go back in our thinking to the account of creation as recorded in the Bible to determine where human sexuality is reported to have originated. There we are told that God made both "male and female" and that he did so in order that man would not be "alone."

Men and women need each other. They provide companionship, support, and fulfillment to each other's lives. This does not mean, of course, that men or women can never be complete entities in themselves without the other sex, but it does mean that a lifetime of mutual sharing broadens one's experiences and enlarges one's outlook on life.

When God made woman, we are told, he took her from the rib of her husband. According to Bible commentator Matthew Henry the selection of the rib is symbolic. God did not take woman from man's foot so that man could dominate her. Neither did he take her from man's head so that she could dominate him. Instead he took her from man's rib so that they could walk side by side through life, the wife under the protection of her husband's arm, very close to his heart. It is a beautiful concept indeed.

Then the Bible says, "When Adam was presented with his bride, he exclaimed, 'This is it . . . She is part of my own bone and flesh. Her name is woman because she was taken out of a man.'" This explains why a man leaves his father and mother and is joined to his wife in such a way that the two become one person. Then the account reads, "Now although the man and his wife were both naked, neither of them was embarrassed or ashamed." So from the beginning man and woman clung to each other physically and derived mutual satisfaction from doing so.

When we consider the results of the sex act in marriage, we discover several benefits that can come from it. All benefits, however, need to be considered in balance. If you emphasize one at the expense of the other, you get a lopsided view. For example, sex for the sole purpose of reproduction results in the condition that is often derogatorily referred to as "barefoot and pregnant" – most of the time. On the other hand, sex for pleasure only can encourage attitudes of selfishness and personal gratification.

There are at least four benefits of sexual union that we want to consider equally. One is the very practical realization that it provides a proper outlet for our God-given passions. Our sexuality is meant to be expressed in the way God intended, that is, in the life-long relationship of one man with one woman in marriage. God gave us the drive and God gave us the channel for expressing that drive. It is up to us to keep the two together.

Another benefit that sexual union provides is the sense of unity it brings to the marriage relationship. The exchange that is involved is total, a wonder that could never be experienced any other way. Just as the intercourse of minds alone is an incomplete experience, so also the intercourse of bodies alone is equally incomplete. But when the two come together, coupled with the spirit and the emotions, there is total satisfaction and real communion.

A third benefit of sex in marriage is the children that sometimes come from the union. One of the first commands God gave to his newly created couple was, "Multiply and fill the earth." Evidently they took God at his word, for their corner of the world was soon sporting the results of their union. The decision to bear children was a good one at that stage in history because what the world needed most was people. Now, however, the problems couples face are much bigger than the prospect of an unpopulated world. There are wars, famines, poverty, crime, drugs, and disease – all of which are overshadowed by the constant threat of nuclear holocaust. No wonder many couples today decide not to have children. There are also couples for whom children are physiologically denied. So the benefit of childbearing is not enjoyed by all who are married. It is a selective benefit, restricted either by the couple themselves or by God – both for reasons known only to themselves.

There is at least one more benefit of sex in marriage that cannot be overlooked. It is pleasure – pure, unadulterated pleasure. It is a "plus" beyond the other benefits. So enjoy every aspect of your physical union, making sure at the same time that your partner is enjoying it too. Be creative in the way you share your bodies, but never to the point where your partner feels embarrassed or ashamed.

If you have to fit your sex life into a schedule interrupted by the demands of children, work, and other obligations, you are probably smiling wistfully at the thought of creativity in your romance. After all, it's pretty hard to be creative (or even romantic) when Susie knocks on the bedroom door and announces "I have to go potty" or when a call from the boss shatters your bliss on the couch. But keep trying anyway. Romance is necessary to the survival of any marriage.

We commented earlier on reading material and films that degrade the physical relationship in marriage. Let us comment now on a piece of literature we not only approve but highly recommend. It is the biblical poem *The Song of Solomon*, which describes both the pleasure and sanctity of sex. As you read this short account of how one couple expressed their love – an account which is rich in symbolic language – you may pick up some exciting ideas to enhance the richness of your own sexual experience.

A good way to increase the enjoyment of sexual union is to plan your time together. Realize that the culmination of intercourse is not the whole "play" in itself. It is the climax to a play that has many previous acts. And each act has to be carefully staged.

First consider the timing. Take into consideration the events of the day. Remember your partner's frustrated business deal or the hectic schedule with three pre-school children. Don't expect your partner to suddenly "turn on," even though you yourself may be more than ready. There is "a time to embrace and a time to refrain from embracing." If you come home from work to find that the washing machine has spewed suds all over the kitchen floor, the couch you ordered won't be delivered for another month, and the family cat has been run over by a milk truck, maybe now is not the time to embrace – except perhaps to cry on each other's shoulder. But then again, it might be just the thing to restore a sense of proportion!

If you conclude the timing is right, toss out an invitation: "How about dinner tonight – by candlelight?" This early hint of a big occasion to come gives both partners time to make preparations. And it gives you both several hours of anticipation.

When dinner time finally arrives, you'll be able to enjoy every minute of your special time together. The mood will be relaxed and easy. Carefully selected music might add to this. The compliments you give your partner will be genuinely appreciated, so don't hold back on them.

As the evening progresses, there might be gentle caresses. You both know that there is a marvelous world of sexuality to be explored. It is a world which cannot afford to be rushed.

It is also a world in which fair play is absolutely necessary. A sensitive husband would never consider marriage an opportunity to practice legalized rape. Nor would a sensitive wife tantalize her husband to the point of sexual arousal, only to say "Not tonight." Sexual union must be neither forced nor toyed with. It must be an act of mutual consent.

The ground rules having been agreed upon, it is safe for the play to continue. And the rest is up to you and your partner. As you enter the bedroom, the door closes behind you. And so it should. For this is one act in the lives of all marriage partners that is meant to be kept secret.

Mutually agree from the beginning to keep anything that happens in your bedroom private. Make sure the door is closed in both directions. In other words, watch both what comes in and what goes out. The advice and tales of friends, photographs of nudes or of sexual intercourse can be a real threat to your union. Likewise, outgoing reports on performance (or lack of it) and the sharing of agonies and ecstasies carry out with them trust, privacy, and the sanctity of sex.

It is natural that in some bedrooms real problems will arise. You may think, "Am I normal? Is my partner? How do other people solve the problems we seem to be having?" There are several ways you can handle these problems without defiling the sanctity of this, the most sacred act of your marriage relationship. The first is to talk things out between yourselves. If this does not help, seek counsel. But determine first what kind of help you need. If it is medical, seek out a competent doctor. If it is not medical, seek advice elsewhere. But choose your confidant or counselor wisely. You are looking not only for someone with the ability to help, but someone who will be dedicated to the protection of your privacy. See the doctor or counselor together if possible. If not, make sure your partner knows whom you are consulting and how much you are revealing, and approves.

We live in a world where we are told to "let it all hang out." In marriage this advice can be disastrous. If you want your marriage to last, keep the special secrets of your sexual relationship between just the two of you.

This pattern for maintaining privacy is based on our observation that God reserves to himself the right to have "secret things." These "secret things" include information concerning sacred events. In fact, the more sacred the event, the less information we seem to receive about it. Take, for example, the fact that there are virtually no details given concerning either the conception of Jesus by the Virgin Mary, or the work of atonement on the cross. In fact, the latter event was so holy that physical darkness surrounded it. It was as if God the Father was saying, "This is between just Jesus and me. I can't share any details of this event without degrading the sacredness of it." Marriage partners take heed.

Marriage is not like two cats with their tails tied together, bickering at each other and struggling to be free. Marriage is enjoying being as close to your partner as possible, communicating to each other the warmth of a very tight fellowship and protecting that fellowship with everything in you.

HOW DO YOU RATE?

1. The following are hindrances to communication in our home: □ *television;* □ *radio;* □ *the newspaper;* □ *children;* □ *family schedules;* □ *the silent treatment from my partner;* □ *the silent treatment from me;* □ *all of the above.*

2. Feelings I have shared with my partner are: □ *fears;* □ *frustrations;* □ *aspirations;* □ *discouragements;* □ *hatred;* □ *all of the above.*

3. Feelings I have never shared with my partner are: □ *fears;* □ *frustrations;* □ *aspirations;* □ *discouragements;* □ *hatred;* □ *all of the above.*

4. My partner and I communicate most effectively: □ *by words;* □ *by actions;* □ *by looks;* □ *other.*

5. My partner and I experience quiet communion of spirit: □ *never;* □ *once in awhile;* □ *frequently.*

6. I pray to God: □ *only in my thoughts;* □ *aloud;* □ *by myself;* □ *with my husband/wife;* □ *with my family.*

7. I confess my sins: □ *not to anyone;* □ *only to God;* □ *to God in front of my partner;* □ *to God and to my partner.*

8. I believe that sexual union before marriage is: □ *a violation of God's commandment;* □ *permissible during the engagement period;* □ *acceptable if both parties agree;* □ *expected as an important part of the relationship.*

9. If I decide to seek advice regarding sexual compatibility and fulfillment I believe in going to: □ *sexually explicit books;* □ *only wholesome books;* □ *pornographic movies;* □ *my physician;* □ *my pastor;* □ *my partner;* □ *the Bible;* □ *nobody;* □ *my friends;* □ *marriage counselor;* □ *my parents.*

10. In the sexual aspect of our marriage relationship the following are usually part of our sexual union: ☐ *mental preparation;* ☐ *mood setting;* ☐ *tender caresses;* ☐ *visual teasing;* ☐ *interruptions;* ☐ *compliments;* ☐ *satisfaction;* ☐ *frustration;* ☐ *ecstasy;* ☐ *warmth;* ☐ *a feeling of spiritual oneness.*

11. In our marriage sexual union is used for the purpose of: ☐ *reproduction;* ☐ *pleasure;* ☐ *deepening the bond between us;* ☐ *all of the above.*

12. To improve my own part in our sexual union I need to work on: ☐ *gentleness;* ☐ *timeliness;* ☐ *monitoring what I read and see outside the bedroom;* ☐ *watching what I say to others about our sex lives.*

13. If I were to rate the sexual aspect of our marriage I would call it: ☐ *excellent;* ☐ *good;* ☐ *fair;* ☐ *poor;* ☐ *unacceptable.*

14. To improve it I will:

4

Learning to Forgive

In every marriage there are bound to be times of difficulty, times when bitterness begins to eat away at your togetherness and one of you has to be the first to say, "I'm sorry." The longer you wait to swallow your pride and take that first step toward reconciliation, the harder it will be to restore your relationship. So, if there is a problem in your marriage today, don't wait. Do something about it right away.

Bitterness is a killer. Not only will it destroy your marriage, but it will destroy each one of you as well. Bitterness, by definition, is a feeling of resentment that builds inside you until it pours out in some very destructive ways.

Some people handle bitterness by giving their partners the silent treatment, sticking their supercilious noses high in the air and sealing their lips as tightly as an angry child does. If they speak at all, it is only to carry on the necessary business of the day, never to encourage conversation.

Others explode in fury, saying things they are sorry for later. Yet the explosion does not release all their bitterness; it continues to fester in their hearts.

Still others withhold the sexual relationship, lying in bed stiff as boards, as far over to their edge of the bed as possible, maybe even hanging *over* the side. Every once in awhile they let out a martyr's sigh, sending a message that cannot be misinterpreted: "Don't touch me or come anywhere near me. I can't stand to have you around."

There are always a few who drag their bitterness out over

days, weeks, or even months. The messages they send to their partners are more subtle, to be sure, but certainly no less destructive. The distraught wife serves her husband soggy eggs, knowing he hates soggy eggs. He gets back at her by tossing her a burnt piece of toast, knowing she likes her toast lightly browned. She brings the car back nearly empty even though he asked her to fill it up. So he countermoves by failing to take a phone message because "it wasn't that important."

However the bitterness is expressed, the objective is the same: "I will make him pay for the way he treated me" or "I will get even with her for that."

What causes bitterness in a marriage relationship? Many things. It can arise from circumstances outside the marriage itself, such as a job loss, being passed over for a promotion, a failure to receive proper recognition or praise, or learning that your partner has been unfaithful. Or it can arise from inside the marriage – from angry or hurtful words that have passed between you, or from a feeling that you're being used as a doormat. It can even arise from a growing dissatisfaction with yourself: your appearance, your handicap, your lot in life. What is most important is not where bitterness originates but what you do with it once it is there.

Bitterness is like a weed in your garden. Once the seed takes root, you have a definite choice: you can either pull it out before it gets big, or you can water it, feed it, and encourage it to prosper, knowing all the while that it will eventually take over your garden, choking life from all the other plants. When you keep mental lists of the wrongs done against you and pull those lists out periodically to review them, even adding new offenses as they arise, you are nurturing the seeds of bitterness in your life.

WHAT BITTERNESS DOES

Who will be affected by your bitterness? Many, many people – but, most of all, you. You will be troubled, chewed-up inside, slowly poisoned and filled with inner turmoil.

The question is, how will you handle that turmoil? Part of you will say, "This is stupid. Why don't I just get on with it, swallow my pride, and ask for forgiveness?" But another part of you will say, "I'm enjoying this pity party. So I'm going to keep it up a little longer." If you choose to pursue the second option, watch out! Your marriage may be in trouble sooner than you think.

Bitterness rarely affects only one person. It usually touches everyone in the family – and often those outside the family as well. Consider a hypothetical situation (at least we *hope* it is hypothetical):

Tension has arisen within a family and everybody is handling it by taking it out on somebody else. The irate wife screams at her husband...the husband then kicks the dog ...the dog chases the family cat...the cat in turn springs at the bird...the bird waits patiently until the wife is in range and then lets loose on her head...the irate wife reacts by screaming at her husband again...the husband again kicks the dog...and the whole scenario keeps repeating itself, as the frustration of one passes to another to another to another.

How do you stop such displaced behavior from happening? How do you combat bitterness in your life? Through the act of forgiveness. Notice we said "act." Though bitterness is a feeling, forgiveness is an action. You rid yourself of the feeling of bitterness by practicing the action of forgiveness. So if resentment is tearing you up on the inside, you need to *do* something about it – as quickly as possible.

THIS IS NOT FORGIVENESS

What exactly do you *do*? Well, it's easier to understand forgiveness if you realize what you must *not* do. So we'll approach the subject of forgiveness from that point of view, discovering what it is *not*.

A conditional release
Forgiveness is not a conditional release. You must never say to your partner, "I'll forgive you *if*..." or "I'll forgive you

but..." For example, "I'll forgive you *if* you promise never to do it again" or "I'll forgive you *but* I want you to know how much you've hurt me." Forgiveness is a very complex issue, making all of these statements valid in certain situations, but forgiveness itself must never be conditional upon the other person's behavior. That is *not* forgiveness.

The Bible has a great deal to say about forgiveness. It tells us that we all need God's forgiveness: we have failed to keep his standards, we have gone our own way regardless. God sent his Son, Jesus, to make our forgiveness possible, to bring us good news of a new life. When one of his followers asked how often we must forgive one another, Jesus said that we must forgive the offender "seventy times seven," – in other words, an infinite number of times. If one partner were to commit the same offense 490 times, we would tend to become a little exasperated with his or her lack of sincerity – understandably so. But if our forgiveness is dependent upon our partner's sincerity or change of behavior, it is not true forgiveness. True forgiveness knows no conditions.

As far as trust is concerned, you may indeed be tempted to be cautious about ever fully trusting your partner again, and you may even take precautions to guard against the repetition of some offense. But if you forgive a past offense while stipulating that it must never occur again, you are not forgiving completely. You are forgiving partially.

The subject of hurts is harder to deal with, for a deep wounding of the spirit often accompanies a breach of trust. In order for there to be a full restoration to a trusting relationship, those hurts have to be discussed so that a greater sensitivity can be developed for the future. But the discussion of those hurts fits into the restoration stage of the healing process, not into the forgiveness stage. Forgiveness is the *beginning* of healing, not the end. For the end to follow, no strings can be attached to the beginning.

Excusing the wrong

Second, forgiveness is not excusing the wrong. Don't say "He couldn't help it," when you know he could, or "Let's just forget the whole thing, it really doesn't matter," when it matters a great deal. Some people even try to smooth things over with remarks like, "It wasn't that bad." But in their hearts they know it *was* that bad. Face your problem squarely and determine to *do* something about it, rather than offer paltry excuses.

Ignoring the incident

Third, forgiveness is not pretending that the incident never happened. The incident *did* happen. So come to grips with reality and take positive steps toward restoration. A broken bone, set properly, can end up stronger than if it were never broken in the first place. Take the proper steps of forgiveness and restoration, and your marriage could end up stronger than it was before the breach occurred.

Simply forgetting

Fourth, forgiveness is not to be equated with forgetting. Our brains are marvelous computers, capable of storing a life-time's memories. While those "files" can never be erased, they can be classified "inactive" and put in a cabinet marked "Do not open." If an unpleasant incident is not replayed for a number of years, certain details do become fuzzy, maybe even forgotten. In fact, the whole incident may be forgotten if it is not too serious.

But if the incident *is* serious, it is doubtful that it will ever be completely forgotten. However, it *can* be forgiven. You can determine in your heart never to replay the details of that incident, or to get back at the offender for committing it.

THIS IS FORGIVENESS

That statement brings us to a working definition of what forgiveness is. Forgiveness is an act of the will, whereby you throw away your list of grievances, release the offender from payment, and willingly bear the consequences of the offender's action. This may well seem impossible, but those who have experienced God's forgiveness, made possible through Christ, are assured of God's help when it comes to forgiving others. This help is available to all who ask.

Something we do

First of all, forgiveness is an act. It is something that you *do*, not something that you feel. You may not feel like forgiving your partner (in fact, you probably won't), but if you want to restore your relationship, you will do it – whether you feel like it or not.

An act of the will

Second, forgiveness is an act of the *will*. You must come to that point in your life when you determine to do something about your resentment. And the sooner you decide to forgive, the better off you will be.

Something which needs God's help

Forgiveness is hard. There are circumstances in which it may be impossible without the help of God. It goes against the grain, since we are all by nature self-centered. It is only God who can effect that radical turn-around which we call "conversion": turning away from self and centering our lives on him. We fragile human beings get hurt very easily and sometimes those hurts run so deep that, by our own efforts, it is quite impossible to do anything about them except nurse them along. We need the help of God. He loves us and longs for us to turn to him. What is more, he specializes in doing for us what it is impossible to do on our own.

Christians find that because they themselves have been forgiven by God it is easier for them to forgive others. The key to this is what they believe happened on a cross raised on a hillside on the outskirts of Jerusalem 2,000 years ago. There, God took the list of offenses committed against him by men and women throughout the ages of history, and nailed them to the cross on which his Son Jesus died. Jesus freely paid the penalty for all those sins with his own life. All who believe in Christ and accept what he has done for them receive God's pardon and forgiveness – and his help to live a new life.

Forgiving others does not come automatically. Christians still have a choice: they can obey or disobey God's command to forgive those who offend them. Choosing to forgive means saying to God, "I have a mess in my marriage, God. Please help me. I cannot forgive my partner. But I know you have that kind of power. I'm asking you right now to do through me what I cannot do myself. Help me to forgive." If we are willing, the miracle will happen.

Throwing away your list of grievances

This brings us to the fourth facet of forgiveness – what you actually do when you forgive your partner. You throw away your mental list of grievances and vow in your heart never to approach the wastebasket that contains it.

"Stop being mean, bad-tempered and angry. Quarreling, harsh words, and dislike of others should have no place in your lives. Instead be kind to each other, tenderhearted, forgiving one another, just as God has forgiven you because you belong to Christ" (so Paul wrote in the New Testament letter to the Ephesians, chapter 4, *Living Bible* version).

Notice the phrase "just as God has forgiven you." You are expected to do with your partner's offenses the same thing God has done with yours – discard them forever, never to be retrieved or recycled.

Releasing the offender from payment

As you throw away your list of grievances, you must also release your partner from the obligation to pay for them. Whereas bitterness says, "Make him/her pay, make him/her pay, make him/her pay," forgiveness says, "Release him/her from payment once and for all."

The Bible teaches that just as those who have been forgiven by God will never face God's condemnation, so also those who are forgiven by you must never face *your* condemnation. That means no more soggy eggs, no more burnt toast, no more bringing the car back nearly empty, no more refusing to take phone messages, no more hanging over the side of the bed in retribution, no more silent treatment or loud outbursts, and, above all, no more reliving the incident and nursing your own deep hurt.

In fact, true forgiveness means never mentioning the incident again.

Bearing the consequences

All of these actions are important in the process of forgiveness, but if you are going to go all the way, you have to be willing in your heart to bear the consequences of the offender's actions. That means that if your partner has embarrassed you in front of your friends and family, you will willingly bear that shame for love and harmony's sake. You will tolerate the raised eyebrows, the whispers behind your back, or even the verbal attacks. You will bear them because you have chosen to forgive and you intend to carry that forgiveness all the way.

Forgiveness is a personal action. It is possible to forgive in your heart without ever confronting the one who has hurt you. But although this silent forgiveness frees you personally from the bitterness that has been binding you, it will never heal the breach in your marriage. To accomplish that, you have to take a step beyond forgiveness – into the process of restoration.

RESTORING YOUR RELATIONSHIP

Restoration is a function involving the whole person. It involves every part of you – from the brain at the top of your head to the feet at the other end. It requires disciplining yourself to be positive – in everything you do.

Positive thinking

When your partner commits an offense against you, your first responsibility – after releasing him/her from the obligation of paying for the offense (which, you remember, is forgiveness) – is to discipline your mind to concentrate on positive thoughts when thinking about your partner. The mind is like a mental battleground where victories or defeats are determined. Which of those victories or defeats you experience is up to you. If you choose to emphasize negative thoughts about your partner, you will experience defeat. If, on the other hand, you choose to emphasize positive thoughts, you will experience victory.

Bringing out the good

Second, look for the potential in your partner. And after you have found it, dedicate yourself to bringing it out. Bitterness can make you so negative that you see only evil – and that magnified. But remember, you *did* choose to marry this person who has offended you. There must have been something of worth to attract you. Rediscover that worth and put all your efforts into bringing it to the forefront again.

Listening for subtle messages

Third, listen for the cry of your partner's heart. Beneath those exaggerated threats or that biting remark is a person in pain. That pain is the cause of the tongue lashings and of the hurt that is being misdirected toward you. So discipline yourself to listen – not so much to the words being spoken as to what is *beneath* the words being spoken – to the cry of need from the heart.

Controlling your tongue

Fourth, control what comes out of your mouth. It is a hard discipline indeed to return a kind remark in exchange for a bitter one, or to keep absolutely quiet when something preposterous happens. Yet that is the route to victory.

When your husband drags mud onto your newly waxed kitchen floor, don't say what you are thinking. Tell him you love him – dirty boots and all. Or when you learn your wife has just dented the family car by entering the garage too far to the right, bite your lip. Don't explode. Don't explode even if she explodes at you (for buying a house with a garage that's too small). Explosions won't help the situation at all. They will just make matters worse.

Determine ahead of time to hold your tongue, not exploding when the crisis comes and not rubbing it in when the crisis is long past. This takes discipline – and lots and lots of practice. Your marriage will offer you the opportunity to practice. But the discipline must come from you.

Feeling what your partner feels

Fifth, involve your heart in the process of restoration. Try to *feel* what your partner is feeling. Crawl inside your loved one's heart and discover what emotions are lurking there. Is there turmoil, or frustration, or inferiority, or defeat? What is causing such outbursts?

When two people are thinking and feeling together, the partners enjoy a oneness in every aspect of life. They weep together, laugh together, agonize together, and triumph together. But when one partner gets out of sync, acting unpredictably without thinking of the other partner, there is an interruption in that feeling of oneness. The more consistent partner then has a responsibility to encourage him/her back into perfect rhythm.

Touching and hugging

Touch has a restorative power in healing broken relationships. Sometimes you don't need to say a word. A touch will say it all. Whether it is an embrace which sobs, "I'm sorry," or a pat on the back which whispers, "You're forgiven," make use of the healing properties of a caring touch. Like the bumper sticker that reads, "Have you hugged your kid today?" we should have a sticker that says, "Have you hugged your husband/wife today?"

Praying for your partner

We've dealt with the role of the mind, eyes, ears, mouth, heart, and hands in the healing process. But for the Christian, there are also the knees! They were made for good old-fashioned prayer.

It is almost impossible to harbor bitterness toward someone for whom you have been praying. If you don't believe that statement, try it. When you pray, however, pray not only for the offender and the offender's need, but also for yourself and your response.

If you and your partner have established a time for praying together, keep it up. You need it now more than ever. And what an opportunity it will give you. What you may not be able to say to your partner directly, you may be able to say to God – in front of your partner. And the process of restoration has begun.

Making the first move
Last in our list (though it may be the first thing needed), get your feet involved in the restoration process. Be the first to go and say, "I'm sorry."

"But what if my partner offended me?" you ask. "Am I still the one to take that first step toward reconciliation?"

Yes, you are. Why? Because you're the one who is being made aware of the responsibilities of making your marriage work.

"But that's not fair!" you protest. "It's not fair to put the whole responsibility on me."

Fair or not, that's the way it is. If you and your partner were both equally sensitive about the right thing to do, you would meet half-way. But that ideal situation almost never occurs in real life. In real life, one person has to care enough about his or her marriage to take that first step, maybe even going all the way to meet the other partner. Since you are the one who is reading this book, the responsibility falls on your shoulders.

You probably have a question at this point: is it *always* right to go to the other person, even if it causes an unpleasant confrontation?

We believe the answer to that question is no, especially if you have committed an offense that your partner is unaware of and perhaps may never become aware of. Remember the purpose of going to the partner is to make things better, not worse. Some information is better not shared, especially, perhaps, information about your escapades before you were married. Some of us bruise very easily, and it is better to avoid the pain.

When you do decide that it is right to bring things into the open, go to your partner with three purposes in mind: to face him/her with the problem (if this will help); help to bear his/her burden (if indeed there is a burden); and to make restitution (if restitution is required).

First, face your partner with the problem. But do so with as much love and tenderness as you can muster. Remember, the tables could be turned. *You* could be the one being confronted. Say to yourself, "There but for the grace of God go I," letting go of any superior attitude you might have been harboring. Then confront your partner in love and with the utmost humility.

Second, go with the expectation of helping to bear your partner's burdens. Breakdowns in relationships often occur because one marriage partner is struggling with a load too heavy to carry. If it is an emotional burden, it may have a physical root. Just temporarily relieving your partner of some burdensome physical chores could bring real relief. But *showing* your partner that you care is even more important than how you show it. With your physical and emotional support, your partner's damaged emotions can begin the healing process and the entire marriage relationship will benefit.

Third, make restitution as necessary. Keep short accounts with your partner – and this includes the little things. If you borrowed something that was jointly owned, for instance, and it was damaged, replace that item with something of equal or greater value. Above all, be considerate of each other. Your thoughtfulness will be appreciated and your love reinforced.

When you determine to move forward in love, be prepared to go the extra mile if necessary. And be ready to go *now*, not next month, not next week, not tomorrow. The Bible says, "Don't let the sun go down with you still angry – get over it quickly," and that is wise advice. Determine to settle your differences the same day.

LACK OF RESPONSE

So much for how to deal with the roots of bitterness in the marriage relationship. Does following these principles guarantee success?

We wish we could answer yes to that question, but unfortunately the answer is "not necessarily." Any steps you personally take in the hopes of bringing about restoration will certainly help ease the tension between you, but total success will come only if *both* partners work at restoration. Suppose you are diligent in doing everything required of you, but your partner is totally unresponsive. What then?

The marriage will still need healing, but you yourself will have peace. When you know you have done everything possible to restore a broken relationship, your obligation has ended. You are not responsible for the outcome of your efforts. Your partner is responsible for that. You personally have been set free.

The world says, "Look out for number one. You have rights. Stick up for those rights." Don't listen. The Bible's advice, on which our suggestions are based, is far wiser. Although you may indeed be number one, there is another number one at your side. You are important indeed, but you are no more important than your husband or wife. If you think so, you'll never restore your relationship. And as for rights – think rather of privileges. It is a privilege to forgive and to be part of the restoration process. It is even a privilege to make yourself vulnerable – vulnerable enough to be hurt again. Why? Because your marriage is at stake.

HOW DO YOU RATE?

1. At the present time I am harboring bitter feelings toward: □ *myself;* □ *my partner;* □ *a parent;* □ *a child;* □ *a relative;* □ *a friend;* □ *a business associate;* □ *my pastor;* □ *a neighbor;* □ *a teacher;* □ *God;* □ *nobody;* □ *everybody.*
2. I usually handle my bitter feelings by: □ *giving the silent*

treatment; ☐ *exploding verbally;* ☐ *withholding privileges;* ☐ *waging a cold war;* ☐ *other.*

3. When it comes to forgiveness, I usually: ☐ *attach conditions to my forgiveness;* ☐ *look for ways to excuse the wrong done to me;* ☐ *try to ignore the incident;* ☐ *have trouble forgetting the incident;* ☐ *forgive easily.*

4. For me the hardest part of the forgiveness process in marriage is: ☐ *coming to the place where I'm willing to forgive;* ☐ *confronting my partner in a positive way;* ☐ *throwing away my list of grievances;* ☐ *releasing my partner from payment;* ☐ *being willing to bear the consequences of my partner's actions;* ☐ *admitting my own wrong in the incident;* ☐ *all of the above.*

5. To restore a working relationship with my partner I really want to: ☐ *discipline my thoughts so they're positive;* ☐ *look for the good in my partner;* ☐ *listen to what my partner is really saying;* ☐ *be positive in what I say to my partner;* ☐ *try to feel what my partner is feeling;* ☐ *reach out and touch my partner;* ☐ *pray for my partner;* ☐ *confront my partner positively;* ☐ *be at peace, even if I've done all of the above and my partner reacts negatively.*

5

The Insult of Infidelity

"Have an affair and it will improve your marriage."

There's advice for you – quoted in one of our major newspapers by a counselor speaking on the topic of troubled marriages. Can you believe it? Not only is it a dangerous statement, it is an outright lie.

Infidelity is probably the greatest threat a marriage could ever encounter. Even the slightest hint of it sends icicles through the warmth of an intimate relationship. It involves a breaking of the marriage vow, results in a breach of trust between partners, sends a sword through the heart of the one who has been wronged, and becomes one of life's ultimate insults.

WHAT IS INFIDELITY?

In its broadest definition infidelity is anything that robs one partner of the other's affection. That could be a job, a sport, a hobby, some consuming interest, an inordinate affection for a parent, or a fixation on another individual. Some people are "married" to their jobs. Others are "married" to their mothers. Still others are "married" to football, golf, or oil painting. None of these individuals can at the same time be properly married to their partners. For when you unite with someone you love, you promise to "keep yourself only unto him/her as long as you both shall live."

Although these broader aspects of infidelity are serious,

they can be dealt with simply by introducing more balance to the marriage relationship. There is one form of infidelity, however, that balance will never help. That is sexual infidelity. In the sexual area you are either faithful or you are not. There is no middle ground.

Unfortunately, every single one of us is capable of becoming unfaithful to our partner. We all have passions, we all have minds, and we all have wills. We all find certain members of the other sex attractive: marriage does not put an end to that. Our passions say, "It would feel good to have a relationship outside of marriage." The mind adds, "I will think about that for awhile." Then the will comes along and clinches it, "What in the world are you waiting for? Go ahead and do it." Is there anyone who is never tempted?

IT BEGINS IN THE MIND

Infidelity begins in the mind – with the fascinating pastime called fantasizing. Fantasizing itself is not wrong. In fact, it can be beneficial – if the one you are fantasizing about is your partner. But that is a very big "if." If it is someone other than your partner, watch out!

It has been said that victory or defeat begins in the mind. That is certainly true when it comes to passionate desires. If you are having trouble in this area, stop a moment and take a personal inventory. Who has been the object of your fantasies lately?

One word of caution before you dredge up your innermost thoughts: don't feel guilty about what you cannot control. Lustful thoughts can pop into anybody's mind at any moment of any day – unannounced and often unwelcome. If you were asked to reveal every thought you ever had about every person you ever met or wished you had met, you would probably blush with embarrassment. So would everyone else. People simply cannot control what comes into their heads. But they can control what they *do* with what comes into their heads.

With every thought that flashes past, you have a choice:

you can either hold on to it and dwell upon it, or you can send it merrily on its way. Unwholesome thoughts are relatively harmless if they are dismissed immediately. It is only when they are entertained that they become dangerous. As the old proverb goes, "You can't stop the birds from flying over your head, but you can stop them from making a nest in your hair."

Infidelity usually begins the same way a roller coaster ride begins – with plenty of time to think about it. You have to stand in line to purchase a ticket. While waiting, you have the opportunity to weigh the pros and cons of taking the ride. It promises adventure beyond the ordinary, to be sure, but there are risks to be considered too. "Do I really want to go on this ride? Everybody says it's exhilerating, but I may get hurt. Do I want to run that risk? Should I purchase a ticket or not? Aw...what have I got to lose? I will buy it..."

Now you are committed – but not irrevocably. You don't have to get in that car. You could consider your purchase a passing whim and leave the adventure to those behind you. Once you do climb into the car, however, turning back becomes more difficult – still not impossible, but certainly more difficult.

As the car makes its way up the hill, laboring cog by cog, you can leap to safety if you wish. Granted, it will be embarrassing to get out of the car at this point, but you *can* do it. You still have a chance to reverse your decision – at least for a little while longer.

With the crest of the hill, however, comes the end of your choices. You reach the point of no return. Down the car goes – in a terrifying plunge to the bottom. The ride you anticipated so long is over in a matter of seconds.

"Wow! My heart is pounding," you say. "What an experience! What a ride!"

"Umm...Should I stand in line again?"

How easily riding roller coasters becomes a habit! The same is true with extra-marital affairs. And it all begins in the mind. Therefore, we must learn how to deal with our thoughts the instant they enter our minds – *before* they are entertained. For the longer they are entertained, the more we are at home with them. The more we are at home with them the harder they are to dismiss.

TEMPTING THOUGHTS

Don't you find that the harder you try *not* to think about something the more you actually *do* think about it?

This is why you must never leave a void in your mind. When you *do* dismiss a lustful thought, replace it with a wholesome one. Say to yourself, "I refuse to think about that. I will think about this instead." Then do it.

Think about your partner. Forget the quarrel you had last night. Instead, entertain only positive thoughts. Go back to your dating days if necessary and make a mental list of pleasing character traits and personal attributes. Think about some of the good times you have shared together. Even think about what you might do today to show your partner the extent of your love.

Physicians tell us that the mind, physically speaking, can focus on only one thought at any one instant of time. Assuming that statement is true, then if you are thinking about the virtues of your partner, you cannot possibly be thinking about anything else, not at that moment anyway. Practice this discipline long enough and you will eventually win the battle against your mind.

Neglect it and you will find yourself taking a series of very small steps from a thought entertained to an action committed. If you have ever been on a diet and, while trying to practice good discipline, were tempted to eat a piece of apple pie, you know exactly how subtle the steps are that lead from thoughts to actions.

"I just love apple pie," the dieter thinks. "I can't have any – doctor's orders, you know – but *I sure do love apple pie* . . .

"Maybe I'll make one. Not to eat, you understand. Just to smell. I'll make one for my family's dessert. They can eat it. I'll just smell it . . .

"There, a cup of sugar, a sprinkling of cinnamon, several pats of butter. Looks great! Into the oven she goes...

"The aroma...umm...like a magnet. It was worth making that pie just to smell it...

"Done! Gently now, lift it out carefully. Beautiful! And that smell...isn't it absolutely marvelous?...

"I wonder if it tastes as good as it smells. I don't dare take a bite...do I? Well...certainly won't hurt if I stick my fork in the middle and then lick it...

"Wow! That is the best pie I ever made. Maybe a small piece won't ruin my diet. I'll pass up my meat at dinner...

"That was fantastic! Now let me just trim up this side a bit...There...now the other side needs a little trimming too...

"Uh oh! I can't believe I ate the whole thing. I'd better wash that plate before anybody discovers it. Oh brother, I thought I had more control of myself than that..."

So it is with infidelity. The thought enters just as temptingly, is entertained just as subtly, and becomes translated into action just as readily as the thought of the dieter's apple pie. The best place to stop this seductive progression is with the first hint of temptation. Let's crawl into a couple of minds.

One day a husband, who has been a model of faithfulness, thinks to himself, "I wonder what my secretary's like in bed. I would never think of committing adultery, you understand. I'll just look...and appreciate...and imagine...and fantasize...

"The way she looked at me today...I wonder if she'd consider having dinner. There can't be any harm in just a dinner. I'll tell my wife I'm working late tonight.

"She really turns me on. Much more exciting than my wife. Maybe if I went over to her place..."

We'll let you end the progression in your mind. But then that's not really the end, is it? There's guilt and confession and lawyers and tears. And children with scars for a lifetime.

All because a thought was entertained instead of being dismissed.

Husbands are not the only ones capable of infidelity. Wives can fracture a relationship too. And the thought patterns are every bit as dangerous as the ones the husband entertains.

"That new salesman the boss hired yesterday is a real good-looker. I wonder if I can get him to notice me. Just 'notice,' you understand. I would never think of being unfaithful to my husband...

"Maybe if I wore my low-cut blouse to work tomorrow, I could get him to look at me...

"I *will* wear my low-cut blouse tomorrow. The routine in this office needs a little shaking up.

"Here I am world! Good...he's looking my way. I think he's noticed me. Here he comes. He really is handsome!

"He wants to go for dinner? Why not? There's no harm in having dinner. I could meet him the night my husband goes bowling..."

Infidelity happens just as subtly as this – with the entertainment of a thought you know is not right. Then it turns to action, often before you are ready to handle it. In no time at all your "innocent" flirting has turned into a full-fledged affair. And you are faced with the problem of how to extricate yourself from it.

THE HAZARDS OF INFIDELITY

Before you give in to these temptations, here is a warning. Infidelity has its hazards – more than the obvious ones like veneral disease or possible divorce.

Guilt
There is the hazard of guilt, that nagging feeling that follows you everywhere, especially into your bedroom and into the intimacy of your marriage relationship.

The feeling of being used

There is also the hazard of feeling you have been used – not for who you are but for what your sexual partner can get out of you. It will sweep over you at the most unexpected times with its unsettling, creeping feelings of disgust.

The risk of discovery

In addition, there is the hazard of unexpected exposure. We heard of a couple who were having a supposedly clandestine affair. The wife drove her husband to the plant for work each morning, then met her lover coming off the midnight shift. Why they chose the wife's small car for their lovemaking is beyond us, but that is what they did.

One morning while locked in a feverish embrace, the lover threw his back out of joint. He discovered he could not move. Neither could the unfaithful wife. After tapping on the window for some time, she finally caught the attention of a passerby.

How she explained her dilemma we do not know. But we do know the passerby ran to the nearest telephone and, as a result, what started out as a secret rendezvous ended up as a spectacle of flashing lights, sirens screeching, and two very embarrassed individuals. These words from the Bible proved all too true: "Be sure your sin will find you out." It will indeed – one way or another, sooner or later, here or there.

Insatiability

There is yet another hazard to infidelity – the frustration of insatiability. Those who are not sexually satisfied within the marriage relationship rarely find satisfaction outside it. That is why those who choose to be unfaithful often go from partner to partner to partner.

If you are presently seeing someone who is promising to leave his or her partner for you, do yourself a favor. Stop and ask, What makes me think that I in my turn won't get left for yet another lover? There is no security in infidelity – none.

There is no fulfillment either – at least not lasting fulfillment. For it is not in getting that we find satisfaction. It is in giving. So why not put aside any self-fulfilling notions you have been entertaining and give more of yourself to your partner? You will get more in return – that's guaranteed. What you get may not be what you think you should be getting. But it will be something of significance, something that contributes to making you a better person.

REPERCUSSIONS

There is another question that must be considered by those who are contemplating an extra-marital affair. When the affair is exposed – and it probably will be – how many lives will be affected by your indiscretion? Infidelity is like a stone dropped in a placid stream. The ripples get bigger and bigger until they reach the shores of the opposite bank. Every person who knows you or knows about you will be affected to some degree by your unfaithfulness.

Your partner will be hurt the most. He or she will start to come apart at the seams, frayed by your betrayal and wounded by your breach of trust. Your children too will be hurt, especially if the infidelity leads to divorce. But there are others you may not have considered. What about your parents, relatives, friends, business associates, and neighbors? What about your own good name in your church, in your community, or in your ministry (if you have one). What will *they* think about what you have done? "No man is an island." What each one of us does affects many, many lives.

GOD'S STANDARDS

There is one more question to ask. And for the Christian it is the most important of all: "What will God think if I have an affair?" Those who married in church took a vow before God and witnesses to be faithful to their partner as long as both lived. You are about to break that vow.

The sexual relationship is such that by God's design it

bonds the two people concerned in a way which changes their relationship and cannot be undone. What will God think about one who tries to "put asunder" what he has joined together?

One of the principles God gave his people for their good reads, "You must not commit adultery." In Old Testament times adultery was considered so serious a crime that the law demanded capital punishment. "But that is way back in the annals of history," we say. "Times have changed." Indeed they have. But has God's standard of morality changed? Find out before you decide to break it.

The New Testament teaches that God himself in the person of his Holy Spirit takes up residence in the life of every Christian. Our bodies are, to use the Bible's picture, his "temple." What will he think about the impurities we have brought to his dwelling place?

People will tell you that the polluting influence of a sexual relationship outside your marriage will do you no permanent harm. Some people said the same thing about environmental pollution, and look where that got us! It doesn't matter what people say. What matters is what is right. Infidelity will never be right, no matter how you may rationalize it. Come to grips with the facts as they are and stop playing a game where the stakes are so high. You're setting yourself up for a real disaster.

THE ROOT CAUSE

So much for how infidelity begins and what its hazards are. But what is its root cause?

The answer is selfism. It is the enemy of real marriage. When two people come together for the purpose of feeding their own egos, there is trouble from the beginning. Each partner goes his/her own way and does his/her own thing, regardless of how it affects the other. Many marriages break on this: two selfish people wanting to get, not give.

The desire for self-fulfillment is not all bad. It is a natural drive, common in everyone. It is only when the drive gets out of hand that there is a problem. When self-fulfillment becomes the reason for living instead of life's result, it has been misplaced.

When marriage works as it should, the result is a tremendous sense of personal fulfillment. But that comes not because we are striving to receive it but because we are working at giving it to our partners. Saint Francis of Assisi was imparting good advice when he observed, "It is in giving that we receive." When you live to give, you do receive. When you live to receive, you often don't – not anything of lasting significance.

The drive to satisfy self begins very early in life. The Minnesota Crime Commission reports: "Every baby starts life as a little savage. He is completely selfish and self-centered. He wants what he wants when he wants it – his bottle, his mother's attention, his playmate's toy, his uncle's watch. Deny these and he seethes with rage and aggressiveness, which would be murderous were he not so helpless."

Unfortunately this drive plagues the child throughout his growing up years. The words *I*, *me*, *my*, and *mine* are dominant in his vocabulary. Whether expressing inferiority ("I'm not good enough, have pity on me") or superiority ("I have made it, please notice me"), the emphasis is on the personal pronoun. In both cases he is saying, "I am living for myself. I have rights. Serve me, give me, fulfill me."

When a person comes to the realization of what selfism is, however, he faces a choice: give in to it or not? For example, in the process of selecting friends, do we choose those who will benefit us or those to whom we can contribute? At times like these it is advisable to remember a biblical proverb which reads, "Be with wise men and become wise. Be with evil men and become evil." Friends help shape our character so we need to choose them carefully.

Another decision point comes when we are faced with the accolades of personal success. It is very easy to cross that fine line from self assurance to arrogance. You may find yourself thinking, "I got to where I am because I worked at it. How much more is there out there for me? Do I want it whatever the cost? Or am I willing to be content with what I have?"

Entry into middle age presents its own special set of problems. It is then that you realize your grandest dreams may never be fulfilled. You begin to wonder if you can do anything really well. You also notice the effects of growing older. It is natural to wonder, "Am I still attractive at 45? Will someone still turn for another look?" You are particularly vulnerable at this stage because selfism has taken on a new approach. Whereas before it presented itself as "desires," now it is presenting itself as "needs." Will you allow yourself to be deceived or will you fight back?

Yet another decision point comes when we are faced with leisure time we don't know what to do with. How do we handle it? Do we spend our evenings watching soap operas on television? Do be wary of such forms of entertainment! These shows suggest that everybody and his uncle are out to satisfy their own personal desires, regardless of who gets hurt in the process. Furthermore, they present self-gratification as the "normal" way to live. An even more dangerous pastime is leafing through pornographic magazines. Such publications are designed for one predominate purpose: personal sexual arousal, selfism at its worst.

You can choose instead to spend your leisure time helping others. How many people do you know who could use a helping hand – the sick, the poor, the handicapped, the elderly, or the emotionally distressed? When you are busily involved in the lives of other people you don't have time to think about yourself.

We feel good about ourselves when we make the right choice. But how often is our choice the wrong one? It seems as if we are constantly battling the base desires within us. Even the apostle Paul, regarded by many to be one of the real saints of the ages, wrote of an inner battlefield: "I don't understand myself at all, for I really want to do what is right, but I can't. I do what I don't want to – what I hate. I know perfectly well that what I am doing is wrong, and my bad conscience proves that I agree with these laws I am breaking. But I can't help myself. . ."

The good news, however, is that Paul did gain victory. It began with his admission of failure. "I can't help myself," he had said. It was this admission that drove him to God. There he found the power to change and the resources to sustain his new life.

So it can be with us. We too can have a new beginning – one that can profoundly affect our marriage. It involves turning to God and asking him to give us higher desires, then putting those desires to work.

Let's begin afresh in our marriages. The best way to combat infidelity is with a strong outward look rather than a strong preoccupation with oneself. It is probably safe to say that many give in to the temptation of infidelity because of a dissatisfaction at home. They feel there is little to lose in having an extramarital affair. If this is true, we need to work more on building our marriages than we do on putting up our guards. If a marriage is on solid ground, then the temptations that come will be really no more than passing thoughts.

The basis for any good relationship is people – not deeds or misdeeds – but people. Love your partner for who he/she is and don't stop loving your partner for what he/she does or doesn't do. When a couple has been together a long time there is a tendency to take each other for granted. You say things you wouldn't say and do things you wouldn't do if you were newly married. Then your relationship was fresh; now you feel yourself getting stale. Then your partner was young; now he/she is showing signs of age.

Listen. Have you looked in the mirror lately? You too are growing older. Yet you are the same person you always were – with the same sensitivity and vulnerability. Do you want to be considered less than desirable? Realize your partner is going through some of the same struggles you are. You both need reassurance that you are loved, and constant reaffirmation that your love is growing deeper with the years. Help each other through the crises of middle age. Be there when needed to remind your partner of past successes and the lifetime of experiences that has made your marriage what it is. Take an inventory of everything for which you are thankful — and don't forget to mention each other. There are many partners who enter the later years alone.

Work at building up each other's self-esteem. Whereas selfism erodes marriage, healthy self-esteem builds it up. Accept yourselves for who you are and be content to build on that base. Avoid the extremes of both self-inflation, which makes a person out to be something he/she isn't, and self-deprecation, which dwells only on the negative. Be realistic. Adopt the healthy attitude that the apostle Paul had. Remember, he had weaknesses too, yet he said, "By the grace of God I am what I am." What a statement! It reflects not only self-acceptance but also gratitude for having found his worth in God.

It is in God's love that we can *all* find ourselves. That is why we keep emphasizing the importance of the vertical relationship. It helps us reach out properly on a horizontal plane. Remember to pray together too. It's pretty hard to cheat on someone with whom you have just joined in prayer.

And don't forget your sex life. It can get better as the years go by. Someone has suggested that having sex for the umpteenth time with your life partner is like rereading a very familiar book. Although the pages are not as fresh as they once were, there is a thrill in turning every one. Since you already know the end of the story, you can pay more attention to detail. But you still look forward to the climax. One of the best ways to combat the threat of infidelity is to make your sex life so exciting your partner doesn't have to look elsewhere for fulfillment.

RESTORATION

Suppose you are the guilty party in a marriage that has been torn by infidelity, and you want to make things right. What is your responsibility?

First, give up the relationship which is threatening your marriage. Don't just think about it. Do it! Then confess your indiscretion to your partner and ask for unconditional forgiveness. Strengthen your resolve by calling to mind all that has been good in the marriage, and by planning some special times together as soon as possible. From that point on give all your attention to your husband or wife. And take a vow before God never to let yourself get into such a mess again.

If you are the one who has been wronged by your partner, be ready to offer forgiveness. If any coldness or indifference on your part contributed to your partner's need to look elsewhere for fulfillment, ask him/her to forgive you. Then renew your vows and begin again. The goal of any breach within the marriage should be restoration.

Restoration will take work – lots of it. You must resolve not only never to discuss the issue once it's been forgiven, but also not to make your partner pay for hurting you. Who is up to such a task? Few of us. Again we need help from outside ourselves – the help God will give if we ask him.

Those who have gone to God with their problems testify to the way he is able to change their whole attitude: to replace hurt and bitterness with love. God does through them what they could never do without him. These are people who have received God's forgiveness for their own sins first and have then become channels for that same forgiveness, allowing it to flow through them to cover the sins of their partners. They know there can be forgiveness and covering for personal indiscretions, because they themselves have experienced it.

A GUARD AGAINST INFIDELITY

The best way to deal with infidelity, however, is to determine never to let it happen in the first place. Then you will not be pre-disposed to it. You will not be setting the stage for it to happen. And you will not be entertaining thoughts that could lead to actions you might be sorry for later.

If temptation does come – and it will – be prepared to say no and run. The Bible offers two examples of sexual temptation, and how those temptations were handled – one unsuccessfully and one successfully. King David was the unsuccessful one. Affluent, idle, and in the wrong place at the wrong time, he saw a woman bathing on a neighboring roof. I must have her, he thought. And he got her. After she informed him she was pregnant, he moved swiftly to have her husband killed in battle. But the baby born to them died. Quite a price to pay for a moment of indiscretion! Yet the price didn't stop with these physical hurts. The inner hurt was greater. Haunted, King David cried, "My sin is ever before me!" Was his momentary pleasure worth the cost? Only the king can answer.

The Hebrew teenager Joseph may have been a lot younger than the mighty King David, but he was certainly more in control of his own actions. Sold by jealous brothers into the strange land of Egypt, far enough away from home that "nobody would ever know," he was tempted to sleep with the wife of Potiphar, a high Egyptian official. Day after day she tried to seduce Joseph. One day, pressed almost to exasperation, Joseph fled, leaving his garment in the hands of the seductress. Frustrated, she cried, "Rape!" and Joseph was promptly thrown into prison. But Joseph knew inner peace.

Which of these two will you be? The one who got what he wanted when he wanted it – and paid dearly? Or the one who said no and had peace? Is there really a choice?

HOW DO YOU RATE?

1. If anything breaks up our marriage, it will probably be:
   ☐ *a job;* ☐ *a sport;* ☐ *a hobby;* ☐ *a consuming interest;* ☐ *an in-law problem;* ☐ *a romantic interest.*
2. Of all of the stage setters for infidelity to occur I would probably fall prey most easily to:☐ *forgetting how good I have it now that I'm married;* ☐ *having time on my hands;* ☐ *being wrapped up in myself;* ☐ *choosing the wrong companions.*

3. Of all of the repercussions of infidelity I would rate the following the most difficult to deal with: ☐ *personal guilt;* ☐ *the feeling of being used;* ☐ *the moment of exposure;* ☐ *the hurt my partner would experience;* ☐ *the hurt my children would endure;* ☐ *the guilt of having broken one of God's commandments.*

4. To keep infidelity from happening in my marriage I will: ☐ *be sensitive to my partner's needs;* ☐ *keep the lines of communication open;* ☐ *discipline my thoughts;* ☐ *shun compromising situations;* ☐ *get involved in activities where I'm helping others;* ☐ *consider the benefits of remaining faithful to my partner;* ☐ *review my wedding vows;* ☐ *review every motive that appears to benefit only myself.*

6

Establishing Roles and Responsibilities

Another great threat to modern marriages is the failure to establish roles and responsibilities. What a problem this can create. If it is not understood who is to do what or who is responsible for which area of the marriage, there will be trouble from the beginning. For example, who will make breakfast today? Will anybody? Who will fill up the car and get it serviced? Who will pay the bills and monitor the budget? Who will do the weekly food shopping or clean the house? Who will cut the lawn or trim the bushes? Who will be the primary breadwinner and who will stay home with the children? Will anyone?

FLEXIBILITY

It is important to remember that every situation is different. The fact that you will be deciding roles and responsibilities does not mean that you will be assigning first and second class positions. Nor does it mean that you will never be able to switch roles.

On the contrary. Because each role must be filled, each is equally important. But regardless of how you have agreed to divide responsibilities in your marriage, do stay flexible. Sometimes it is more important that a job gets done than it is who finally decides to do it.

INDIVIDUAL TALENTS

But how do you go about deciding what your roles and responsibilities should be? There are several important factors to consider.

First, take into consideration each partner's individual talents and areas of expertise. For example, whoever is gifted with figures or enjoys looking at numerals for long stretches of time should certainly pay the bills and balance the books. Your family's finances will be "safer" that way. Likewise, whoever is the best chef will probably be unanimously elected to cook the meals. The one with the flair for decorating will undoubtedly opt for that particular service. And the best bush trimmer will snip away at the shrubbery and delight everyone with his/her neatness and precision.

It is important to remember, however, that even if you are *not* the gifted one in any of these areas you not only support your partner in his/her responsibilities, but you also lend a hand now and then. Not only will you appreciate the role your partner is fulfilling but you may even like the experience of trial and error enough to take on the task seriously in the future.

EMOTIONAL MAKEUP

Next consider your emotional make-up. By nature, some people are more expressive and others more clinical. These differences readily show when it comes to decision making. Whereas some tend to bring feelings, tenderness, and tears to the bargaining table, others bring facts, a certain toughness, and a rather detached approach. Because of these natural differences some can more easily see the whole forest of ramifications while others get hung up on the trees. We need to learn how to complement each other as we fulfill our selected responsibilities.

CULTURAL MANDATES

Another consideration when choosing roles and responsibilities is the culture of which you are a part. Whereas in some cultures it is expected that the woman till the ground, in others that role falls to the man. Likewise, in some cultures the woman takes an assertive role in decision making and in others she is expected to be a silent witness to the process. But in all cultures women bear the children and are equipped by God to nourish them. So the role of child rearing has traditionally fallen to them. Almost every culture, however, produces some who examine the constraints they find themselves in and decide to break out of the mold.

In biblical times women had no education and therefore limited qualifications to do much outside the home. There were, however, a few women who rose to importance in spite of the confines of their culture. One was Deborah, a prophetess who assumed the position of judge and along side of Barak led the Israelites in a successful campaign against their oppressors the Canaanites. Another was the woman in Proverbs who symbolizes the ideal for women everywhere. In addition to carrying out her domestic duties, she "buys imported foods...goes out to inspect a field and buys it... plants a vineyard...and makes belted linen garments to sell to the merchants." She is wise as well as practical – earning respect within and outside the family.

In the New Testament we find Jesus running counter to the culture of the time and giving women an equal place with men. It is Christianity that has given women the position they rightly deserve. Despite some lamentable failures it is still true to say that everywhere Christianity has spread, a more liberating attitude toward women has followed. Today in most of the western world the woman can pursue a good education, be afforded equal rights and privileges, enjoy freedom of expression, be genuinely appreciated for who she is, and command respect for what she has accomplished.

EQUALITY

In God's sight men and women are created "equal." They come from the same stuff and carry the same potential.

Neither can boast superiority over the other – not in intelligence nor in ability. Both exhibit certain strengths and, if pressed, have to admit to certain weaknesses. Both have intrinsic worth – to God and to each other. Both are entitled to develop their gifts and talents. In other words, both have a claim on the meaningful life. But both also have a real dependency (whether they realize it or not). They need to love and be loved.

THE MERGER

It is this dependency that drives them to establish meaningful relationships, the most intimate of which is marriage. In marriage those whom God created "male and female" take a vow to merge their lives. They become "one flesh," as the Bible says – a term which suggests that after they make the physical union they are, in a sense, incomplete without the other.

This in no way suggests that single persons cannot be whole people in themselves. They can be. And they will be – up until they decide to get married. Once the physical merger of sexual union takes place, they can never again be complete in themselves in the same sense they were before the union. The most intimate part of each partner has been joined with the most intimate part of the other. They are now in a sense "incomplete" without each other. Perhaps this explains to a certain degree the tremendous sense of loss that is experienced in either the death of a partner or divorce. Part of yourself is gone.

The idea of "one flesh" also connotes a mutual ownership. In a sense each partner becomes the "peculiar property" of the other, with certain claims on each other's time, talent, and love. But with the claims come responsibility – weighty responsibility. Someone now belongs to you – someone who needs love, protection, sensitivity, and concern. Some people take better care of their cars (or boats or pets) than they do of their partners in marriage – a sad commentary indeed.

When two persons merge in marriage they are required

to make a life-changing decision. They are asked to take their talents, which up to this time may have been used primarily for personal satisfaction, and invest them in the growth of the merger. They must yield their strengths to cover each other's weaknesses and not mind becoming vulnerable when the warts of their own personalities begin to show. But most important of all, they must be willing to give up certain individual rights, to surrender certain personal claims, and from this point on to share each other's responsibilities. They must decide, in essence, to surrender their own freedom that their partner might enjoy his/hers.

Before marriage you are an entity unto yourself, the king or queen of your own domain. Without consulting anyone you are free to choose the clothes you wear, the food you eat, the type of home you live in, the company you work for, the entertainment you enjoy, the way you worship, and the schedule you keep.

But when you marry, there is someone else involved in each of these decisions. It is usually a jolt to discover that your ties or earrings are being selected *for* you. And early on, you are struck with the awareness that the menu has to satisfy the tastes of two of you (no more peanut-butter sandwiches or canned soup). The selection of home furnishings must receive dual input too. Two schedules now have to be dove-tailed into each other. Any decision to change jobs must be reviewed together. Also where you will worship and what type of entertainment you will enjoy is a decision for the double-unit. The key to making it work is mutual submission, each partner in deference to the other.

MUTUAL SUBMISSION

What is "mutual submission"? Perhaps it will help to determine first what it is not. Mutual submission is not the arbitrary dominance of one person over the other. Nor is it a grovelling subservience of one to the other. While in "submission," no one is required to become a slave or a martyr. Nor is anyone called upon to offer him/herself as a doormat to be walked all over. And certainly it does not mean the disparagement of any one sex.

Quite the contrary, mutual submission is a give and take relationship, an affectionate, voluntary subjection. It means putting the other person first, weighing his/her desires and being sensitive to his/her needs. It means bearing the other's burdens, rendering assistance when needed, and lending support to the achievement of your loved one's goals.

This may take sacrifice, but personal sacrifice is what mutual submission is all about. Its pattern is in the kind of love Jesus Christ displayed when he was willing to go to the cross to ensure a meaningful life to those who follow him. The apostle Paul exhorts, "Honor Christ by submitting to each other...And you husbands, show the same kind of love to your wives as Christ showed to the church when he died for her..."

So you suffer a little as you give up, give in, and give out. The result is worth it. You will find yourself establishing a duality of partnership that cannot come any other way. You will have strived toward a more intimate union and succeeded.

ESTABLISHING PRIORITIES

Before roles and responsibilities can be properly established, priorities need to be set. Some good principles to remember might be these:

1. God deserves first place in your life.
2. You can't effectively meet the needs of others until you personally "get it all together."
3. Put the needs of your family before the demands of work, community, or church.
4. When your home is in order, you are ready to branch out into your world.

Any disruption of this order will bring chaos to your life. For example, leave God out of the picture or make him an asterisk to your plans and nothing you do will really count in the long run. Get so involved in the needs of your family and friends that you neglect your own needs and you will soon find you have nothing left to contribute. Take on the concern of others at the expense of your husband, wife, or family and you'll run the risk of losing your marriage and your home.

When faced with a decision about how many activities to become involved in, we suggest the following personal inventory:

1. Can I take on this added responsibility without neglecting my own personal development?
2. Can I take on this added responsibility without neglecting my husband, wife, or my children?
3. Can I take on this added responsibility and still keep my home in order?
4. How will I feel at the end of every day? Fulfilled? or frazzled?

Some people can handle more responsibility than others. Just remember as you make your decisions to keep people primary. They are more important than money, prestige, or power. And don't be deceived by the lure of the business world or the promise that your sense of identity will come from career achievement. It comes from inside yourself. A sense of personal significance begins where you are, right inside your soul. And with it comes inner confidence, self-knowledge, and a personal settling. So work out your relationship to God first, your relationship to your husband/wife and children next, and *then* branch out into a wider world.

Once you have established personal priorities you are ready to decide how your home will be run. Because of the personal assessment you have taken, and the demands of each of your lives, you will find yourselves falling into certain functions. This difference in function is absolutely necessary to the establishment of a harmonious home. It will help give structure to what may become a confused "battle of the bosses." Create a framework in which you are comfortable, then move within that established framework. If a role needs to be changed, feel free to change it. If not, be thankful things are running smoothly and fulfill the roles you have chosen and the responsibilities you have been given to the best of your ability.

NECESSITIES

In addition to house cleaning, cooking, taking out the trash, cutting the grass, maintaining the car, and a myriad of other routine tasks that have to be performed in every home, there are others, much more weighty, that should be addressed. They include such things as teaching moral values, praying for family needs, and caring for family members.

Teaching moral values

It is important that each family member becomes aware that he/she is part of an onflowing stream of history, both as a receiver of that history and as a vehicle through which it will continue to flow. Individuals receive from their parents and will impart to their children certain distinctives. These include recognizable physical traits and unmistakable tendencies. But even more important are the cultural traditions, family history, and moral values that come with belonging.

King David of old had a good sense of his responsibility in the flow of generations. He said:

"Oh my people, listen to my teaching... For I will show you lessons from our history, stories handed down to us from former generations. I will reveal these truths to you so that you can describe these glorious deeds of Jehovah to your children, and tell them about the mighty miracles he did. For he gave his laws to Israel, and commanded our fathers to teach them to their children, so that they in turn could teach their children too. Thus his laws pass down from generation to generation."

What a beautiful way to guarantee the survival of family history, family traditions, and moral values. Make sure it happens in your family, even if there are only two of you.

Praying for family needs
Another task that needs to be performed is praying for family needs. We have already addressed praying with your partner as a means of fostering closer communion. Now we want to address praying *for* your partner and for other family members. This type of prayer is for the purpose of bringing family needs to God. The book of Job speaks of the ancient patriarch as "getting up early in the morning and offering a burnt offering for each of (his children). For Job said, 'Perhaps my sons have sinned and turned away from God in their hearts!' This was Job's regular practice." How wonderful to make it our regular practice too – to show God how concerned we are for those we love.

Caring for the family
A third task that needs doing is caring for those who are under your roof. Although this certainly entails such expressions of love as administering medicine to the sick or rubbing the feet of the weary, it means much, much more. It means listening for words both spoken and unspoken, being accessible no matter how busy you are, being willing to offer advice in the difficult process of decision making, imparting discipline when necessary but doing so in love, making sacrifices of time and self and doing so willingly, and providing a place of safety where every family member is free to be himself – warts and all. That means accepting each individual just as he is now, not after he has proven himself. It also means forgiveness for every demeanor, no matter how great the offense. These are weighty roles indeed but to establish a home that runs smoothly they have to be performed.

To make all these tasks meaningful there has to be a proper atmosphere in the home. To help Christians build harmonious family relationships the apostle Peter wrote:

"You should be like one big happy family, full of sympathy toward each other, loving one another with tender hearts and humble minds. Don't repay evil for evil. Don't snap back at those who say unkind things about you. Instead, pray for God's help for them, for we are to be kind to others, and God will bless us for it."

Send your partner off to work with joy and your children off to school with a sense of well being. Welcome each other at the end of the day with genuine concern and a desire to become involved in each other's world. And make the time you do spend together the stuff from which memories are made.

HEADSHIP

You may be asking at this point, "What if all these tasks don't get done? Whose fault is it?"

The fault lies with both of you, of course, because these are joint responsibilities. However, the ultimate accountability lies with the husband. He is the "head of the home," and as such is accountable to God for order in his home. It does not necessarily follow that if the husband is accountable for jobs getting done, then he himself must do them. That is as absurd as saying that the head of a corporation must do the work of the entire company. On the contrary, it is his responsibility to see that the jobs are delegated. Whoever carries out a responsibility the best should be the one who does it most regularly. It is the husband's function to see that each job is effectively carried out by *somebody* but not necessarily by himself.

Headship also does not connote tyranny. No husband has the right to become a fire-breathing dragon. Some husbands, especially those who take biblical passages out of context, ride the concept of headship for all it is worth – and more. They exaggerate it to mean power, oppression, and the license to abuse. What a sad misinterpretation of biblical authority. When the Bible speaks of man as being "head of the home" it compares the position with the one Christ has as "head of the church." Being a "head" is then defined as being a "savior," a humble servant, one who is willing to lay down his life for his bride. A husband who wants to be true to biblical principles will give and give and give again – till there's no more left to give.

The husband who has a proper view of headship is not threatened by his wife's abilities. In fact, he appreciates them and actively nourishes them. What is important to him is not any outward status she may attain but the inward status of a stable relationship. If she wants to pursue a career or become involved in a ministry, he encourages her, provided the timing is right and they agree on their priorities. And you may need that second income!

When it comes to decision making, there must be a dual effort. Each partner not only has a right to put in his/her two cents, but also a responsibility to listen carefully to the other's line of reasoning. Since the decision affects both of you it has to be made with the interest of both of you in mind. If in the process of talking things out there is a "draw," there must be some pre-determined structure to pull the decision makers out of the stalemate they find themselves in. It is at times like these that you become grateful for the concept of headship. The husband should make the decision. But he should make it with the interest of his wife foremost. What a responsibility goes with headship!

The wife has a responsibility in return. In the same biblical passage that tells the husband to "love his wife as part of himself," there is the following admonition: "The wife must see to it that she deeply respects her husband – obeying, praising, and honoring him." If she does her job as she is supposed to, then she is qualified to teach the younger women to "love their husbands and their children, spending their time in their own homes, being kind and obedient to their husbands, so that the Christian faith can't be spoken against by those who know them."

The apostle Peter echoes the admonitions of the apostle Paul with an added emphasis: it is the godly wife's behavior that will speak louder to her unbelieving husband than her preaching. "Wives, fit in with your husband's plans; for then if they refuse to listen when you talk about the Lord, they will be won by your respectful, pure behavior . . . Be beautiful inside, in your hearts, with the lasting charm of a gentle and quiet spirit which is so precious to God." A woman who so responds is truly fulfilling the functions she was originally designed for: to be a "helper suited to (her husband's) needs."

The conclusion of the matter, then, is that although men and women are equal in essence, they are different in function. One is to serve as a head while the other supplies a support structure. Together they form a partnership within which they are free to choose their own roles and responsibilities. While fulfilling these duties they remain flexible, submitting to each other "in the same way (they) submit to the Lord."

As you are reviewing all this remember two things: God ordains the functions (headship or support) and he does so according to sex. But *you* determine how you will carry out your functions and you do so according to personal ability (roles and responsibilities). Remember too, when you are newly married, some of these roles and responsibilities may seem strange. So give space to your partner to grow. Give space to yourself too.

HOW DO YOU RATE?

1. In our home roles are: □ *well established;* □ *flexible;* □ *interchangeable;* □ *totally undetermined.*
2. We have assigned our roles according to: □ *individual talents;* □ *respective physical, emotional, or spiritual make-up;* □ *cultural dictates;* □ *Biblical principles;* □ *all of the above.*
3a. I discuss moral values with my children: □ *frequently;* □ *occasionally;* □ *never.*
  b. I pray for my family: □ *frequently;* □ *occasionally;* □ *never.*
  c. I do the following:
      □ *listen for words spoken and unspoken*
      □ *try to be accessible to hear problems*
      □ *am willing to offer advice when asked*
      □ *impart discipline in love*
      □ *make sacrifices of time and self*

☐ *allow family members to be themselves*
☐ *accept family members just as they are*
☐ *forgive family members readily*

4. Put the following in the order of priority in which they occur in your life:

☐ *self*   ☐ *neighbors*
☐ *God*   ☐ *job*
☐ *children*   ☐ *church*
☐ *partner*   ☐ *hobbies and interests*

5. Now put them in the order in which you feel they should occur in your life:

6. In our home loving deference to the other's desires is practiced: ☐ *frequently;* ☐ *occasionally;* ☐ *never.*

7. In our roles and responsibilities we are: ☐ *supportive;* ☐ *satisfied;* ☐ *disenchanted;* ☐ *in need of improvement.*

7

Building a Successful Partnership

Have you ever seen a successful partnership in which each member determines to do his/her own thing, and to do so whenever he/she feels like it? Of course not. Yet how many marriages try to run on that same principle? It will never work. We must present a unified front to our critics (and there are many critics of marriage), adopting the same goals, striving together to meet those goals, and taking time every so often to evaluate our efforts and to see whether or not we are succeeding.

For a partnership to succeed there is usually one dominant contributing factor: teamwork. Both partners are doing their best, not for individual victory but for the victory of the two of them together. Marriage is like that. It is togetherness all the way. It is walking through life hand in hand, stopping to lift the one who falls and picking up speed as your strides are synchronized. It is sharing each other's defeats and rejoicing over each other's victories. It is mutual submission and exaltation, mutual sacrifices and praise. Self glory is subordinated to the achievements of the partnership, self fulfillment to fulfillment as a couple.

How do you take two people who come from entirely different backgrounds and who have diverse talents and abilities and make them into a partnership like that? Not easily. It takes practice – years and years of practice.

STEPPING OUT ON YOUR OWN

One of the first challenges is becoming independent of parental influence. The Bible speaks of "leaving" parents before there can be a "cleaving" to husband or wife. From observation of others and from personal experience we know this leaving must take place not only physically but emotionally and spiritually as well. Then the cleaving to each other can fill the voids of the leaving in your respective lives.

Physical leaving
When you decide to get married, it is best to make plans to move out of your parents' home. Because of the financial burdens many young couples face today, this may seem impossible. But it is better to scrimp and save to support yourselves in one tiny room that is away from your parents, than to start your married life well catered for and free of charge, in their home. You need to set up a home of your own right away, breaking the pattern of proximity to them. You must realize that you are now independent, a separate entity from those who brought you to this point.

Emotional leaving
Some couples manage to leave their parents physically but fail to do so emotionally. Even though they now have partners to help share their burdens, they still go to their parents when they need a shoulder to cry on. Some even try to cling both to their parents *and* to their husband or wife. Even though they may have moved some distance from home, there is probably a telephone at their fingertips, a car in their garage – even a plane at a nearby airport. When feelings need to be shared the first thing they think of is their parents. Can you imagine how this makes the partner feel? Don't let it happen to you. Failure to leave your parents emotionally can drive a real wedge between you and your husband/wife.

Spiritual leaving

You also need to leave your home spiritually. A Christian couple needs to find their own place of worship, to determine their own church involvement, and to develop their own prayer and study time as a couple. You may want to visit several different churches before you settle into one. Since the two of you probably come from different religious backgrounds anyway, choosing a new church where you are both comfortable will help prevent the feeling that one has imposed his/her religion upon the other. If you come from a warm and enthusiastic spiritual background, you are very fortunate. But now is the time to make that heritage really your own.

It is hard to leave a family that has been involved in your whole life. If either partner is "tied to Mama's apronstrings," then leaving will be doubly hard. But it *must* occur if the marriage is going to survive.

By "leaving" we do not mean that you are never to visit your parents again, never to ask their advice, never to tell them you love them. On the contrary, you should visit, seek the wisdom only they can offer, and show them your love in many tangible ways.

"Leaving" is not severing all contact with your parents. "Leaving" is severing the old dependent relationship with them and realizing it can never be that way again. You, as well as they, must come to grips with the fact that you are now an adult, responsible for establishing your own home, planning your own activities, and making your own decisions. It is true that leaving your parents can cause a physical, emotional, and spiritual void in your life, but it is also true that cleaving to your partner will fill that physical, emotional, and spiritual void.

THE OTHER SIDE OF THE COIN

When children leave home to go out on their own, they are not the only ones who experience a void. Their parents do too, perhaps even more so.

We'll never forget the precious moments we shared as a family when our oldest son left home to set up on his own. Upon finishing college, he secured a job 500 miles from us. He was thrilled with the possibilities of an exciting future, and so were we. But that didn't make his leaving any easier.

When the big day came, we made sure we were both home. Slowly the clock ticked away while everybody did "routine things," trying not to focus on what we all knew was inevitable. Finally the hour of departure arrived. Into the car went all his belongings – not much, but everything he owned: a trumpet, a stereo, some books, and a sleeping bag. On his head went a baseball cap, and then he shot out a hand to meet his father's. He said only one word, "Bye," but that said it all. Father and son grabbed each other in a tight hug, unashamedly letting their love spill out. Then we prayed together for God's guidance, protection, and blessing.

God answered those prayers. Our son made it safely to his destination, found himself an apartment, spread his sleeping bag on the floor and began to set up housekeeping. In due time his engagement period ran out and the girl of his dreams became his wife. Now he had someone to share the void that was caused when he made the break from us.

This experience taught us something we wish we had known when we were starting out as a couple. We wish we had realized that someday we too would be left, we too would become in-laws, we too would have to settle back and watch another generation start out. This is never easy, because the kids that are getting married today seem so much younger than we were. How can they possibly handle life? But we did, didn't we? And just in case you think you were mature when you started out, get out those wedding photographs and take a look at how young you really were!

WHERE TO SPEND THE HOLIDAYS?

In the course of teaching a class of young married couples several years ago, we asked each of them to tell us what they considered to be the greatest hurdle of their first year together. Can you guess? It was the problem of where to spend the holidays.

Each partner is filled with sweet memories of special family traditions that now have to be incorporated with the other partner's traditions and made their own.

Although it is perfectly all right to continue to fit into your parents' festivities for a while after you are married, you should start planning for the time when your marriage has turned into a family and you won't always "go home" for the holidays. What will you do then? That can be an even bigger problem than the one facing you when you are newlyweds. Team up for the holidays and plan on making them uniquely yours.

GETTING THE PARTNERSHIP TOGETHER

Forming a partnership means sacrifice, a real "giving" kind of love. It is the kind of love that pours out until it hurts, the kind of love that has the other person's interests at heart.

Husbands, do you know anything of this kind of love? Test yourself. Have you ever given up a night out with the boys to stay home with the children so that your wife can have *her* night out with the girls? Have you ever given up your Saturday round of golf to clean out the basement in preparation for a garage sale? Do you ever relieve your wife of the baby's night feedings, or is this *too* great a sacrifice to ask for? Remember, the baby belongs to *both* of you, not just to its mother. Do you help with the washing up after meals, or ever prepare the meal yourself? Although partners usually perform those functions for which they are best equipped, they are not above filling in for the other member when there is a real need. And it's a debatable point who's best equipped for washing dishes!

Wives, how are you doing as a partner? Do you ever mow the lawn, change the oil in the car, or help with the family business? Maybe performing some of these functions is a routine practice for you. If so, great. You are contributing to the welfare of the partnership, doing what needs to be done regardless of whose "job" it is to do it. And chances are, you have a good feeling about the contribution you are making.

Enjoying chores together

Helping each other with the housework gets the work done, and at the same time makes it a lot more fun and rewarding. You can choose separate tasks if you want to, but some can be accomplished together. Take the task of window washing. One of you could do the outside, while the other does the inside. That way you can smile at each other through the glass! Or if you are washing down the bathroom tiles, you can start back to back and then meet face to face as you move around the room. Painting and decorating, too, can be companionable team jobs. Some great discussions can be had when you work in close quarters like this.

Take your partnership outside too. One of you can rake the leaves while the other bags them. One can trim the shrubs while the other picks up the clippings. Or both can paint the house together perched on ladders side by side. Not only is it fun to work together, but you get a feeling of having accomplished something together.

Parenting together

Perhaps the greatest challenge of your dedication to together-ness will be childrearing. Who will change the baby *this* time? Who will get out from under the warm covers for the two o'clock bottle tonight? Of course, if you are breast-feeding, there is no question as to who will make the move.

If you are the one to volunteer, think of the marvelous adventure awaiting you. You will have the thrill of heating the bottle to room temperature, of testing the milk on the inside of your wrist to see if you did your job correctly, of positioning the nipple inside those hungry lips, of trying to keep your eyes open until the last drop is gone, of gently rubbing the baby's back, and then watching in horror as the whole meal comes back up. Oh the agonies of shared parenting! But it's worth it when you see that little tyke look up at you and grin. You can go from agony to ecstasy in a second. Don't miss either emotion.

Having fun together

Athletics is another area where togetherness can be promoted. Play tennis together, go golfing together, bowl together, or go jogging together. Once you have completed the chores of the day you need a little time for relaxation. Let your emotions loose. Have fun. But do it together.

Entertaining is another thing that you can have a lot of fun doing together. One way to show your friends that you are a partnership is by opening your home to them. It is fun to cooperate in tidying up the house and preparing the food, then serving your guests and doing the dishes afterwards. But perhaps the most fun of all is entering into the dinner conversation together.

Making decisions together

The partnership however, does not apply only to physical activities. It applies to mental activities as well. Working together as partners is essential in the decision-making process. Take, for example, the following decisions that you'll most likely face at some time during your marriage: what job to take, what home to buy, whether or not the wife should work, what school to select for the children, how much insurance to carry, even where to go on a vacation. Although the husband is ultimately responsible for the decision that is made, he does not make it alone. You two are in this thing called marriage together. So both of you need to learn how to express your feelings freely. Your thinking, emotional reactions, and perspectives on life are bound to be different. That's good. When both sides of an issue are evaluated, a better decision can be made. So challenge each other's reasoning and point out faulty logic. Then make your decision and abide by it.

Budgeting your money

Another area where cooperation is vital is the area of budgeting and finance. Determine how much money will be left after taxes, savings, and giving are taken out, then budget a certain amount for each fixed expense (like rent, mortgage or goods bought by instalment) and for each estimated expense (like food, housekeeping, heat, electricity, clothing, and entertainment). Don't forget to put aside some money for emergencies. Once you have determined how much you can spend, stay within the budget. Neither of you has the freedom to splurge without consulting your husband/wife. You are a partnership, remember?

Planning your purchases

Work as a partnership, too, in making your purchases. Major expenditures like carpets, curtains, and furniture take a lot of planning and a fair amount of looking until the right item appears for what you can afford. Choosing together is fun, and very satisfying. Where tastes differ you'll look for things you both like. And you'll talk about the kind of values your home will express. Is cost what matters most, or looks, or durability? Do you want a home to impress your visitors or to spell out welcome and relaxation?

But shopping for smaller items like clothing can also be a cooperative effort. If, for example, your wife is better at matching fabrics and colors than you are, then ask her advice on shirts, ties, and socks. If your husband has an eye for what looks best on you, weigh his advice very carefully.

Dressing on a modest budget does not mean looking drab. Even on the tightest budget you can look good. Frequent the discount stores or the charity shops, or wait for the sales in the regular stores. Then make your selection carefully, remembering that anything you wear on the outside is meant to compliment your personality on the inside. So choose your clothing the way an artist chooses a frame on his painting. He looks for something that will bring out the best in his creation, never anything overpowering or distracting. If an artist overhears a viewer say, "Wow! Look at that frame," he knows he has made an error in judgment. So rely upon your partner to guide you as to what looks best on you.

Growing spiritually

Commit yourselves to spiritual maturity. If you have found a church you feel comfortable in, get involved. As you choose your areas of service, make sure you choose to do at least one activity together. Sing in the church choir, work in the nursery, teach a Sunday school class, or open your home to a group. Don't get so involved with others, however, that you forget your growth as a couple. Read the Bible together; share a challenging book. Then discuss what you have read. You will love the peace and confidence this brings to your marriage, and the deepening oneness.

Getting involved in the community

Many couples today want to get involved in their community. Do you? Together, you may get involved in helping with local elections, serving in the parent-teacher organization, or petitioning for worthwhile causes. In a world of shifting values (morally, educationally, and politically), we need couples of strong moral convictions willing to work together, making an impact for what they believe.

There is a need for people to stand up and be counted on moral issues, to say: "We are concerned about what you are teaching our children. We are concerned about what our theaters are showing and our local stores are selling. We are concerned! Furthermore, we are willing to do whatever we can to restore solid values to our community. We are available for service." There is a need for more voices like that. But those voices will count for much more if they are backed up by the way we live. If you are going to get involved in your community, you will certainly need to practice what you preach, both personally and as a couple.

DOING YOUR OWN THING

Pause for a moment to let us introduce you to a free-thinking modern couple. Like many of their peers, they fell in love, in due time they got married, and now they are in the process of setting up housekeeping. They share the same apartment, share their take-home pay, and even share the same name, but that is where their sharing ends.

Each day they go their separate ways. The wife is working at the same job that she had when she was single, still working the same long hours, still missing the evening meal at home. On Tuesday night she rushes directly to her pottery class. And on Thursday night she does her aerobics.

Her husband's schedule only adds to the problem. His business trips take him out of town a couple of nights a week. When he *is* home, he is often home by himself, for his wife is busy pursuing her own interests. On Saturdays when the two of them could be together as a couple, he plays golf. He has *always* played golf on Saturdays. He would think of doing nothing else. This attitude is a carry-over from his carefree single days. On Sundays they go to church together, but by then the companionship is empty. They are not really one in spirit because they haven't allowed themselves the opportunity to develop a spirit of unity all week long.

Commitment to companionship is vital in any marriage. The married male must realize that when he takes on the responsibility of a wife, some of his "single" activities may have to go (unless, of course, his wife likes to play golf or tennis or racquetball). The married woman should ask herself not, "How can *I* develop *my* potential as a person?" but "How can *we* develop *our* potential as a couple?" If there are problems in this area, they should be discussed.

If you want to build a lasting marriage, social activities, athletic activities, personal development activities, and religious activities should be enjoyed as a couple if possible. This is not to say that you can never have a night out with the boys/girls, or that you can never take a class in basket-weaving, music appreciation or real estate. But only with the support and approval of your partner.

MEALTIMES TOGETHER

Arrange your schedules so that you can eat together. The dinner hour is one of the focal points of true companionship. Establish a mutual dinner hour right at the onset of your marriage and then guard it jealously throughout the years. With the entrance of children, companionship around the dinner table can be easily stolen by music lessons, sports, scout activities, and a host of other things – all of which compete with the business trips of one parent and the business appointments of the other.

RESERVING YOUR INDIVIDUALITY

Togetherness, of course, can be overdone. You never want to get to the place where you are driving each other crazy by always tagging along. Nor do you want to lose your own individuality or your own interests. If the concept of partnership is functioning properly, you won't. You will find that the encouragement you receive *from* your partner and the sacrifice you make *for* your partner will make you a better person. The members of a partnership can blossom as individuals as a result of their togetherness.

So get busy organizing your partnership today. Make an effort to be more supportive of the activities your partner is already pursuing as an individual. Also choose an activity you have never participated in as a couple and try it. You may find you like it. In fact, you may discover a whole new world of adventure just waiting for you to become part of it. But as you are contemplating all of this, a word to the wise: when you think of the opportunities open to you, think "ours" instead of "mine"; and when you receive praise for something you have done, let it go to "us" instead of "me."

This way you will experience the ultimate satisfaction that togetherness has to offer.

Sometimes such oneness takes years to develop, probably because people by nature seem to be obsessed with self-promotion and self-fulfillment. Certainly our culture encourages this philosophy. But the more you experience the joy of "giving that another might receive," the more you begin to realize that this is what life is really all about: not gathering but giving, not accumulating but dispensing, not waiting for others to sacrifice for you but sacrificing for them – whether that sacrifice is appreciated or not.

A couple who have grown together over the years are like glowing embers on a hearth. Side by side they draw from the warmth of each other's presence. The intensity of their original fire may come and go, but the glow continues – warm, soft, and very, very constant. If the embers are thrust apart, the warmth quickly dies. And if one is used to spark a new fire elsewhere, it will be consumed in the flame. But close together the coals feed one another's life. They will keep on glowing for a long, long time, as long as the tiniest spark endures.

HOW DO YOU RATE?

1. I feel I have left my parents' home: ☐ *physically*; ☐ *emotionally*; ☐ *spiritually*; ☐ *none of the above*; ☐ *all of the above*.
2. My relationship with my parents now that I am married is: ☐ *poor*; ☐ *fair*; ☐ *good*; ☐ *excellent*.
3. My relationship with my in-laws is: ☐ *poor*; ☐ *fair*; ☐ *good*; ☐ *excellent*.
4. When I hurt, I go first to my: ☐ *partner*; ☐ *friend*; ☐ *pastor*; ☐ *parents*; ☐ *God*.
5. My partner and I participate in: ☐ *no*; ☐ *few*; ☐ *many*; ☐ *all activities together*.
6. We function as a team in: ☐ *housework*; ☐ *outdoor work*; ☐ *childrearing*; ☐ *athletics*; ☐ *entertaining*;

☐ *decision-making;* ☐ *budgeting money;* ☐ *making purchases;* ☐ *spiritual growth;* ☐ *community involvement;* ☐ *educational pursuits;* ☐ *career;* ☐ *all of the above;* ☐ *none of the above.*

7. I pursue the following activities alone: ☐ *housework;* ☐ *outdoor work;* ☐ *childrearing;* ☐ *athletics;* ☐ *entertaining;* ☐ *decision-making;* ☐ *budgeting money;* ☐ *making purchases;* ☐ *spiritual growth;* ☐ *community involvement;* ☐ *educational pursuits;* ☐ *career;* ☐ *other.*

8. My partner pursues the following activities alone: ☐ *housework;* ☐ *outdoor work;* ☐ *childrearing;* ☐ *athletics;* ☐ *entertaining;* ☐ *decision-making;* ☐ *budgeting money;* ☐ *making purchases;* ☐ *spiritual growth;* ☐ *community involvement;* ☐ *educational pursuits;* ☐ *career;* ☐ *other.*

9. In the future I would like to join my partner in the following activity:

8

The Spice of Life – Those Little Things

It is the little things in life that make or break a marriage. While we may handle major crises quite effectively, no one is above falling apart at minor annoyances. A rush to the local emergency room may find us calm and collected. Yet once we're back home trying to recover and are interrupted by the family dog, barking feverishly to be let outside, we yell our frustration at the cowering animal and would kick him through the door if we could. What complex beings we humans are!

Recognizing our weaknesses, however, can be the first step in dealing with them. Just waking up each morning and reminding ourselves that "What I say, how I act, and how I react will make a difference in the kind of marriage I am building" will begin to interject a partner-consciousness into our relationship. This partner-consciousness, a moment-by-moment awareness that your partner is there – with his or her special needs – is a necessary ingredient in any lasting marriage.

COMMON COURTESY

One way to establish partner-consciousness is to seize opportunities to practice common courtesy in word and deed. Unfortunately, courtesy is one of those niceties that often ends with the courtship and never finds its way into actual marriage. Once our vows are exchanged, a strange thing happens. We start taking our partner for granted. Consciously or subconsciously, we think, "He/she will always be there no matter what kind of treatment I dish out." How sad! And what a lie we're using to deceive ourselves. It doesn't take any more to break a marriage than it does to break a camel's back – just one straw too many. That's all. Just a straw.

We often treat our guests with more courtesy than we treat the members of our family. For example, when a guest spills a cup of coffee all over our clean white tablecloth, we say, "Think nothing of it, my dear, I'll have it cleaned up in a jiffy." When, however, a family member spills coffee on the same tablecloth (assuming we even use a tablecloth for family), we retort, "Clumsy! What's wrong with you? Why can't you be more careful?"

Words

As you can see, the words that we speak are some of the "little things" that must be monitored very carefully. They have the power either to destroy a relationship or to build it up – and to do so in a very short period of time. The frightening thing is that words are ours to control. We can let them out, keep them in, or change them. And the choice we make may determine the course our marriage takes.

Someone wisely said, "Before you speak a word, you are its master. After you speak a word, it is *your* master." How true! How many of us have spent hours, even days, trying to ease the hurt that a hastily spoken word has inflicted? Scientists tell us that the average person speaks about 30,000 words a day. Indeed, some of us do better than average! No matter how you compare to that average, in your lifetime you will speak a staggering number of words. And words are a bit like toothpaste. They come out in a torrent, but they're almost impossible to get back in.

Perhaps that is why King David of the Old Testament prayed, "Help me, Lord, to keep my mouth shut and my lips sealed." Perhaps that is why our mothers advised us, "Think before you speak." And perhaps that is why the Bible warns, "A man's heart determines his speech. A good man's speech reveals the rich treasures within him. An evil-hearted man is filled with venom, and his speech reveals it. And I tell you this, that you must give account on Judgment Day for every idle word you speak."

Some of us have to give an account before Judgment Day for the words that we have spoken (to other people as well as God), and that can be very painful. It's wise, then, to watch what we say. Although we may have been told as children that "Sticks and stones may break my bones but names will never hurt me," as adults we have learned how false that statement is. We have all been hurt by the unkind words of others, and with our tongues we have hurt others more than we care to admit.

As you communicate with your partner each day, you face a series of choices: What do I say? How do I say it? And what do I keep to myself? The Bible says, "If anyone can control his tongue, it proves that he has perfect control over himself in every other way."

Before we think about how to control our tongue, however, let's consider the various things the tongue can do. It can determine the direction your marriage will take, for good or for bad; it can start a fire within your marriage, either to enflame you or to warm you; and it can either kill a relationship altogether, or give it new life. In every case the choice is yours.

Charting your course
First, the tongue determines the direction your marriage will take. Like the bit in a horse's mouth or the rudder on a ship, its tiny but powerful influence can steer the whole relationship.

For example, suppose you've been having a rocky time in your marriage lately, and your partner surprises you one day with, "I talked to a lawyer today. I'm going to move out for a while." Shocked, you shout back, "Go ahead. See if I care. It's been a lousy marriage anyway." By your words, you are committing yourself to the break-down of your marriage. Although actions may follow (securing your own lawyer, determining who gets what, deciding what to do with the kids, putting the house up for sale, withdrawing money from the joint account, and so forth), the actions do not chart the course of your lives – they reinforce it. Your words chart it, the moment they are spoken. And you will continue in that direction until more words turn you in a new direction.

Suppose, on the other hand, your partner makes another kind of suggestion, like, "Let's go to the pastor for counseling," and you agree, "Okay." This time your words will commit you to a course of healing rather than of hurting. Again many actions will follow, actions like attending weekly sessions, doing constructive homework, planning activities together, maybe even getting involved in a ministry of the church together.

When the healing has taken place, stop and ask yourself, "What started our marriage in this new and challenging direction?" The counseling? No, that was only a reinforcement. The decision to go to the counseling did. You have experienced an interesting phenomenon – once an idea is verbalized it is not long before it is actualized.

Starting a fire

Second, the tongue is a starter of fires. It can enflame a hurt or warm a heart. Again the choice is up to you. Say things like "I'm telling you this because I love you" or "My mother put basil leaves in *her* spaghetti sauce" or "Can't you ever do *anything* right?" and watch the flames of anger start. You'll be able to observe the fire in progress: the slow smoldering in the pit of the stomach, the fanning of the fire with quick breaths, the reddening of the neck as anger builds up, and finally the frenzied explosion as the mouth opens and exposes the inferno inside.

But words don't have to enflame. They can be controlled to give a very warm glow to your marriage. Try saying things like "I love the way you look, even when you're angry" or "Thanks for backing me up – I just want you to know I appreciate it" or "Thanks for pointing that out. I didn't realize. Will you help me work on my weak areas?"

Responses like these are geared to evoke positive reactions.

When you say words like these, make sure you do so with a smile. It's possible to smile with your voice so that even when you are talking with your partner on the telephone, he/she can "hear" that smile. We are not talking about a sugar-coated, everything-is-all-right-even-when-it-isn't kind of approach. We are talking about genuine communication that warms the heart. It can all begin with your tongue.

Death or life sentence

Third, your tongue can kill your marriage relationship or it can give it new life. Biting words are like poison. It's amazing how little is needed to do a deadly work. Take just a few one-word statements and look at what those words can kill in your marriage:

1. "Stupid!" (self-worth)
2. "Never!" (hope)
3. "Cheater!" (trust)
4. "Later." (present opportunity)
5. "God!" (reverence)

Quite a graveyard from only five words!

There are other one-word statements, though, that have just the opposite effect. Think about these and add them to our list:

1. "Thanks." (appreciation)
2. "Beautiful!" (compliment)
3. "Delicious!" (praise)
4. "Better!" (encouragement)
5. "Of course." (assistance)

Just another five words, but what a difference in outcome!

It's not just one-word statements that can make or break a relationship. There are certain three word statements that can also have powerful effects, for bad or for good. The words "I hate you" are some of the most devastating that will ever reach the ears of the one who stood before witnesses and you vowed to love for life. What heartache, what failure, what frustration they evoke. Avoid them at all cost. They have no place in a marriage relationship that hopes to endure.

Instead say "I love you." Say it over and over again. Don't worry about repetition. Your partner will *never* get tired of hearing those words. As long as you mean them they will not become trite, canned, worn-out or old. On the contrary, they will give new life to a tired relationship and soothing reassurance when someone is hurt. Say them today. In fact, say them now.

The power of praise

Another type of expression that will bring out the best in your marriage is praise. Remind yourself daily to say something complimentary to the one you love. These compliments are not to be contrived or to be used in a manipulative manner. They are simply to be an expression of encouragement from one heart to another. We all feel tired, discouraged, and ready to give up at times. We need a special boost from our partner.

Not only should you praise your partner to his/her face, you should also praise your partner in front of others. For too long the wife has been referred to as "the little lady back home." She should never be so degraded. Men – your wife is your companion, your encourager, your support, and your strength. She is the joy of your life. Tell your business associates that – if it is true. Tell your neighbors how she stuck by you when your world started falling apart. Tell your friends how she buoyed you up when you felt you were drowning. As we noted earlier, there is a place for a confidant in talking out frustrations, but even then choose your words carefully. Also make sure you are genuine in what you say. Don't let your praise sound "fake."

Likewise, women – when you are tempted to participate in a negative conversation over coffee, say only positive things about your husband. Remember why you married him. If you have cause for displeasure, talk it out with him, not with the gossip group at the office or elsewhere. In front of them, highlight his good points. In front of him, remember to praise too. It's amazing how what we say establishes what we believe. So, if you want to have a lasting marriage, speak positive words both *to* your partner and also *on behalf* of him/her. Positive words are "little things" that determine really big things in the course of your marriage.

WORDS TELL A STORY

...about character

Did you ever stop to think that what comes out of your mouth is an indication of what kind of person you are? It's true. Bitter words come from bitter people and encouraging words come from people who are at peace. Also, how we react to the words that are spoken to us indicates the kind of person we are. For example, when criticized adversely, our natural reaction will probably be to lash back in defense of ourselves. But people to whom God has given a new orientation are able to access God's power, helping them to react in a more loving manner. The Christian's goal is to be able to say, "Thank you for the criticism. I will take it into consideration and apply it where needed." Human nature has been given a new capacity.

...about God's presence

That kind of change is possible for anyone. "Never," you protest. "I could never react like that. It goes against everything that's in me."

We're sure it does. In addition to indicating the type of person you are, words also indicate the presence or absence of God in your life. Without God's help to control your tongue, you will continue to experience defeat. This defeat is expressed in a quip that Peg's mother has taped to her refrigerator:

> *I did it again today*
> *I guess I'm in a rut*
> *I missed an opportunity*
> *To keep my big mouth shut.*

Best intentions at personal reform fail again and again and again. But they do not have to fail. The God who made you can help you. He knows your frailties and shortcomings, and he cares. He wants to come into your life and effect a change.

Furthermore, he has the power where we do not. That's important.

When he takes up residence within you, you may not notice any change in your circumstances. But your reactions to those circumstances now have the power to improve. You can express your frustrations to God, not just to your partner, and then call on him to help. He will. Say, "I've had it with _____, God. I'm going to explode in anger. But I don't want to. At least I *think* I don't want to. You're going to have to perform a miracle here, God. Say through me what I could never say myself." Now you're ready to watch the miracle occur.

It will come through your obedience to God's advice found in the New Testament letter to the Ephesians: "Stop lying to each other; tell the truth, for we are parts of each other and when we lie to each other we are hurting ourselves. . . Don't use bad language. Say only what is good and helpful to those you are talking to, and what will give them a blessing. . . Quarreling, harsh words, and dislike of others should have no place in your lives. Instead, be kind to each other, tenderhearted, forgiving one another. . ."

Here we have the victorious principle of substitution. When you are about to tell a lie, stop the lie before it comes out and substitute the truth, leaving the results to God. When you feel a derogatory remark coming from deep within you, put your hand over your mouth until you have control of yourself and then substitute a compliment instead. When you know you are about to explode in anger, refuse to give way to the degenerative force within you and substitute, "I love you, I really do." You may say, "But I can't say something I don't feel. That would be hypocrisy." No it wouldn't. That would be maturity. Hypocrisy involves the intent to deceive. Maturity involves the desire to grow.

. . . about maturity

Marriage is a growing process. A test of real maturity in the marriage relationship can be the degree of control you have over your tongue. Maturity means knowing when to keep silent as well as knowing when to speak. It may mean holding your tongue while your partner is shouting at you, knowing all the time that it takes a whole lot more strength to be silent than it does to lash back in anger.

Ask Jesus of Nazareth, who "never sinned, never told a lie, never answered back when insulted; when he suffered he did not threaten to get even; he left his case in the hands of God who always judges fairly."

In connection with this statement the Bible tells us: "Follow in his steps." What an example!

It is an example of maturity of character on the very highest level. In marriage this maturity is manifested by not responding to the insult. It is refusing to cut down your partner in order to build yourself up. In fact, it is refusing to say anything that would cause strife or division, but rather making an effort to be a peacemaker. Maturity in marriage, above all, is being honest with God. Don't be afraid to say to him, "I blew it today. I'm sorry. Help me tomorrow to control my tongue, to think before I speak, and to measure what I say." Then add, "Thank you for hearing my prayer," for you can be sure that he has heard – every little word.

. . . about health

The tongue is a very little thing when it comes to building a happy marriage, yet it is an indicator of the condition of your relationship. Just as a physician can tell by looking at your tongue whether you are a healthy patient or a sick one, so those who hear the conversation that passes between the two of you can tell whether your marriage is in good condition or bad. "Stick out your tongue," the physician says. "Examine your words," we echo him. They will tell you what kind of marriage is in the making.

ACTIONS SPEAK LOUDER

As important as words are, actions speak louder. As with words, it is the little ones that add up to make a big impression. They reassure your partner of the constancy and warmth of your love. Words sometimes come cheap but there is a higher price tag on actions. They require us to put feet to our promises and hands to our intentions. Good intentions which are expressed but never carried out are hollow. And promises whispered in the heat of passion become quite cold when there is no action to back them up.

Someone once said, "Act the way you want to become and you will become the way you act." True. If you want to become a loving person, then act in a loving way toward your partner. If you want to be considerate, then go out of your way to do a favor. If you want to become more empathetic, then take time to weep with one who is weeping or to rejoice with one who is rejoicing.

Actions which count in a marriage need to be planned and they need to be frequent. When is the last time you surprised your partner with a kindness? Perhaps you could think of something right now that you might do tomorrow. And after you have completed tomorrow's task, plan for the following day. Make a habit of bringing happiness to the one you love.

Hide a note

Notes are one way many people use to brighten their partner's day. Write short expressions of appreciation or love (leave the long ones for special days), then hide them all over the place – in different spots each day.

When your note is found, be prepared for a reaction: a hug, a squeal, a phone call, or another note in return. Also be prepared for no reaction at all, at least not immediately. It could be some time before your note is discovered. When it is, however, it will bring joy. A "little thing" will have earned rich dividends.

A word of caution may be in order here. When notes become "expected," perhaps it's time to switch to another type of surprise. Be creative. The object is to bring a little sunshine into your partner's life.

Offer a helping hand

Helping your partner with a burdensome task is another

special way of expressing your love. If there is typing to be done and you can do it, sit down and relieve him/her at the typewriter. If there are leaves to be raked and bagged and you have an extra hour, take your turn at this outdoor exercise and let your partner enjoy a much-needed rest. If you are expecting company for dinner, offer to set the table or stir the gravy. Your help will ease the tension of last minute preparations. Or if there is a huge mailing to be done, such as sending out Christmas cards or invitations to a party, offer to write some of the notes, address some of the cards, or lick some of the stamps. Get used to saying "I'll help," – then prove that you mean what you say.

Little kindnesses
In these days of business women and house-husbands, chivalry need not be declared dead. In fact, without degrading either one of the sexes, it can still be very much alive and functioning. Husbands, you might open the car door for your wife – the way you used to do when you were dating. In fact, open *every* door for her. Not only is that chivalry, it is common courtesy. When you see her come home with the groceries, meet her outside and help carry in those bags. Move the furniture for her when you know she is planning to shampoo the rug. Check out her car and fill it up before she goes on a trip. Send her flowers when she least expects them. Bring home a tiny gift from your travels. Rub her feet after a long hard day! It is the little things, not the big extravaganzas, that matter in the long run.

Wives, you can get into the action too. An errand run (one that he would normally do) can make his homecoming an event. A sewn button, a pressed suit, clean towels, and a relaxing back rub – all do the job of reminding the one you care about that love is a moment-by-moment concern. And don't forget a spontaneous hug. It will squeeze the words "I love you" right into his heart.

In short, plan to demonstrate your love. Figure out what you might do in the next few days then make a note in your daily planner or on your monthly calendar to do it. Never do anything that would nurse a hurt or inflict a new one. Do only those things that produce happiness and joy. Much of life is routine. We get up in the morning, shower and shave or apply our cosmetics, dress, eat breakfast, take the kids to school, drive to work, vacuum the carpet, take the kids to their after-school activities, pick up the kids, prepare dinner, clean up afterwards, watch the evening news, read the sports section of the paper, write a couple of letters or pay a few bills, and fall into bed exhausted. This routine can be the same, day after dreary day – *unless* it is broken by small unexpected kindnesses. Then the day brightens up, the anxieties take on a new perspective, and there's a tug at the heart that says, "you're loved."

Little kindnesses are like small pearls. Alone they may not amount to very much. But strung all together they are exquisite. Every time one pearl is added to the string, the value of the necklace goes up. It goes up and up and up until the owner of the necklace would not trade it for anything in the world. He can't afford to. It is too valuable. It has become a treasure of inestimable worth.

HOW DO YOU RATE?

1. I handle major crises: □ *poorly;* □ *fairly well;* □ *extremely well.*
2. I handle minor annoyances: □ *poorly;* □ *fairly well;* □ *extremely well.*
3. I try to be aware of my partner's needs: □ *never;* □ *seldom;* □ *most of the time;* □ *all of the time.*
4. I try to be courteous to my partner: □ *never;* □ *seldom;* □ *most of the time;* □ *all of the time.*
5. I am in control of what I say: □ *never;* □ *rarely;* □ *most of the time;* □ *all of the time.*
6. I praise my partner: □ *never;* □ *rarely;* □ *most of the time;* □ *all of the time.*
7. I praise my partner in front of others: □ *never;* □ *rarely;* □ *most of the time;* □ *all of the time.*

8. I draw on God's power to help me control my tongue: □ *never;* □ *seldom;* □ *most of the time;* □ *all of the time.*

9. Little kindnesses I perform for my partner (list):

10. Judging by the words that pass between us, I would rate our marriage: □ *poor;* □ *fair;* □ *good;* □ *excellent.*

Total Commitment

Of all the ingredients that make up a successful marriage, commitment is perhaps the most important. For without that the others could never be developed at all. For example, without commitment you could be under no obligation to live out your vows, to communicate your feelings, to be faithful to your partner, to care enough to forgive, to carry out your designated responsibilities, to work at building a winning partnership, or even to think about the little things that make a marriage special. Commitment is the glue that makes everything else stick together.

WHERE HAVE WE GONE WRONG?

Yet commitment is the quality most lacking in so many marriages today. This lack is mirrored in other relationships too – at work, in school, in church, and in the community. Why is that? Is it because as human beings we find it difficult nowadays to be committed to anything? We doubt that. For there does seem to be *something* that almost everybody is committed to. Too often that *something* is the fulfillment of our own desires.

Consider the degree of diligence with which the enthusiast pursues a hobby. Give a golfer the opportunity to play an unexpected round of golf and he'll meet you at six o'clock in the morning – no questions asked. That's commitment.

Or present a fisherman with the chance to catch a trout and he'll be up even earlier, never thinking twice about the sleep he's losing. That's commitment. The same degree of dedication is true of the sailor, the jogger, or the garage sale addict. They have no trouble at all sacrificing for the activity to which they have committed themselves.

A similar type of commitment shows up in spectator sports – but with a different twist. Let a local team show promises of winning the championship and the "commitment" of the townspeople rises with each victory. But let the same team do badly the following year and watch the number of "committed" followers drop significantly. Why is that? Maybe the commitment is not really to the team but to the thrill of being part of something that is successful – to fulfilling a selfish desire within.

WHAT IT REALLY MEANS

We suggest that this is not commitment at all. Commitment is not throwing yourself into a project only when that project is going well, or when you can derive personal benefits from it. No. Commitment is sticking with a project whether that project is going well or not. It is seeing the project through to completion, even at great personal cost.

If we have made no other point clear in the previous chapters of this book, let us make this one as plain as possible. If you go into marriage only for what you think you can get out of it, you are almost certainly programming yourself for failure. If, on the other hand, you go into marriage determined to put everything into it that you can, you are laying the foundation for a lasting relationship.

Take a personal inventory right now to check on the health of your marriage. Are you out for yourself, or are you out for the two of you as a partnership? Which is more important to you: the promotion of your personal image, or the development of the relationship with your partner? Ask these questions very seriously, because they may determine

whether you are "together tomorrow" or "split tomorrow."
Seriously.

HOW FAR DO I HAVE TO GO?

There is no question, then, that commitment is a necessary
ingredient in a successful marriage. The next concern is, how
"total" must it be? To find out, let's state the problem
mathematically. Out of a numerical base of 100%, what
percentage is each partner required to give to ensure the
success of the marriage?

Pitfalls of a 50%-50% arrangement
Did you say 50%? Why not? After all, two 50s add up to
100. And certainly that would be a fair distribution of
responsibility. It sounds good in theory. But does it work
in practice?

Let's see. Bob and Sue will serve as our model couple. Each
enters the marriage relationship with the intention of giving
only 50%. No problem, they think. And they are right –
for the first few days. Then one day Sue wakes up feeling
irritable. She cannot give any more than 35% of herself that
day and even that much takes a little doing.

Now Sue is a lucky girl, for Bob, her husband, is very
"giving" by nature. He doesn't mind giving 65% that
day. In fact, he feels kind of heroic playing the martyr
to Sue's passing whims. So their marriage survives its
first crisis.

But what about the second? By now Sue has been doing
some thinking: "If I can get away with giving only 35%, do
you think I can get away with 25% – or maybe even 15%?
After all, Bob is a super guy. I'll see how much he loves me.
I wonder how far he'll let me go. Let's see..."

Attitudes like Sue's breed disaster. If you *begin* with
only a 50-50 commitment to each other, you will run into
trouble much sooner than the couple that begins with a total
commitment to each other of 100-100. But more devastating
than the percentage factor is the degenerative mind-set this

reasoning fosters. Instead of thinking, "How much more can I give to this relationship to make it work?" you will be thinking, "How little can I get away with and still remain 'happily married'?" In a few years you may find that neither partner is interested in giving anything.

Benefits of 100%-100% commitment

In order for a marriage to survive and be productive, the commitment of each partner must be a full 100%. That way there is a guarantee of total commitment all the time from at least one partner. You need that base of security. Let's face it, even the best intentions to promote marital bliss get foiled by health problems, interpersonal tensions, and emotional upheavals. If this happens to the best intentioned, what happens to those with lesser intentions?

There will be days when you yourself, no matter how "committed" you are, will be able to contribute very little, if anything, to the growth of your marriage relationship. On those days your marriage will be in trouble – unless your partner is covering your inadequacy with his/her adequacy. If 100% comes in from any source, it is there – in all of its fullness. But if you start with less than that, there will be a gap in the total count at times.

So plan on the inevitable. There will be days when you will have to contribute everything to see your marriage through. There will be other days when your partner will be the one to contribute everything to see your marriage through. On those days, however, when you *both* are contributing everything, there will be so much love abounding in your marriage that it will spill over to your children, to your place of business, to your church, and to your community. And when it flows out, it will flow back a thousandfold. Give 100%, receive 1000% – a good investment by anybody's book. But even if the return is less, it will be worth it. For you will have proved in your life the biblical principle that in giving you receive, in pouring out you are filled.

THREE KINDS OF MARRIAGE

One author suggested that marriage is like two hands approaching each other hesitantly, yet wanting to form a strong bond. Each hand is made up of both finger tips and finger "valleys" (the space between the extended fingers). The tips represent the strengths of each partner and the valleys represent the weaknesses. As we have already stated, opposites seem to attract. That can be a healthy challenge, for in the merging of opposites lies the potential for a very strong union. But to realize its strength, the union has to be made properly.

The painful union
There are three ways that the two hands can come together. The first way is to approach each other "at sword's points," the only contact being between the tips of the extended fingers. There's not much interaction in this type of relationship, and what contact there is is painful. Unfortunately, too many marriages try to make it work this way, with each partner forcing his/her strengths upon the other and inflicting wounds in the process.

The formal union
The second way the hands can come together is formally, with the palms touching each other lightly and the fingers extended in selfish points to the sky. Too many marriages fit into this category also. The partners hold back on letting their weaknesses show. Although their strengths are not actually fighting each other, they are not helping each other either. They are just existing side by side, linked in a cold, ungiving, self-serving union.

In both of these relationships, separation is easy. The extended fingertips pull away and the pressed palms simply become unpressed. Gradually there is a drifting apart.

The "unbreakable" union
There is only one union that can really be called a merger.

In fact, once formed, it is so strong that it takes a conscious effort to break. It is the clasping of the two hands with the fingers intertwined. Consider what happens in this type of union. The strengths of the fingertips fill the weaknesses of the valleys. Isn't this a beautiful picture of what marriage is all about?

Not one of us is so strong that we never need the help of another. And there is no one without weaknesses that need a little covering from time to time. This is marriage as God meant it to be: two individuals merging their respective strengths and weaknesses, one so totally covering the other that the outside sees only the strength of the union, not the individual weaknesses, and one so wrapped in the other's warmth that it's hard to tell where one's identity leaves off and the other starts, though the identity is clearly there when they are apart. This is a union that takes a mutual effort to break.

A break will be accomplished only at the determined effort of both hands. Finger by finger must be pulled apart until the two hands emerge, separated. But when you think about it, who wants to break it? If the merger has been as warm and as comforting as it is supposed to be, the hands will be restless when alone. They will yearn to move back toward each other again and re-establish the rewarding relationship that was once uniquely theirs.

LEARNING TO FIT

Fitting Physically

Husbands and wives were created by God to "fit" into each other's lives – physically, emotionally, and spiritually. Physically, each one of us is uniquely equipped. Some are short, others are tall. Some are well endowed, others not so well endowed. Some are thin, others are heavy. Some are dark, others are light. Some are strong, others are weak.

Whatever the physical characteristics of your partner, the

important thing to remember is that he/she was made that way to fit into the groove of your life. So stop wishing he were more muscular (or less so) and she had more curves (or fewer – whichever the case may be). Be content with the puzzle as it has been designed. Now commit yourself to fitting the pieces together.

Fitting emotionally
The same truth applies emotionally. There are volatile people who need to be tempered by those who are more stable, and reserved individuals who need to have their personality brought out by someone who is more outgoing. When you give yourself to your partner, you must give *all* of yourself, holding nothing back, not even your weaknesses. Likewise, when you receive your partner, you must receive *all* of him/her, leaving nothing out, especially the obvious short-comings. Once you know each other and have identified each other's points of vulnerability (you don't have to make a special effort to do this; in an open relationship the vulner-ability will become obvious), commit yourselves to covering each other's weak spots and strengthening each other's short-comings so that the world outside your home sees only the strength of your commitment.

Fitting spiritually
In addition to committing yourselves to "fit," both physically and emotionally, commit yourselves to fit into each other's spiritual lives. While it is true that each one of us has a very private side that is open to no one except God, it can be really beneficial to let your partner in on some of your thinking on spiritual lines. God has given your partner to you to help share your doubts, your uncertainties and your fears, as well as your "highs." Don't be afraid to open up on the most important level of all. Encourage each other to develop a deeper faith.

Discuss your most private questions. Is God real? How can I know him? Am I accountable for my actions? Do his principles really work? Can we try them together.

Many people have found that the honest sharing of spiritual matters has opened the way for an individual commitment to God. And as that commitment to God grows, your commitment to each other will grow as well. A Christian illustration of this relationship is the diagram of a triangle, with God at the top and the individual partners positioned at each corner of the base. As each partner moves closer to God, the two move closer together. This is a principle that works almost without exception. It has worked in our lives, and we heartily recommend it to anyone who wants to have a lasting marriage.

If you want to know what commitment is all about, ask a Christian. He/she will tell you about a "bridegroom" named Jesus Christ who loved his "bride," the church (that is, everyone who determines to follow him), so much that he went all the way to the cross and died for her. He didn't stop halfway. He didn't stop three-fourths of the way. He didn't even stop seven-eighths of the way. He went *all* the way – even though it cost him his life.

He could have opted out several times: when the religious leaders of the day were after him, when the questioning got hot, when the trial unfairly turned against him, and especially when it seemed that even God his father, had deserted him. He *could* have opted out. He could have thrown up his hands and exclaimed, "I've had enough of this! Who do they think they are anyway? I created these people who have turned against me. They're using the breath I gave them to curse their creator's name. They're using the strength God gave them to nail his son to this cross. I'll show them who's boss around here."

He *could* have said all this. But he didn't. He was committed to the task before him: to take the death penalty each of us deserved and to set us free to serve him.

Every person who has accepted for him/herself the sacrifice and forgiveness of Jesus Christ knows that to be on the receiving end of this kind of commitment requires full commitment in return. Commitment should never be a one-way street. It should give and receive and then give again.

A NEW KIND OF LOVE

A lawyer once approached Jesus and asked, "'Which is the most important command in the laws of Moses?' Jesus replied, 'Love the Lord your God with all your heart, soul, and mind. This is the first and greatest commandment. The second most important is similar: Love your neighbor as much as you love yourself. All the other commandments ...stem from these two laws and are fulfilled if you obey them. Keep only these and you will find that you are obeying all the others.'"

What a challenging answer! Who would ever think that love, which is commonly regarded as an emotion instead of an act of obedience, that *love* is expected to be a response to a command? Who would ever believe that God could say, "Love!" and people would love? Well, we really should consider this possibility, for the way we are loving now (with our emotions only) doesn't seem to be working very well.

What the Bible teaches is a new kind of love. Actually it is as old as creation itself, but it is new to those of us who have been taught that love is a feeling that comes and goes and you'd better enjoy it while you've got it. We need a better kind of love than that. The Bible teaches that love is a commitment rather than a feeling. To quote the King James English, God says, "Thou shalt love." Notice he does not say, "Love if you feel like it" but "love...with all your heart, soul, and mind." Furthermore, this total kind of loving implies not only that we are *doing* it, but that we are giving the effort every ounce of commitment we can muster.

As we keep God's command and focus our entire being and all our energies on him, then the *feeling* of love naturally follows. It is an overwhelming response to all the blessings he pours out upon us as part of his total commitment to us. It evokes commitment in return, which is much easier when we focus on him and not on ourselves. It is only when we change focus and become more self-orientated that our commitment becomes less "total."

THE TEST OF LOVE

The same is true in marriage. Ask yourself, what is the true test of love? Is it how many times she says "I love you"? Is it the amount of time we spend together? Is it the cost of the gifts he gives? Is it the things we do for each other? Is it the intensity of the sparkle in her eyes? Is it the degree of chemistry between us? Is it how much we sacrifice for each other? What *is* the true test of love? Interestingly enough, as we have already seen, to Jesus Christ the test is obedience. He says, "If you love me, obey me." We think that a similar test applies to love in the marriage relationship.

As part of the Marriage and Family Seminars we conduct, we constructed a list of ten guidelines that we think every married couple can use. Based on the famous commandments God gave, these principles have proved to be one of the most popular aspects of the entire seminar. Although the points are very specific, they speak volumes in interpersonal relationships.

It is interesting to observe that when marriages prosper, the partners are either consciously or subconsciously observing these principles. When marriages fail, it is usually because at least one of the partners has broken at least one of the points.

As you read the individual points, which sum up all we've tried to say in this book, pretend your husband or wife is saying them directly to you. Remember that obedience to what you hear will be the test of how much you love. "If you really love me," your husband or wife is saying, "you will want to follow these principles."

But first a word of caution. As you read the following points, you may become acutely aware of how far short your partner has fallen in his/her obligations to you. If possible, refrain from looking at your partner's shortcomings and look instead at your own. After all, you may be focusing on a speck in your partner's eye when you have a log in your own. So look at the principles with the idea of improving your *own* record of obedience. And when you *do* see a failure on your partner's part, cover that failure with love. Remember, love is the greatest command of all.

BETWEEN YOU AND YOUR PARTNER: TEN GUIDELINES

1. **You should hold no other person higher than me in your affection.** Only God should receive more of your love than I. Through the marriage vows I have become the most important person in your life – above parents, children, business associates, and friends. Therefore, I expect you to love me with all your heart and to guard against anyone coming between us. And please, don't ever take my position and give it to another. I could never bear the shame or the void.

2. **You should not fantasize or daydream about any other lovers.** That means no pornographic magazines, books, movies, or shows. For infidelity begins in the mind. So focus your romantic thoughts on me and me only. Remember how attracted we were to each other when we first began going together? We can keep that old flame alive by the proper discipline of our minds. If you think about me and I think about you our romance will continue to take its God-directed course.

3. **You should not talk about me in a derogatory manner.** Praise me and compliment me freely – in public as well as in private. Never criticize me or cut me down in front of others. Call me whatever you want that is loving and kind, but please, don't call me names.

4. **Remember our anniversary and other special days and plan for them ahead of time.** If you don't know what the "other special days" are, let me give you a hint. They are Christmas, my birthday, Father's Day, Valentine's Day, and Mother's Day. You can add a few more if you want to. Observing ordinary days in a special way (when I'm not expecting it) will make me feel appreciated. Send me a card,

put a note under my pillow, call me at work, surprise me
with flowers, bake my favorite pie, or take me out to dinner.
What you do doesn't have to be elaborate. Just let me know
that you care. These expressions of love take planning, so
mark your calendar now. I don't like having to drop hints
as my birthday rolls around.

5. **Honor your father and your mother but don't let them
come between us.** We want to respect them, visit them, ask
their advice, and include them in our family circle. And if
one parent is a widow or a widower, we certainly want to
do everything we can to help that lonely one feel loved. But
let's remind ourselves that when it comes to establishing
policies that affect our marriage and our family, the decisions
that we face are ours, and ours alone, to make.

6. **You should not kill my attempts to express my affection
for you.** When I reach out to hold you, that's my way of
saying "I need you" and that I desire physical contact with
you. So don't withdraw from me, ignore me, shun me, or
say "Don't touch me." You can kill my spirit that way and
destroy the love that we share.

7. **You should not commit adultery.** In the marriage vows
which we exchanged you pledged yourself to sexual fidelity
"as long as we both shall live." As far as I know, your pledge
was made without reservation. In turn, my trust in you is
complete. This sacred bond between us frees me from undue
concern whenever we are apart – a blessing for which I am
grateful. I want you to know how much I treasure this trust
that we share and that I'm counting on your continued love
and unwavering faithfulness always.

8. **You should not rob me of the privilege of communing
on a deep level with you.** Because I love you, I want to share
your dreams, your fears, your aspirations, and your questions about life. So don't spend too much time shopping,
reading, golfing, or watching television. Set some time apart
for talking things over with me. By conversing about important issues now, we will be making a real contribution to
the type of relationship we will share in the future. We need
to remind ourselves continually that there is much more to

marriage than physical togetherness. There should be a blending of minds, of personalities, and of spirits as well.

9. **You should not lie to me**. I need assurance that at all times you are being open and honest with me. For my trust in you is based on your truthfulness. So don't deceive me, mislead me, or tell me half truths or little white lies. If I discover that what you are telling me is not necessarily true, how will I know when to believe you? How will I know which statements to accept and which ones to discard? I want to be able to trust every word that comes out of your mouth. So please tell me nothing but the truth.

10. **You should not covet anyone else's partner, relationship, or situation in life**. I am all that you need. I have been designed by God – just as I am – for the purpose of fitting into your life. So don't create impossible expectations for me to meet. And don't compare me with other people – in appearance, in personality, in business acumen, in social status, or in spiritual maturity. Let's enjoy what God has given us and together let's form a partnership for his glory.

Remember these words from the traditional service: "What God has joined together, let no man put asunder." In this world in which we live there are many, many factors that can become a threat to your marriage. Make sure *you* are not one of them. The best advice we, personally, can leave you with is, "Put God first in your marriage and remember to keep him there." Since he has joined you together, he has the power to perfect your union. Don't hamper his efforts with your own selfish ones. Be committed, be yielding – and *love*!

HOW DO YOU RATE?

1. I am committed to: ☐ *hobby;* ☐ *sports;* ☐ *job;* ☐ *church;* ☐ *community;* ☐ *marriage;* ☐ *God;* ☐ *other*.
2. In my marriage I give: ☐ *50%;* ☐ *less than 50%;* ☐ *more than 50%;* ☐ *less than I should;* ☐ *100%*.

3. My marriage could be described as: □ *painful;* □ *formal;* □ *liveable;* □ *good;* □ *excellent;* □ *ecstatic.*

4. I fit well into my partner's life: □ *physically;* □ *emotionally;* □ *spiritually.*

5. I need to work on fitting into my partner's life: □ *physically;* □ *emotionally;* □ *spiritually.*

6. My commitment to God is: □ *minimal;* □ *adequate;* □ *leaves something to be desired;* □ *as total as I can make it.*

7. With regard to the ten guidelines for marriage I evaluate myself in the following manner:

   a. Putting my partner first: □ *never;* □ *sometimes;* □ *usually;* □ *always.*

   b. Fantasizing about others: □ *never;* □ *sometimes;* □ *usually;* □ *often;* □ *want to stop.*

   c. Being derogatory: □ *never;* □ *sometimes;* □ *often;* □ *want to change.*

   d. Remembering special days: □ *never;* □ *sometimes;* □ *usually;* □ *always;* □ *want to do better.*

   e. Evaluating the relationship between my parents and my partner: □ *poor;* □ *workable;* □ *good;* □ *excellent;* □ *want to improve.*

   f. Accepting affection: □ *never;* □ *sometimes;* □ *often;* □ *always.*

   g. Committing adultery: □ *never;* □ *occasionally;* □ *frequently;* □ *never again.*

   h. Talking things over: □ *never;* □ *occasionally;* □ *frequently;* □ *regularly.*

   i. Lying to my partner: □ *never;* □ *not intentionally;* □ *occasionally;* □ *regularly;* □ *want to change.*

   j. Coveting others' lifestyles: □ *never;* □ *not intentionally;* □ *occasionally;* □ *regularly;* □ *want to change.*

...rtheless, hope that the oracle's message might after all
some significance silenced the royal irritation, and in
too horrible a voice the king told Priestess Shawl the
business, hoping she might throw more light upon it.

'On Globadan I won the shubshub race",' she echoed.
less that was written by another shubshub, it's pure non-
se. *Nothing*, absolutely nothing on legs can beat a shub-
b.'

OK. It's nonsense. Let's go back to bed!' said Swap,
denly tiring of the whole thing. 'It would be me have to
getting tied up with neurotic kings . . .' he reflected.

'You go,' said the king. 'I want to ask the priestess a
uple of questions—'

('I'll wait till *you* go,' said Swap; he wasn't born yester-
y.)

'—are these shubshub races an institution on Globadan?'

The priestess said they were staged every year.

'May anything but a shubshub enter for them?'

A study of criminal punishment throughout the galaxy
yields much interest. On Globadan, according to the priestess, it was the tradition to release certain more harmless
criminals and let them enter for the shubshub races with the
promise of liberty if they won. Some tried hard and died of
heart-failure on the course. This custom added a spice of
humour to the day's events.

'Has any human ever won?' pressed the king.

'As I said, it would be impossible,' said the priestess,
adding somewhat illogically: 'Certainly nobody did it in my
time. But you must remember that Globadan is out on the
rim of the galaxy, and I have been away on missionary work
since I was virtually a child. Can't you imagine just how
excited I am to think I'm on my way back there tomorrow?'

'But nobody *could* beat a shubshub,' pressed the king.

'*Nobody* could beat a shubshub,' agreed the priestess.

'Nobody could beat a *shubshub*,' Swap told them.

They had it straight. All three returned to their separate
beds. King Horace spent a restless night, Swap slept deeply,
Priestess Shawl was gone by morning.

The malady which was never far from the king returned
that day and laid him low. He lay and sweated with a body

King Horace's face twisted bitterly. He stabbed at the
message to pluck it away, but it formed part of the plate.
Tears burned in his eyes: how could that nonsense cure
him? Even as he peered at it again, the wording writhed and
faded till not a trace remained. He stared for a moment
more, then sent the plate scudding far out of the palace
window.

Next morning, King Horace was in poor shape. He appeared obsessed with the idea of leaving for Upotia, sick as
he was: nobody could dissuade him. Swap arrived and was
ordered to escort the king on pain of having his sentence
reimposed. They made for the tiny space port, the king ignoring the glad farewells of his subjects. Once there, he dismissed his courtiers with a glum wave of the hand, and
hobbled into the lift of SS *Potent*. In a moment more he was
whisked up out of sight. Swap, two elderly nurses and a
baggage man followed without enthusiasm; they formed all
his retinue.

Spaceships, it is frequently said, are inventions of the
devil. But in King Horace's day the devil was obviously less
of an engineer than he is now. The ship which bore the king
– not, incidentally, one of his own, for his kingdom was too
small to finance more than moon freighters – belonged to
the Solar-(Upotia-Vegan and All Stations for Andromeda)
Line and was a tub. To be more precise, it was cramped, had
a poor *cuisine* and boasted almost no turn of speed. So the
unpleasant journey was also protracted, the seven light years
taking nearly four weeks to cover.

Nevertheless, Upotia was worth a little discomfort.

For the early part of the journey, the king preserved a
reflective silence. He brooded chiefly on the question of the
oracle, for although his message had been, at best, a con-
undrum, the man himself was as much of a riddle. Was he
genuine or a trickster? The odds seemed evenly balanced.
On the one hand, his complete indifference to the person of
the king argued a certain authority noticeably lacking in all
the quacks who had previously presented their fawning
selves at court; on the other hand, if he had anything of real
value to offer, it seemed likely he would have insisted on

greater reward than he had, in fact, received – his passage paid home, at the least.

Now he had vanished, leaving only a sentence of uncertain meaning.

King Horace was still undecided when they touched lightly down on Upotia.

Most planets, like Earth itself, provide all sorts of weather, although a few like Venus possess only bad: but Upotia enjoys only good. This is due partly to an exceptionally deep atmosphere, partly to its axial inclination and partly to the multiple sun system of which it is the only habitable planet.

'Delightful!' exclaimed the king, inhaling deeply.

'Absolutely!' echoed Swap. His first surliness had long since faded. Once he fully realized what an easy number he had fallen into, he was as agreeable as it was in his uncertain nature to be. The voyage had forced him into the king's company: they were much of an age: when allowances were made for the king's infirmity he was not such a bad chap: he had given Swap the Royal Pardon: they were going on holiday – and the King had told him about the oracle and 'On Globadan I won the Shubshub race'.

'At least we know what shubshubs are,' said Swap, as who should say: '—and a fat lot of good that does us!'

'Do you?' said the king eagerly. 'I don't! I thought it was a bit of gibberish. What are shubshubs? Sweets?'

'Of course you've led a very secluded life,' said Swap, mastering the big word with difficulty. And he explained that shubshubs were rare and expensive animals like six-legged ostriches which ran more swiftly than leopards. Where they came from he did not know, nor had he ever seen one.

Perhaps there *was* something in the message after all. Hope began to circulate again in the king's blood; after all, surely if the oracle had been a fraud he would have taken care to be more ingratiating?

'We may find out more about this on Upotia,' the king said.

But they found out no more on Upotia. For one thing, there was a deal of snobbery among the rich invalids there,

and those who had seen the king land not in but in a common liner cut him dead. So the (and the two elderly nurses) roamed the cou away from the centres of population.

They had been there a fortnight of golden d met the Priestess Colinette Shawl. King Horac grown tired of Swap and the limitations of though at first he had been titillated by the oth of romantic wrong-doing back in the palace soon wearied of what sounded rather an em Accordingly, he was more ready to welcome th

'This is my entourage,' he said, reluctantly i Swap.

'Charmed,' they said together, and Swap reste ful and commanding eyes on the newcomer – for priestess came from priestesses were picked for the to attract the parishioners. That indeed was her bu Upotia: to make converts to her sect. She began away on the king and Swap, and when it grew d pitched her tent beside theirs.

After midnight the third and fourth suns rose. The rth was a glinting speck hundreds of millions of miles away, while the third was a dull, fuzzy giant, trailing over the horizon like a shock of red hair. Together they made little more light than Luna, but the effect was very romantic.

Possibly you recall the old saying about the chlorophyll being greener in someone else's grass. Swap also recalled it as he lay and meditated on the discomfort of his bed; he wa unable to sleep.

At last he rose, and padded out to Priestess Colinette tent. He knocked gently on the wooden door-pole.

'I'm converted!' he whispered.

The priestess, who had heard that one before, came c cumspectly forth and delivered a religious address.

'What is more,' she added, 'it is too late to start anythi Tomorrow I begin the voyage back to Globadan.'

'Globadan!' shouted Swap. 'You mean to say you c from Globadan? There is such a dump! Hey, skipper – up!'

And he pulled the king out of bed, much to the la displeasure. Swap had acted with his usual thoughtless full of cramp, while in his mind he ran in infinitely slow motion through cotton wool mists across an endless plain: in King Horace's deliriums the time was always out of joint. The elderly nurses had a field day.

When he returned to something like his senses, he insisted that they moved to the space port without delay, catching the next ship home. This they did, the king consequently leaving Upotia in worse condition than when he arrived there.

Swap, who was disgusted by illness in any form, took to his berth and avoided his sovereign. But on the second day of the voyage the king burst in on him.

'I have solved another link in our problem,' he exclaimed without preamble.

'*Our* problem?' Swap inquired.

'Listen, man – I was a fool not to think of it sooner. It was something the Priestess Shawl said – I've just been talking it over with the captain. He has confirmed the point . . .'

He stopped for breath, sitting down abruptly on Swap's bed and passing a hand over his brow. Then he explained carefully how the priestess had mentioned that Globadan was on the rim of the galaxy: as he knew and the captain confirmed, the lines of space and time stretch thin on the edge of the great star wheels, just as they are condensed towards the hub. This phenomenon was known even before the age of space travel, and christened – I believe I recall the name correctly – the Döppler effect, although an entirely erroneous construction was put on the facts: some improbable affair about the universe expanding, I believe.

However, to travel outwards is to have one's entire metabolism, physical and psychological, slowed – just as to travel in towards the centre suns is to have it speeded. This effect, since it operates uniformly through all living tissue, is not discernible by human senses. Only instruments can detect the slowing or acceleration.

'Well?' asked Swap.

The king sighed and explained condescendingly: 'Don't you see? If I could somehow be on Globadan with my present metabolism rate, I should be living faster than the creatures of Globadan: *I might even be fast enough to win the shubshub race!*'

87

'Yes . . . And if you'd got a good enough refrigerator suit you could mine hydrogen off the sun.'

King Horace flung himself out of Swap's cabin in disgust – straight into the bony arms of the two elderly nurses, who commenced to lead him back to bed. He cursed them silently and swore to himself he would resolve the oracle's words sooner or later, for the more baffling that sentence became the stronger became his faith that within it lay his cure.

The nurses tucked him between the sheets and retired to play cards with two elderly ship's stokers.

' "On Globadan I won the shubshub race," ' King Horace muttered to himself: ' "On Globadan I . . . zzzzzz." ' He fell into a light doze, snored and woke himself . . . ' ". . . won the" – wait! It is obvious *I* must win the shubshub race, but how did the oracle win the shubshub race? He was a short, heavy man who could hardly have won a tortoise race.'

The agitation of pondering this fresh aspect of the puzzle propelled him again from his bed. Slipping on a robe over his sleeping suit, he paced up and down the narrow, curving corridor of the first class promenade. However much space-ships have changed between those days and the present, the passengers at least are unaltered: King Horace received frosty looks from the well-dressed women and snorts from the impeccable men, as they eyed his dressing-gown.

'A fig for the lot of you!' he thought, but noticing among the array of tailored façades the eldest princeling of one of his neighbouring kings, he decided to retire to a place where he would be less conspicuous, and descended to the tourist class deck.

As he stepped off the escalator, he caught sight of a short, heavy figure in a strange habit . . . It went into Cabin 12. Had it been – *could* it have been—?

'I got to mop here.'

He stepped automatically out of the way of the robot menial who had spoken and took up a position where he could watch Cabin 12. He was sure he had just seen the oracle! That figure was almost unmistakable. The passage swarmed with people and children, but they took little notice of the king.

After an hour, when the king was feeling faint with standing, the stocky figure re-emerged from Cabin 12 and clomped away down the corridor. It *looked* like the oracle, although the king had never seen the oracle's face. Pulses beating madly, he hurried over and tried the door with 12 on it. It was not locked! Daring greatly, he slipped in.

The interior was so bleak he paused astonished. Of course, many of these alien races had odd ideas of comfort, but everything here had been rendered as bleak as possible. Even the foamattress had been stripped from the bunk. Decorations had been removed from the walls, the magnapile rug had been taken off the floor. Yet everything was as neat as a card index, folded and packed and filed out of sight, no easy job in a tourist class cabin.

King Horace shrugged. All he was really interested in was finding his stick. If he could find that, it proved the stocky little man was his oracle. He searched feverishly in a palsy of sick agitation, throwing everything out on to the floor as he worked. But the stick was not hidden. When he opened the guardrobe, there it lay, in full view on a lower shelf. He seized it in ecstasy.

At that exact second he felt the ray gun in the small of his back.

'Ugh!' he gulped.

'Turn around slowly!' said a voice like a car crash.

The king turned slowly, raising his hands trembling above his head. He was confronted by a ship's guard whose face made him long to turn back again.

'I spotted you loitering about in the passage,' the forces of justice snarled. 'Now you can come on down to the lock-up.'

'But please . . . I'm King Able Harkon Horace.'

'Oh, are you? And I'm Queen of all the Fairies. Now just you come on smartly, in case this gun goes off.' And for emphasis he jabbed the king in the kidney and prodded him fiercely from the cabin.

'If you require proof of my identity, ask my two elderly nurses—'

'I'm the only nurse you got now, bud. Come on!'

The bowels of a spaceship . . . hot, noisy, oppressive. And most oppressive of all is the brig, which in the SS *Potent* was situated next to the refuse and sewage disposal plant. King

Horace was pushed, fuming, into a narrow cell. Yet as the tall, barred door clicked into place, in his mind an irrelevant item clicked into place, and he was suddenly calm.

He held the whole secret of the oracle!

That mysterious sentence, 'In Globadan I won the shub-shub race,' was a mystery no longer: but now that he was at liberty to act upon its advice – he was no longer at liberty!

For several hours he rested on a narrow bench in his cell, enduring the heat and ignoring the noise. Then a guard appeared, ushering him into a grey steel office to stand before a guard sergeant who had taken charge of the matter and was preparing the evidence. He wrote down without comment the king's name, and the names of Swap and the elderly nurses who would vouch for him.

'Very good,' said the sergeant, '—or perhaps I should say very bad. You understand this is a serious charge brought against you?'

'Who is bringing it?'

'The occupant of Cabin 12, of course, Klaeber Ap-Eye.'

'I swear to you, officer, I was not going to steal the stick – I was just seeing if it was there.'

'A likely tale! A very likely tale! Take his statement, Corporal Binnith.'

Back in his cell, the king's outlook on life became very gloomy indeed. He resented intensely the indignity and the likely effect on his health ... Not that for one moment he doubted the outcome of this silly business. Directly word got to Swap, he would be freed. And then the ship's lawyer arrived at the cell.

Lawyer Lymune was a *quart*; roughly humanoid in shape, he had a swivel head like a gun turret with five different sorts of eyes and two mouths – the latter a great asset in his profession, enabling him in court to address the judge while conferring with his client. He made it clear to King Horace at once that things were not going to be as easy as expected. Swap and the elderly nurses had denied that he was of the Royal House of Harkon.

'What treachery is this?' gasped the king. 'Anyhow – all my credentials are in a strong-box in my cabin.'

'I took the precaution of looking in your cabin,' said

Lymune, using both mouths for emphasis. 'And there are *no* credentials in there now – if there ever have been.'

'The – the captain!' said King Horace wildly. 'I spoke to him. He can't have been got at! He'll identify me.'

'He may possibly identify you as a man who *said* he was King Horace. Beyond that I fail to see he could possibly go ...'

'Are you meant to be defending or offending me? I'll have you executed along with the rest of them!'

'Delusions of grandeur ...' the lawyer commented. 'Hm – you might plead insanity.'

When, after this unsatisfactory interview, the king was once more left alone, he fell into the most lugubrious of meditations. The familiar sensation of time delayed overcame him, he clutched at his shirt and groaned. He fully recognized that as we are none of us free from Original Sin, so a time comes in even the most sheltered of lives when circumstances arise like an angry sea to overwhelm us.

Until now he had seen himself as an austerely solitary figure, separated from the rest of human kind by reason of his royal blood, and swept by the winds of mortality which blew illness upon him. Now he realized how illusory that figure was; his royalty was in grave doubt, and he was fit enough to stand trial for theft.

What could have induced Swap to turn against him, King Horace could not guess. Finding no particular motive, he could only ascribe the act to a general human baseness.

His melancholy was interrupted by a visitor whom the guards thrust unceremoniously into his cell. He looked up dazedly in the half-light to see a short, clumsy figure standing before him.

'The oracle!' he breathed, sitting slowly up.

'Yes, it is I – Klaeber Ap-Eye. Odd, is it not, that we should meet again like this?'

'Listen – I meant to do you no harm by ferreting in your cabin. I was only looking for the stick to find if you *were* the oracle. You've got to get me out of here!'

'That, my friend, is what I came to talk to you about.' He squatted on his haunches. 'I have you bottled up in a tight spot, my friend, so you had better listen closely to me, see?'

The king wearily nodded agreement, for though he knew more than the oracle credited him with, he wished to hear what the other had to say. Ap-Eye began quietly by commenting on their both being on the SS *Potent* together. When he had delivered the oracle to the king, he said, he had not known of the latter's forthcoming visit to Upotia and had expected him to journey at once to Globadan. Meanwhile, he (Ap-Eye) disappeared on other business and had been – until the king was apprehended in his cabin – on his way back to Earth, expecting to find the kingdom without a king.

'Why?' demanded King Horace.

Ap-Eye spread wide hands. 'I have my own ideas on who should be king . . .'

'So! Ah, I see it all now . . . I was a fool to hope— Then you are just a simple usurper!' He buried his weary face in his hands.

The other touched his shoulder. 'I am not simple, my friend. Nor am *I* the usurper. *Nor* were you a fool to hope. I am – call me the hand of justice. In my own way, my friend, I am dedicated to unravelling past wrongs.'

'Never mind past ones: get me out of this present one.'

'That I cannot do. You should have gone to Globadan, then this would not have happened; when this chance came along – well, my friend, I had to take it. It is more *convenient* to have you here.'

Feebly, but with dignity, the king rose, towering over this strange creature in the twilight.

'Then I will force you to help me. For I have discovered what you are – you are a pseudo-man!'

For a space of seconds Ap-Eye crouched where he was. Expelling his breath in a rush he stood up and inquired softly: 'Well, my friend?'

'If I called to that guard down there that I had a pseudo-man in here with me, they would take you out and throw you through the airlock immediately.'

'And merely because man made my kind with more powers than man himself – and then became frightened . . . Man has never ceased to regret that experiment, has he? It was too successful, eh?'

'We were lenient – you were not exterminated. But you

were confined to Alpha Centauri II, and for you to leave there is to court a death sentence,' the king said sternly.

'Don't talk to me of that dreary world—'

'You deny nothing, Ap-Eye. Do I call the guard?'

The other faced the king's gaze without flinching, letting the light fall on his plain, open countenance: there was little inhuman there. After a moment he chuckled.

'We'd better come to an agreement, my friend. I'll visit you again in the morning.'

'Oh, no you don't. Settle this here and now. Call the guard and tell him who I am, or I'll call him and tell him who you are!'

'No.' He shook his square head in regret. 'The matter is more complicated than you imagine, my friend. But I'll be back in the morning.'

'How do I know?' Even as the king asked, his eyes met the full force of the other's: large eyes, implacable and inhuman, yet with something in them never entirely to be found in human eyes. Justice perhaps.

'I'll see you in the morning,' he said huskily, answering himself.

Ap-Eye nodded casually and whistled the guard.

'By the by,' he asked as that dignitary was lumbering over, 'how did you guess – about what I am?'

'Partly the way your cabin was: disregard of comfort, phenomenal neatness.'

'I must be more careful!' Ap-Eye exclaimed.

'And then I realized – a pseudo-man has the electronic consciousness of an instrument, which would function at one basic rate anywhere in the galaxy. For instance, such a being from Alpha Centauri II could win a shubshub race on Globadan . . .'

SS *Potent* sped on through the eternal interstellar night. Inside the tiny space of its hull, a hundred human beings went through the cosy pretence of day and night, and when their chronometers said day again Ap-Eye returned to the prisoner in the brig.

Not, however, before Lawyer Lymune had called. He announced cheerfully that the court hearing was to follow ship's rounds, in three hours' time. The king wearily refused to plead insanity and dismissed the man. He could conduct his own defence; surely they would *see* he was speaking the truth.

Ap-Eye, when he arrived, was brisk, brief and business-like.

'You're all settled, my friend,' he said. 'I've got all your official papers and credentials, of course – I took care of them directly I heard the guards had taken care of you.

'Now listen, if you just sign this document I have here, my friend, *I'll take you in psi to Globadan*. It is not what I intended, but it can't be helped. You know what I mean by taking you in psi?'

King Horace nodded gravely. The pseudo-men had been created originally without any ancient limbic brain – what was once called 'the subconscious'. They had been provided instead with a second upper brain, which was capable of willing the transference into itself of the entire contents of a man's brain.

'I know you have strange powers,' he said submissively.

'No stranger than some of yours, my friend.'

'What can man do that you can't?' the king asked.

Ap-Eye leant forward and said a word in his ear. King Horace smiled feebly and suggested the oracle consulted Swap about that.

'It's for Swap I wish you to sign this,' the pseudo-man said abruptly, jumping up, clapping his hands briskly and thrusting forward the document under his arm. Wondering what he was going to read, King Horace took it gingerly over to the dim illumination and scanned it.

It declared in florid terms that the undersigned, King Able Harkon Horace, wished to abdicate from the throne of his country, surrendering every claim thereto for himself and his heirs and assigns for ever. He furthermore adjured his court and ministers, as the final prerogative of his reign, that his place as ruler of his aforesaid country be ceded to his companion bearing the distinguishing nomenclature of Swap—

'So Swap's behind all this!' exploded the king.

'Of course not – I thought you were a judge of character? Swap does what I tell him. Now hurry up and sign.'

'I can't—'

But there was a firm hand on his elbow and the grating voice of Ap-Eye whispering urgently: 'Sign, you sick fool, sign and let's be away!'

Hypnosis? 'I can't—' began the king again, but he brought out a pen and signed with an automatic flourish. Next moment, he was lying back on the narrow bench with Ap-Eye bending eagerly over him.

'Come on, old friend, we're going to get you cured. Nothing to worry about any more. Look at me hard now, hurry up . . .'

The eyes, the just eyes, grew suddenly more luminous — then they fell forward on to Ap-Eye's cheeks, dangling springily. In the cavities were more eyes, but these lenses, strange, whirling, flickering, held a power too fearful to be ordinarily revealed. Under their induction, King Horace felt himself fade into a minute pool of being.

And then he was merged into Ap-Eye.

A moment of pain grew and vanished as he fitted into the new brain. His consciousness had been poured from one body into the other as easily as liquid is poured from one vessel to another.

Ap-Eye stood up slowly. The king's body lay breathing shallowly on the bench, relaxed and deserted.

Disturbing though the experience was, it was not unpleasurable. He, his body, his role in life, had always been misfits.

'You'll stay in a trance till I put you safely back there. The body as a body will function more smoothly without your interfering mind in it.'

'I'm frightened.'

'What, because you happen to use the same mouth to eat and speak with as I? You've never been better off, old friend. This body's immortal, you know. And now — to present our document to Swap. Sleep tight, sweet prince!'

There was no interconnection between their minds, or Ap-Eye allowed none. Horace — he could now hardly think of himself as a sovereign — was carried helplessly as the other willed. The odd idea that he no longer had any being obsessed him; still, there was pleasure in savouring the integration of a fit body, although he realized more clearly than

95

ever that his unending illness rode in his mind, as he rode parasitically in Ap-Eye's.

He watched or half-watched helplessly as the spaceship landed on Earth. His old body (the trial had been waived in view of his 'illness' and Swap's promise to take the living corpse into his custody) was shipped home, Ap-Eye collected money from the royal coffers, Swap began a prolonged debate with the court. The two elderly nurses slipped off and married the two stokers.

Their journey to Globadan began almost at once.

It was long, but not monotonous. Gradually, as they wormed their way out through the long light years, towards the rim of the Galaxy, the Döppler effect became noticeable – through those strange optics of Ap-Eye's. The people about them, passengers and crew, began to slow up. It was gradual, very gradual, the dragging of a foot, the faltering flash of a girl's eye. And to this Ap-Eye carefully adjusted his movements, impeding them deliberately, while his made brain functioned as rapidly as usual.

So they came to Globadan.

He stood with another prisoner on the starting line. *That* had been easily arranged: the Globadanians were a primitive people with harsh laws – a window broken at midnight, a flash of moonlight on the shattered glass and he had been hurried enthusiastically to prison.

Now he waited beneath the great grandstand, his ears – Ap-Eye's ears – full of the noise of festival. The yellow sun shone down on banners, bright instruments and feathers. Everyone wore plumage for the occasion: the crowd might have been a flock of birds. And beside him, curbed but snorting, was the line of shubshubs.

The shubshub is native to several planets. It is one of the finest creatures in God's galaxy, tall, fleet, sweet of temper. The specimens entered for this race were all over seventeen hands high, six-legged and shod with steel. Their muscles rippled and their white beaks shone.

The starter's trumpet blared, the clarion note plunging them into gracious action. The treble mile lay flat before them, and they plunged over it like war arrows.

But they ran their splendid race on the slow outer edge of

the galaxy: through their limbs flowed the slur of space-time. To Ap-Eye's unchanged perceptions they merely crawled.

He ran. The course was ochre-coloured.

The great beasts plunging in bright slow-motion, the sun a fervent yellow, the time holding back, waiting for him, waiting . . .

. . . as once before it had waited, over thirty years ago.

The clock on the palace tower had been stopped. It had been stopped deliberately to delay the king and queen, to keep them idling on the summer beach an extra ten minutes. The young guardsman who in fear of his life had stopped it hurried down to the royal nursery.

There was Horace's mother, a gardener's wife at the palace, young, lovely and nervous, with her child clasped in her arms. The child was himself – Horace! She looked up as the guardsman came in and flashed him a brief smile of thanks for his help.

'Quick,' he said. 'Let's go!'

She hurried over to the cot with the crown emblazoned on it and pulled the curtain back. There lay the royal infant asleep, a child of the same age, almost of the same appearance as her own.

'Quick!' urged the guardsman.

Gently, she lifted out the royal babe and put her child in its place. She leant over it lovingly, her eyes filling with tears as it stared solemnly back at her.

'Fear not, my own babe,' she whispered. 'Your mother is a wicked woman. She is going to run away with another man – but at least she has given you a good start in the world. Now you must forget her! Sleep well, my little love, and when you wake you'll be a prince.'

'Quick!' said the guardsman. 'Time is against us, Anne!'

She thrust the royal babe into his arms and said: 'Smuggle this one out to your aunt in the country, then, as we arranged. Tell her to call it – oh, Swap!'

'And I'll see you tonight by the harbour, my love?'

'You have an anxious face, sir!' she said coquettishly.

'You'll be there, Anne, dearest?'

'Have the engine running ready for me.'

'Total recall!' bellowed Ap-Eye's voice in his ear.

From the immensity of space, from the greater immensity of a life's memory, Horace returned. The yellow sun, the slowly plunging line of animals behind, the dun-coloured plain, the gaudy spectators . . . they slipped back into place. Ahead loomed the winning post.

'He kept the engine running but she never came, poor chap,' Ap-Eye said. 'She had really fallen for an ugly little man who promised her the stars.'

'Not . . . you?'

'Yes, I . . . alas! We came here for a honeymoon. When I foolishly confessed I was a pseudo-man – she took a poisoned potion . . . I was too much in love, she had too much pride . . . Ah, it's a long time ago, to human life if not to me. But now finally I hope I have erased the consequences of my folly as well as possible. It's not a perfect world, old friend. How do you feel?'

He could not answer. He knew he was free at last, and the knowledge choked him. Only a few more yards to run – they had won easily.

'How do you feel?' Ap-Eye asked again. 'Looking forward to getting your own body back?'

'Yes,' gulped Horace. 'Yes, old friend.' And as he spoke he noticed Priestess Colinette Shawl standing clapping among the throng.

In a burst of triumph, they flashed past the winning post.

Criminal Record

This must all be written down quickly while I have the chance. Let me see how it began ... Yes, the gramophone record and the smoof. Only two days ago – don't bother to check that word; I will repeat it: smoof. Only two days ago – my name's Curly Kelledew, by the way, and I'd better try and think straight.

Are you fortunate enough to know Cambridge? One of my favourite haunts there is Curry Passage. It boasts three very similar, very satisfactory junk shops (over the three doors the word 'junk' is spelt A-N-T-I-Q-U-E-S). This particular afternoon, I made a find – quite accidentally. I had already bought a three-foot Chinese junk with a high prow and a real lateen sail that I thought would amuse a nephew of mine, and a little eighteenth-century milkmaid in china that was purely for my own gratification, and was just turning to go. Then I saw the pile of records behind a chest.

I put down the junk and the china maid, and began to shuffle through the pile. They were a mixed bunch, some 78s, some LPs, sold probably by hard-up undergraduates at the end of the Trinity term. Jazz – several Louis Armstrong's for those who liked him – dance, Stravinsky, a cracked 'Prize Song' and – I breathed faster! – Borodin's Second Symphony, the Coates recording that is now out of the catalogue. It was in an album, neat and new. I scrutinized the first record, and it looked as if it had never been played. The shop had no player, but the price was low; I wanted that symphony, so I paid my money and carted the album off with the junk and the figurine.

That was how I got it! The next afternoon, Sunday, Harry Crossway came round as usual. That's my definition of a friend, a man you work with all the week and are glad to see on Sundays. After a drink, after he had admired the little porcelain breasts swelling beneath the porcelain bodice, I pulled out the Borodin. We had the first movement on before I got the second record out of its envelope. I knew at once that it was odd, although it bore the correct red labels in the middle; when I touched them, they peeled off easily.

We were left with a chocolate-coloured freak twice as fat as the usual record, only one side grooved and those grooves highly extraordinary looking. Of course, I should have noticed it in the shop, but in my excitement I had only glanced at the labels and that had been sufficient. Clearly, I had been had!

I stated my irritation in very certain terms, and spent five minutes stamping round my room. Only when I had calmed a little did Harry say, in an interested voice: 'Do you mind if I try this on the table, Curly?'

Harry and I work for Cambridge's biggest radio firm, on the experimental side. Discs, tapes, short wave, TV – plain and coloured – we are paid to tackle them all, well paid. Next time you hear of a crease-innoculator on the new TV cameras, think of Harry and Curly, the proud parents. All of which I mention merely to explain why one wall of my lounge is covered with amplifiers and what-have-you and the bureau is full of electric tackle. All my equipment is home assembled, an improvement on the commercial variety. Even so, we did not get anything out of the mystery record. The turntable seemed unable to hold it; it slipped beneath the light pick-up. For one thing, the hole in the middle of the disc was not round but shaped like a star with sixteen points; for another, the groove seemed to be separated by a smooth groove of fair width on which the needle had no grip. We left it, and played 'Pictures at an Exhibition' instead.

But when Harry had gone, I picked the thick disc up again and re-examined it. On the blank side was a small panel. It yielded to my exploratory fingernail and slid up. Underneath was a label which read:

INTERPLANETARY

Cat: Ganymede-Eros-Earth-Venus
Cr: Sabotage. Timesliding. Murder.
Type: Humanoid Venusian experiment: smoof.
Name: Above type use only generic name, smoof.

Filed —/viii/14/305
Rev. 2/xii/12/309

When I had read it, I re-read it. Then I re-read it. Catching sight of myself in a mirror, I saw my features were suffused with an expression of blank imbecility. 'What's a smoof?' I asked the dolt.

'A humanoid Venusian experiment,' it replied.

Was the disc a joke of some sort? And what was a videofile? And what was a videofile doing in my room? I put it on the turntable again and started it up. But again came the trouble of dodging the smooth groove; that one being the wider, into that one the sapphire generally went. Finally I succeeded in hitting the other groove.

There was a high and rapid babble of sound, together with a rasping noise. I switched off smartly. There was no reason why it should have worked. Then it occurred to me that at 78 revs I might have played it too fast. I switched on at $33\frac{1}{3}$. Now the babble resolved itself into a high, fast voice; but still that horrible rasp. Again I switched off. Possibly the sapphire was over-running the grooves; somewhere I had a finer one on a lighter pickup. After searching excitedly through three littered drawers, I found it and attached it. Breathless, setting the speed still slower, I tried again.

This time I had it! I had, to be accurate, a number of things. I soon gathered this disc was only the sound-track for a sort of film. And I knew the police report was no joke; it threw sidelights, tantalizing and confusing, on a complex future world. It threw a searching light on to a smoof that made my hair stand on end . . .

Next day I smuggled the disc down to the works, carefully avoided Harry Crossway, and took a few plates of it under the X-ray apparatus they use for checking valves, etc.

The X-rays revealed an interior that looked at first about as complicated to me as a watch would have done to a primitive who had only just stumbled on to the use of a wheel. But the harder I looked, the more convinced I became that the disc was some sort of television receiver. There were, for instance, the normal horizontal and vertical deflecting systems employed in today's circuits, although infinitely better packed and planned.

The thin spiral that we had called our 'smooth groove' proved to be a vast number of separate but linked rectangular plates. They were made of a glass that seemed infinitely strong and thin. And then I had an idea, and locked myself away from mortal men for a day. Oh, one thing I ought to mention. Foolishly – curiosity plays deadly tricks on a man! – I inserted an ad. in the local paper. It read 'Smoofs welcome here. No spoofs.' And my address. Facetious to the last, that's me.

When I had inserted that ad. I did not fully believe. But at the end of that day and night of figuring, swearing and tinkering, I emerged believing all too fully. I felt grey; I felt bald; I felt scared. With a shaking hand, I phoned Harry. He was still at the workshop, but at the sound of my voice he said he would be over at once. While I waited, I took a drink and composed myself.

Very shortly I heard Harry letting himself in. He climbed the stairs, entered, and said, handing me a note: 'This was tucked in your letter flap.' Then he exclaimed: 'What have you got here?' and went over to my gadgets on the side-table.

'Is this what you called me over for?'

'Yes,' I said.

'Huh! You sounded so excited, I brought my revolver over just in case.'

'We may need it yet,' I answered dazedly, my eyes scanning the note he had brought up. It was a reply to my advert. It merely said: 'I shall be at your house at nine o'clock. Set no traps. Smoof.'

'Oh Lord!' I whispered. It was ten past eight. Outside, the street lamps were on. It was very still.

'What's all the mystery?' Harry asked impatiently. In

some ways he is a queer fellow. Slow and methodical in his work, yet otherwise reckless – a round peg with a square hole somewhere inside him.

It seemed best to tell him everything if he was to be involved in the affair. I crossed to the apparatus. I had a large cathode ray tube resting in front of the radiogram and connected to a specially doctored image orthicon that was clamped to an extremely clumsy bit of mechanism. This last gadget was merely a long-running clockwork motor that moved my image orthicon slowly in towards the centre of the record, keeping its neck constantly in – touching, in fact – the smooth groove.

'I'm going to play that disc to you now, Harry – on this.'

'You got it to work?' he asked.

'Yes. It's a telefile from the police records in some future time.' I paused for comment, but he made none.

'How far in the future I don't know. Perhaps two hundred years ... not less. You'll be able to judge. You'll see vast technical ability going hand in hand with the death of conscience – the sort of thing a pessimist might predict today. Not that there's much room on this record for more than guesses, which seems to make it more hauntingly dreadful; and although I've got it to work, it doesn't work well.'

'Surprised you got it to work at all!' he said.

'I don't know. Supposing Edison got hold of one of our present-day recordings. He'd soon fathom it.'

'You're some Edison!'

I saluted snappily and said: 'Thank you. Actually it's quite simple. At least, my part of it is. Up to a point, in fact, the whole thing is easily understandable, if not duplicatable, by modern knowledge.'

'Up to which point?' Scepticism in his voice.

'Harry, we've got hold of a television record from the future. It's certainly more compendious for short documents than a roll of film. The unusual feature in it is a frozen signal. It seems the signal is shot from transmitter into a video memory circuit; or perhaps the ability lies in the transmitter, in which case duplication will be more difficult – I'll have it all worked out, if it takes a lifetime. If I've got a lifetime ...'

'Go on about the record.'

103

'Oh yes. I've had to take the turntable pin off the radiogram and install an insulated cog in its place, over which the record just fits. As you can see, two brushes are in permanent contact with the top of the cog; they're plugged into a transformer off the mains, so that a permanent current of 40 watts is fed into the record as it revolves. Shall I switch on?'

He did not know what was coming and his scientific interest was aroused, so he said – still clinging to disbelief: 'What sort of a circuit have you got inside the record?'

As I described, I sketched on a bit of paper. 'Some of the circuitry I can't understand,' I confessed. 'The frozen signal feeds to a video amplifier and then splits into restorer circuits – you'll see if you don't think them the sweetest little jobs you've ever set eyes on! – and the ordinary synchronizing separator and horizontal and vertical deflecting circuits (which, by the way, are self-controlled on a fluid-drive principle).

'Here the two circuits join on to what acts, as far as I can see, as the hind part of an image orthicon. There's a photocathode to take the light image and a quite ordinary electron lens system which focuses the electrons on to the target, the target being this superfine "film" glass which is our smooth groove. From then on it's all my own work. As you can see, I've broken down one of our image orthicons and fixed it up so that when the turntable turns the fine-mesh screen is touching the smooth groove the whole time.'

'In other words, you've got half the image orthicon in the record and the rest outside?'

'Exactly. Unfortunately it meant a much smaller fine-mesh screen to get in the groove, so that the signal is chopped. However, you'll see enough to get a good scare. From there, it's plain sailing. These are the leads to the cathode ray tube—'

'What about your sound circuit?' he asked.

'Same as normal – our normal. Grooves run between the video grooves. They're insulated, of course. Featherweight pickup. Twenty-eight revs per minute. I've just had to put a little boost on the amplifier. Shall I switch on?' My palms were sweating.

Harry stared blankly out of the window and whispered to

himself: 'A television recording!' Then he said: 'Seems a funny thing to want to have.'

'It comes from a funny civilization,' I answered.

'Switch on,' he said.

The screen came alive with a shot of the police station in which the evidence on the smoof had been gathered. What a station it was, an ugly saucer-shaped metal affair built into and round the asteroid Eros, which had been pressed into a new orbit to swing it as far out as Jupiter and as near in as Mercury. Lord, but it looked dismal – and half-finished. Perhaps, after all, I had not fixed the disc up too well, because we got a flicker of stills, some discontinuous, and most with a shower of 'noise' across them, so that you could not help getting the idea that our descendants were slipshod, imagination outriding inclination, invention outpacing execution.

We flicked inside the Eros station. Dirt, peeling walls, and a great bank of instruments a block long, before which a broken-nosed officer slouched. 'Exterminate der wrong-doer!' he said, as a voice announced him as High Space-Dick Hagger. He had been in charge of this smoof's case since—

Grimy sheds that only on this second showing I realized to be dwelling quarters. This time I caught a name too. Bristol. Pronounced Brissol. Or perhaps it was Brussels, after all. Either way – ugh! Just a lot of giant shanties with ugly plumbing, stretching out to a mile-wide desert, after which they began again and spread to the horizon. The desert was a landing-ground for rockets after their long supersonic glide in from space. We saw one come in – and plough straight into the shanties. Explosion. Fire. 'Dis was smoof work,' said the terse commentator.

We saw the shanties up again. There was a shot of the inside of somewhere, and then more shanties; they flickered – vanished, and there was a forest there instead. 'More smoof work. Timesliding . . .'

'Good for them!' I whispered. Those trees were the first bit of beauty we had seen.

Venus next. A human settlement, half underground, on a mountain range. Clouds, desolation. The commentary was desperately hard to follow, the language sounding like some kind of verbal shorthand. We were evidently having a flashback. Men crawled in the muck of a ravine, erecting more buildings, drilling, blasting, and all the while weighed down with space suits. 'Foul atmosphere. Carbon dioxide 'n' bacillae,' the commentary grunted.

Inside this outpost, we saw colonists living like animals and scientists living like tramps. Atomic lighting and straw beds. A crude sort of vivisection was going on – and the subjects were human beings. A snow shower of static blurred the image. Then we were peering from the outpost across the dreary gulches of Venus. A chain of human beings passed the window in single file. They were poorly clad and wore no space suits; a close-up showed us, sickeningly, why. They could breathe the unbreatheable Venusian air. An operation had been performed; their nostrils were blocked with living flesh, and a complex, multi-flanged nose was grafted into their windpipes.

'So were first smots created,' said the commentator. 'Dey never returned. Dey multiplied in hidden recesses o' planet. Some o' dem cross-bred with true Venusians and formed smoofs. Smot and smoof greatest menace . . .'

We were shown pithily just what a menace they were. They started as a new race without background or tradition, loathing the planet that was now their home, but with the knowledge of hate and of the weapons of science, to which they speedily added a few kinks of their own. In five generations they had space travel and in seven they had split the space-time band and were able, in space, to travel for some distance back and forward in time. Our commentator barked an explanation of all this that seemed to consist mainly of formulae, but it was obvious that humanity had been unable to duplicate the discovery of the semi-human race. Fortunately, the smot and smoof were able to time travel only from space, which meant that their big, rickety spaceships moved a century back and then released a scout which could blast down and land, wreaking what havoc it could, and later rejoin its parent ship; but the warp effect involved was only operative in free space and by the enormous nuclear directors that needed a giant vessel to carry them. So the police forces of Earth, spread out in grim fortresses over the whole barbarous ring of inner planets, were given sitting targets – provided the targets would sit in the present.

Under a state of affairs where your yesterday might hourly be cut from under you or your future be already shattered, humanity and its concerns suffered a staggering blow. Ethics, logic, the sane comforts of a continuous memory, were now swept away. Rigid martial law was universally declared, air, army and space forces turned into an ubiquitous police force.

Harry and I sat helpless before this glimpse into chaos, where tomorrow flickered helplessly to keep up with the brutal revision of yesterday. It was by these stab-in-the-back methods that Bristol or Brussels was demolished, and other centres followed the same fate. The forces of the smoof seemed to be spreading destruction everywhere; the only hope for man was that the semi-humans seemed to have run into another race in their future who possessed weapons the smoof could not withstand.

We saw a smoof ship captured by Earth's police, and its crew, with one exception, massacred without mercy on the spot, the exception, a smoof of some importance, being taken to Eros station. He was the subject of our criminal file; his wan, noseless features slid across the screen. There was an interval – an explosion – the station crumbled into ruin – smoofs appeared from a giant ship visible through a gaping hole – the hole disappeared, the station re-integrated – the smoofs vanished – reappeared – were shot down – vanished. Timesliding – an earthquake in human metabolism. The scene blurred and trembled, filmed crazily from a high angle on automatic; Hollywood's patient art of focus and composition has been lost in this dizzy totalitarian future. Abruptly there was nothing.

'Time lines crossed?' Harry asked from a wrinkled face.

'Yes,' I said. 'It comes on again in a minute.'

It did. It was quite different. Still squalor, still Eros, but all changed. Other men carried on the hunt. High Space-Dick Hagger had a good nose but freckles and a bald head. The very symbols on his uniform had changed.

'Der smoof was rescued. Gone into der past – noo machines carrying them further back than ever,' the commentator grunted. 'Record revideoed 2/xii/12/309 – we hope.'

There it ended. It had only taken about twenty minutes, but in that time I suppose we had both lost something of our souls – the same something those unhappy descendants of ours had long forgotten amid kaleidoscoping events. And in the last seconds of vision a detail I had not noticed before: across that dreary new instrument room a man walked, near enough to the recording eye for us to see his face clearly. It was Harry Crossway.

And that changed the whole meaning of the whole affair. It meant that my finding the record was not an accident, but something planned by beings with a knowledge of our future; it meant the smoofs were pressing even further back in time for – what? – technicians like Harry and me? And it gave, above all, a ghastly sense of predestination: and predestination is something you can't level a gun at. Harry at least was going to be – was it *certain*? – kidnapped into that Frankenstein world; the videofile proved that.

And me? I can only guess, and it gives me the shakes.

Now it is five minutes to nine. I have phoned the unbelieving police, more in anger than hope. One lurks downstairs, one in the bathroom – neither is armed. Harry, a man with a fear on his back, crouches behind the curtain that screens off my bed. He is nursing his revolver. I scrawl this down – it may help, somehow.

Outside, dear old Cambridge is silent. No, a car pulls round the corner. It draws up outside. A man climbs out, a man with a light scarf round his throat – no, no, it's not a man! His nose—

I reckon we haven't got a chance.

The Failed Men

'It's too crowded here!' he exclaimed aloud. 'It's too crowded! It's too CROWDED!'

He swung round, his mouth open, his face contorted like a squeezed lemon, nearly knocking a passer-by off the pavement. The passer-by bowed, smiled forgivingly and passed on, his eyes clearly saying: 'Let him be – it's one of the poor devils off the ship.'

'It's too crowded,' Surrey Edmark said again at the retreating back. It was night. He stood hatless under the glare of the New Orchard Road lights, bewildered by the flowing cosmopolitan life of Singapore about him. People: thousands of 'em, touchable; put out a hand gently, feel alpaca, silk, nylon, satin, plain, patterned, or crazily flowered; thousands within screaming distance. If you screamed, just how many of those dirty, clean, pink, brown, desirable or offensive convoluted ears would scoop up your decibels?

No, he told himself, no screaming, please. These people who swarm like phantoms about you are real; they wouldn't like it. And your doctor, who did not consider you fit to leave the observation ward yet, he's real enough; he wouldn't like it if he learnt you had been screaming in a main street. And you yourself – how real were you? How real was *anything* when you had recently had perfect proof that it was all finished? Really finished: rolled up and done with and discarded and forgotten.

That dusty line of thought must be avoided. He needed somewhere quiet, a place to sit and breathe deeply. Everyone must be deceived; he must hide the fused, dead feeling inside from them; then he could go back home. But he had also to try and hide the deadness from himself, and that needed more cunning. Like alpha particles, a sense of futility had riddled him, and he was mortally sick.

Surrey noticed a turning just ahead. Thankfully he went to it and branched out of the crowds into a dim, narrow thoroughfare. He passed three women in short dresses

109

smoking together; farther on a fellow was being sick into a privet hedge. And there was a café with a sign saying 'The Iceberg'. Deserted chairs and tables stood outside on an ill-lit veranda; Surrey climbed the two steps and sat wearily down. This was luxury.

The light was poor, Surrey sat alone. Inside the café several people were eating, and a girl sang, accompanying herself on a stringed, lute-like instrument. He couldn't understand the words, but it was simple and nostalgic, her voice conveying more than the music; he closed his eyes, letting the top spin within him, the top of his emotions. The girl stopped her singing suddenly, as if tired, and walked on to the veranda to stare into the night. Surrey opened his eyes and looked at her.

'Come and talk to me,' he called.

She turned her head haughtily to the shadows where he sat, and then turned it back. Evidently, she had met with that sort of invitation before. Surrey clenched his fists in frustration; here he sat, isolated in space and time, needing comfort, needing . . . oh, nothing could heal him, but salves existed . . . The loneliness welled up inside, forcing him to speak again.

'I'm from the ship,' he said unable to hold back a note of pleading.

At that, she came over and took a seat facing him. She was Chinese, and wore the timeless slit dress of her race, big daisies chasing themselves over the gentle contours of her body.

'Of course I didn't know,' she said. 'But I can see in your eyes . . . that you are from the ship.' She trembled slightly and asked: 'May I get you a drink?'

Surrey shook his head. 'Just to have you sitting there . . .'

He was feeling better. Irrationally, a voice inside said: 'Well, you've been through a harsh experience, but now you're back again you can recover, can't you, go back to what you were?' The voice frequently asked that: but the answer was always No; the experience was still spreading inside, like cancer.

'I heard your ship come in,' the Chinese girl said. 'I live just near here – Bukit Timah Road, if you know it, and I was at my window, talking with a friend.'

110

He thought of the amazing sunshine and the eternal smell of cooking fats and the robshaws clacking by and this girl and her friend chattering in her apartment – and the orchestral crash as the ship arrived, making them forget their sentences; but all remote, centuries ago.

'It's a funny noise it makes,' he said. 'The sound of a time ship breaking out of the time barrier.'

'It scares the chickens,' she said.

Silence. Surrey wanted to produce something else to say, to keep the girl sitting with him, but nothing would dissolve into words. He neglected the factor of her own human curiosity, which made her keen to stay; she inquired again if he would like a drink, and then said: 'Would it be good for you if you told me something about it?'

'I'd call that a leading question.'

'It's very – *bad* ahead, isn't it? I mean, the papers say . . .' She hesitated nervously.

'What do they say?' he asked.

'Oh, you know, they say that it's bad. But they don't really explain; they don't seem to understand . . .'

'That's the whole key to it,' he told her. 'We don't seem to understand. If I talked to you all night, you still wouldn't understand. *I* wouldn't understand . . .'

She was beautiful, sitting there with her little lute in her hand. And he had travelled far away beyond her lute and her beauty, far beyond nationality or even music; it had all gone into the dreary dust of the planet, all gone – final – nothing left – except degradation. And puzzlement.

'I'll try and tell you,' he said. 'What was that tune you were just singing? Chinese song?'

'No, it was Malayan. It's an old song, very old, called "Terang Boelan". It's about – oh, moonlight, you know, that kind of thing. It's sentimental.'

'I didn't even know what language it was in, but perhaps in a way I understood it.'

'You said you were going to tell me about the future,' she told him gently.

'Yes. Of course. It's a sort of tremendous relief work we're doing. You know what they call it: The Intertemporal Red Cross. It's accurate, but when you've actually been –

ahead, it sounds a silly, flashy, title. I don't know, perhaps not. I'm not sure of anything any more.'

He stared out at the darkness; it was going to rain. When he began to speak again, his voice was firmer.

The IRC is really organized by the Paulls (he said to the Chinese girl). They call themselves the Paulls; we should call them the technological *élite* of the Three Thousand, One Hundred and Fifty-Seventh Century. That's a terribly long way ahead – we, with our twenty-four centuries since Christ can hardly visualize it. Our ship stopped there, in their time. It was very austere: the Paulls are austere people. They live only on mountains overlooking the oceans, and have moved mountains to every coast for their own edification.

The Paulls are unlike us, yet they are brothers compared with the men we are helping, the Failed Men.

Time travel had been invented long before the age of the Paulls, but it is they who perfected it, they who accidentally discovered the plight of the Failed Men, and they who manage the terrific business of relief. For the world of the Paulls, rich as it is – will be, has insufficient resources to cope alone with the task without vitiating its strength. So it organized the fleet of time ships, the ITR, to collect supplies from different ages and bear them out ahead to the Failed Men.

Five different ages are co-operating on the project, under the Paull leadership. There are the Middle People, as the Paulls call them. They are a race of philosophers, mainly pastoral, and we found them too haughty; they live about twenty thousand centuries ahead of the Paulls. Oh, it's a long time . . . And there are –but never mind that! They had little to do with us, or we with them.

We – this present day, was the only age without time travel of the five. The Paulls chose us because we happen to have peace and plenty. And do you know what they call us? The Children. The Children! We, with all our weary sophistication . . . Perhaps they're right; they have a method of gestalt reasoning absolutely beyond our wildest pretensions.

You know, I remember once on the voyage out ahead, I asked one of the Paulls why they had never visited our age before; and he said: 'But we have. We broke at the nine-

112

teenth century and again at the twenty-sixth. That's pretty close spacing! And that's how we knew so much about you.'

They have so much *experience*, you see. They can walk round for a day in one century and tell you what'll be happening the next six or seven. It's a difference of outlook, I suppose; something as simple as that.

I suppose you'll remember better than I when the Paulls first broke here, as you are actually on the spot. I was at home then, doing a peaceful job; if it hadn't been so peaceful I might not have volunteered for the IRC. What a storm it caused! A good deal of panic in with the excitement. Yes, we proved ourselves children then, *and* in the adulation we paid the Paulls while they toured the world's capitals. During the three months they waited here while we organized supplies and men, they must have been in a fury of impatience to be off; yet they revealed nothing, giving their unsensational lectures on the plight of the Failed Men and smiling for the threedy cameras.

All the while money poured in for the cause, and the piles of tinned food and medical supplies grew and filled the holds of the big ship. We were like kids throwing credits to street beggars: all sorts of stuff of no earthly use went into that ship. What would a Failed Man do with a launderer or a cycloview machine? At last we were off, with all the world's bands playing like mad and the ship breaking with noise enough to drown all bands and startle your chickens – off for the time of the Failed Men!

'I think I'd like that drink you offered me now,' Surrey said to the Chinese girl, breaking off his narrative.

'Certainly.' She snapped her fingers at arm's length, her hand in the light from the restaurant, her face in the gloom, eyes fixed on his eyes.

'The Paulls had told you it was going to be tough,' she said.

'Yes. We underwent pretty rough mental training from them before leaving the here and now. Many of the men were weeded out. But I got through. They elected me Steersman. I was top of their first class.'

Surrey was silent a moment, surprised to hear pride in his own voice. Pride left, after that experience! Yet there was no pride in him; it was just the voice running in an old channel, the naked soul crouching in an ancient husk of character.

The drink arrived. The Chinese girl had one. too, a long one in a misty glass; she put her lute down to drink it. Surrey took a sip of his and then resumed the story.

We were travelling ahead! (he said). It was a schoolboy's dream come true. Yet our excitement soon became blunted by monotony. There is nothing simultaneous in time travel, as people have imagined. It took us two ship's months to reach the Paulls' age, and there all but one of them left us to continue on alone into the future.

They had the other ages to supervise, and many organizational problems to attend to: yet I sometimes wonder if they did not use those problems as an excuse, to save their having to visit the age of the Failed Men. Perhaps they thought us less sensitive, and therefore better fitted for the job.

And so we went ahead again. The office of Steersman was almost honorary, entailing merely the switching off of power when the journey was automatically ended. We sat about and talked, we chosen few, reading or viewing in the excellent libraries the Paulls had installed. Time passed quickly enough, yet we were glad when we arrived.

Glad!

The age of the Failed Men is far in the future: many hundred millions of years ahead, or thousands of millions; the Paulls would never tell us the exact number. Does it matter? It was a long time ... There's plenty of time – too much, more than anyone will ever need.

We stepped out on to that day's earth. I had childishly expected – oh, to see the sun stuck at the horizon, or turned purple, or the sky full of moons, or something equally dramatic; but there was not even a shadow over the fair land, and the earth had not aged a day. Only man had aged.

The Failed Men differed from us anatomically and spiritually; it was the former quality which struck us first. They just looked like a bunch of dejected oddities sitting among piles of stores, and we wanted to laugh. The humorists among us called them 'the Zombies' at first – but in a few days there were no humorists left among us.

The Failed Men had no real hands. From their wrists grew five long and prehensile fingers, and the middle digit touched the ground lightly when they walked, for their spines curved in an arc and their heads were thrust far forward. To counter this, their skulls had elongated into boat shapes, scaphocephalic fashion. They had no eyebrows, nor indeed a brow at all, nor any hair at all, although the pores of their skin stood out flakily, giving them a fluffy appearance from a distance.

When they looked at you their eyes held no meaning: they were blank with a surfeit of experience, as though they had now regained a horrible sort of innocence. When they spoke to you, their voices were hollow and their sentences as short and painful as a child's toothache. We could not understand their language, except through the electronic translator banks given us by the Paulls.

They looked a mournful sight, but at first we were not too disturbed; we didn't, you see, quite grasp the nature of the problem. Also, we were very busy, reclaiming more Failed Men from the ground.

Four great aid centres had been established on the earth. Of the other four races in the IRC, two managed sanitoria construction and equipment, another nursing, feeding and staffing, and the fourth communication, rehabilitation and liaison between centres. And we – 'the Children!' – our job was to exhume the Failed Men and bring them to the centres: a simple job for the simple group! Between us we all had to get the race of man started again – back into harness.

All told, I suppose there are only about six million Failed Men spread over the earth. We had to go out and dig them up. We had specially made tractors with multiple blades on the front which dug slowly and gently into the soil.

The Failed Men had 'cemetery areas'; we called them that, although they had not been designed as cemeteries. It was like a bad, silly dream. Working day and night, we trundled forward, furrowing up the earth as you strip back a soiled bed. In the mould, a face would appear, an arm with the long fingers, a pair of legs, tumbling into the light. We would stop the machine and get down to the body, digging with trowels round it. So we would exhume another man or

115

woman – it was hard to tell which they were, their sexual features were not pronounced.

They would be in a coma. Their eyes would open, staring like peek-a-boo dolls, then close again with a click. We'd patch them up with an injection, stack them on stretchers and send them back in a load to base. It was a harrowing job, and no pun intended.

When the corpses had had some attention and care, they revived. Within a month they would be up and walking, trundling about the hospital grounds in that round-shouldered way, their great boat-heads nodding at every step. And then it was I talked to them and tried to understand.

The translator banks, being Paull made, were the best possible. But their limitations were the limitations of our own language. If the Failed Men said their word for 'sun', the machine said 'sun' to us, and we understood by that the same thing the Failed Men intended. But away from the few concrete, common facts of our experience, the business was less easy. Less synonyms, more overtones: it was the old linguistic problem, but magnified here by the ages which lay between us.

I remember tackling one old woman on our first spell back at the centre. I say old, but for all I know she was sweet sixteen; they just looked ancient.

'I hope you don't mind being dug – er, rescued?' I asked politely.

'Not at all. A pleasure,' the banks said for her. Polite stereotypes. No real meaning in any language, but the best machine in the world makes them sound sillier than they are.

'Would you mind if we discussed this whole thing?'

'What object?' the banks asked for her.

I'd asked the wrong question. I did not mean thing = object, but thing = matter. That sort of trip-up kept getting in the way of our discussion; the translator spoke better English than I.

'Can we talk about your problem?' I asked her, trying again.

'I have no problem. My problem has been resolved.'

'I should be interested to hear about it.'

116

'What do you require to know about it? I will tell you anything.'

That at least was promising. Willing if not co-operative; they had long ago forgotten the principle of co-operation.

'You know I come from the distant past to help you?' The banks translated me undramatically.

'Yes. It is noble of you all to interrupt your lives for us,' she said.

'Oh no; we want to see the race of man starting off again on a right track. We believe it should not die away yet. We are glad to help, and are sorry you took the wrong track.'

'When we started, we were on a track others before us – you – had made.' It was not defiant, just a fact being stated.

'But the deviation was yours. You made it by an act of will. I'm not condemning, mind; obviously you would not have taken that way had you known it would end in failure.'

She answered. I gathered she was just faintly angry, probably burning all the emotion in her. Her hollow voice spanged and doomed away, and the translator banks gave out simultaneously in fluent English. Only it didn't make sense.

It went something like this: 'Ah, but what you do not realize, because your realizing is completely undeveloped and unstarted, is how to fail. Failing is not failing unless it is defeat, and this defeat of ours – if you realize it *is* a failing – is only a failure. A final failure. But as such, it is only a matter of a result, because in time this realization tends to breed only the realization of the result of failure; whereas the resolution of our failure, as opposed to the failure—'

'Stop!' I shouted. 'No! Save the modern poetry or the philosophical treatise for later. It doesn't mean anything to me, I'm sorry. We'll take it for granted there was some sort of a failure. Are you going to be able to make a success of this new start we're giving you?'

'It is not a new start,' she said, beginning reasonably enough. 'Once you have had the result, a start is no longer a result. It is merely in the result of failing and all that is in the case is the start or the failure – depending, for us, on the start, for you on the failure. And you can surely see that even here failure depends abnormally on the beginning of the result, which concerns us more than the failure, simply

117

because it is the result. What you don't see is the failure of the result of the result's failure to start a result—'

'Stop!' I shouted again.

I went to one of the Paull commanders. He was what my mother would have called 'a fine man'. I told him the thing was beginning to become an obsession with me.

'It is with all of us,' he replied.

'But if only I could grasp a fraction of their problem! Look, Commander, we come out here all this way ahead to help them – and still we don't know what we're helping them *from*.'

'We know *why* we're helping them, Edmark. The burden of carrying on the race, of breeding a new and more stable generation, is on them. Keep your eye on that, if possible.'

Perhaps his smile was a shade too placating; it made me remember that to him we were 'the Children'.

'Look,' I said pugnaciously. 'If those shambling failures can't tell us what's happened to them, you can. Either you tell me, or we pack up and go home. Our fellows have the creeps, I tell you! Now what – *explicitly* – is or was wrong with these Zombies?'

The commander laughed.

'We don't know,' he said. 'We don't know, and that's all there is to it.'

He stood up then, austere, tall, 'a fine man'. He went and looked out of the window, hands behind his back, and I could tell by his eyes he was looking at Failed Men, down there in the pale afternoon.

He turned and said to me: 'This sanatorium was designed for Failed Men. But we're filling up with relief staff instead; they've let the problem get them by the throats.'

'I can understand that,' I said. 'I shall be there myself if I don't get to the root of it, racing the others up the wall.'

He held up his hand.

'That's what they *all* say. But there is no root of it to get at, or none we can comprehend, or else we are part of the root ourselves. If you could only *categorize* their failure it would be something: religious, spiritual, economic . . .'

'So it's got *you* too!' I said.

'Look,' I said suddenly. 'You've got the time ships. Go back and *see* what the problem was!'

118

The solution was so simple I couldn't think how they had overlooked it; but of course they hadn't overlooked it.

'We've been,' the commander said briefly. 'A problem of the mind – presuming it was a mental problem – cannot be seen. All we *saw* was the six million of them singly burying themselves in these damned shallow graves. The process covered over a century; some of them had been under for three hundred years before we rescued them. No, it's no good, the problem from our point of view is linguistic.'

'The translator banks are no good,' I said sweepingly. 'It's all too delicate a job for a machine. Could you lend me a human interpreter?'

He came himself, in the end. He didn't want to, but he wanted to. And how would a machine cope with that statement? Yet to you and me it's perfectly comprehensible.

A woman, one of the Failed Men, was walking slowly across the courtyard as we got outside. It might have been the one I had already spoken to, I don't know. I didn't recognize her and she gave no sign of recognizing me. Anyhow, we stopped her and tried our luck.

'Ask her why they buried themselves, for a start,' I said.

.The Paull translated and she doomed briefly in reply.

'She says it was considered necessary, as it aided the union before the beginning of the attempt,' he told me.

'Ask her what union.'

Exchange of dooms.

'The union of the union that they were attempting. Whatever that means.'

'Did both "unions" sound the same to you?'

'One was inflected, as it was in the possessive case,' the Paull said. 'Otherwise they seemed just alike.'

'Ask her – ask her if they were all trying to change themselves into something other than human – you know, into spirits or fairies or ghosts.'

'They've only got a word for spirit. Or rather, they've got four words for spirit: spirit of soul; spirit of place; spirit of a non-substantive, such as "spirit of adventure"; and another sort of spirit I cannot define – we haven't an exact analogy for it.'

'Hell's bells! Well, try her with spirit of soul.'

Again the melancholy rattle of exchange. Then the commander, with some surprise, said: 'She says, Yes, they were striving to attain spirituality.'

'Now we're getting somewhere!' I exclaimed, thinking smugly that it just needed persistence and a twenty-fifth-century brain.

The old woman clanged again.

'What's that?' I asked eagerly.

'She says they're still striving after spirituality.'

We both groaned. The lead was merely a dead end.

'It's no good,' the Paull said gently. 'Give up.'

'One last question! Tell the old girl we cannot understand the nature of what has happened to her face. Was it a catastrophe and what was its nature? OK?'

'Can but try. Don't imagine this hasn't been done before, though – it's purely for your benefit.'

He spoke. She answered briefly.

'She says it was an "antwerto". That means it was a catastrophe to end all catastrophes.'

'Well, at least we're definite on that.'

'Oh yes, they failed all right, whatever it was they were after,' the Paull said sombrely.

'The nature of the catastrophe?'

'She just gives me an innocent little word, "struback". Unfortunately we don't know what it means.'

'I see. Ask her if it is something to do with evolution.'

'My dear man, this is all a waste of time! I know the answers, as far as they exist, without speaking to this woman at all.'

'Ask her if "struback" means something to do with a possible way they were evolving or meaning to evolve,' I persisted.

He asked her. The ill-matched three of us stood there for a long time while the old woman moaned her reply. At last she was silent.

'She says struback has some vague connection with evolution,' the commander told me.

'Is that *all*?'

'Oh, God, man! Far from it, but that's what it boils down to! "Time impresses itself on man as evolution," she says.'

120

'Ask her if the nature of the catastrophe was at least partly religious.'

When she had replied, the commander laughed shortly and said: 'She wants to know what "religious" means. And I'm sorry but I'm not going to stand here while you tell her.'

'But just because she doesn't know what it means doesn't mean to say the failure, the catastrophe, wasn't religious in essence.'

'Nothing means to say anything here,' the commander said angrily. Then he realized he was only talking to one of the Children; he went on more gently: 'Supposing that instead of coming ahead, we had gone back in time. Suppose we met a prehistoric tribe of hunters. Right! We learn their language. We want to use the word "luck". In their superstitious minds the concept – and consequently the word – does not exist. We have to use a substitute they can accept, "accident", or "good-happening" or "bad-happening", as the case may be. They understand that all right, but by it they mean something entirely different from our intention. We have not broken through the barrier at all, merely become further entangled in it. The same trap is operating here.

'And now, please excuse me.'

Struback. A long, hollow syllable, followed by a short click. Night after night, I turned that word over in my tired mind. It became the symbol of the Failed Men: but never anything more.

Most of the others caught the worry. Some drifted away in a kind of trance, some went into the wards. The tractors became undermanned. Reinforcements, of course, were arriving from the present. The present! I could not think of it that way. The time of the Failed Men became my present, and my past and future, too.

I worked with the translator banks again, unable to accept defeat. I had this idea in my head that the Failed Men had been trying – and possibly involuntarily – to turn into something superior to man, a sort of super-being, and I was intensely curious about this.

'Tell me,' I demanded of an old man, speaking through

121

the banks, 'when you all first had this idea, or when it came to you, you were all glad then?'

His answer came: 'Where there is failure there is only degradation. You cannot understand the degradation, because you are not of us. There is only degradation and misery and you do not comprehend—'

'Wait! I'm *trying* to comprehend! Help me, can't you? Tell me *why* it was so degrading, why you failed, how you failed.'

'The degradation was the failure,' he said. 'The failure was the struback, the struback was the misery.'

'You mean there was *just* misery, even at the beginning of the experiment?'

'There was no beginning, only a finish, and that was the result.'

I clutched my head.

'Wasn't burying yourself a beginning?'

'No.'

'What was it?'

'It was only a part of the attempt.'.

'What attempt?'

'You are so stupid. Can you not see? The attempt we were making for the resolution of the problematical problem in the result of our united resolve to solve the problem.'

'Which problem?'

'*The* problem,' he said wearily. 'The problem of the resolution of this case into the start of failure. It does not matter how the resolution is accomplished provided all the cases are the same, but in a diversity of cases the start determines the resolution and the finish arbitrarily determines the beginning of the case. But the arbitrary factor is itself inherent in the beginning of the case, and of the case itself. Consequently our case is in the same case, and the failure was because of the start, the start being our resolution.'

It was hopeless. 'You are really trying to explain?' I asked weakly.

'No, you dull young man,' he said. 'I am telling you about the failure. You are the struback.'

And he walked away.

* * *

Surrey looked hopelessly across at the Chinese girl. She tapped her fingers on the table.

'What did he mean, "You are the struback"?' she asked.

'Anything or nothing,' he said wildly. 'It would have been no good asking him to elucidate – I shouldn't have understood the elucidation. You see it's all either too complex or too simple for us to grasp.'

'But *surely*—' she said, and then hesitated.

'The Failed Men could only think in abstractions,' he said. 'Perhaps that was a factor involved in their failure – I don't know. You see, language is the most intrinsic product of any culture; you can't comprehend the language till you've understood the culture – and how do you understand a culture till you know its language?'

Surrey looked helplessly at the girl's little lute with its own trapped tongue. Suddenly, the hot silence of the night was shattered by a great orchestral crash half a mile away.

'Another cartload of nervous wrecks coming home,' he told her grimly. 'You'd better go and see to your chickens.'

NATHANIEL
and other people

Supercity

Fear not, Nathaniel, that you are about to hear a far-flung fantasy extolling the gigantic, the terrific or the tremendous. This is no fable about one of the monstrous cities of our universe, a megapolis covering an entire planet. No, if that is what my heading led you to expect, you were mistaken, Nathaniel.

Supercity (emphasis on the second syllable: su*per*city) is a word coined by Alastair Mott, the greatest supercitist of them all, to denote the art of becoming indispensable through being thoroughly useless: or, as he phrased it himself, more gracefully, 'the easiest way to the highest point'. From the ancient Latin, *super*, above, and *cito*, easily.

Alastair was born to power, although, as we shall see, he was later ousted from it. At twenty-one he was created Protagon of the Territory of Sconn of the planet Earth, a state about the size of North and South Dakota put together; in fact, it was North and South Dakota put together; and was later to become Division III of the United Parastates.

Alastair's life was a carefree one. His health was good, his face handsome, his wealth unlimited. Also he owned a little love nest on Ganymede and (because this last remained a deep secret) was at present wooing, with every omen of future success, the Virgin Rosalynd Staffordshire III. Also – this above all, Nathaniel – he had no social conscience, so that the hardships of his underlings at no time affected his sleep or cooled his natural ebullience.

Away from the frequent parties and carnivals which the loot of a thousand-odd planets provided for his social set, Alastair studied fitfully. He became a dilettante philologist, partly because of a certain genuine interest in language, partly in an attempt to provide himself with a little character, which he knew he lacked.

Philology is a nice, safe pastime, party-going is not. (Indeed, how gratifying to scholars it must be to reflect that in Alastair's case party-going brought his downfall and philology his regeneration. But we precede ourselves.) Foolishly, Alastair, on the fourth night of a punitively merry and wicked party, became involved in a small triangle, the other two angles of which were occupied by the Virgin Vera Manchester IXA and the Court Procreator.

As soon as the party was over, Alastair realized his mistake; he awoke and found the dawn was grey, for the Virgin Vera, by forfeiting her title, had placed his own status in jeopardy. The Court Procreator was not a man to be trifled with: it lay within his power to elect one to the August Order of Eunuchs at a moment's notice. Alastair blenched at the very thought and ended the affair forthwith. He ended it, unfortunately, with more precipitance than tact. Quite justifiably, the Virgin Vera Manchester IXA was offended, reading in his sudden withdrawal a mute criticism of her charms; for ladies, in those days as now, prefer to be taken to bed than to task.

The Virgin Vera nursed her spite in secret while Alastair returned to wooing the Virgin Rosalynd. All might have been well had there not occurred at Court – as have occurred at Courts from time immemorial – several fortunate deaths among the highest in the hierarchy. At the drop of a hat, the Virgin Vera had been acclaimed Ultimate Lady, a title which to the ears of that century held a sinister ring in it, and so the Territory of Sconn and its Protagon came under her jurisdiction.

Almost at once Alastair was promoted.

He received the news in his afternoon bath.

'I have been elected Resident Governor of the planet Acrostic I!' he said with some astonishment, scanning the telecoder above the bath taps. 'What does that mean? And where in Jake's universe is Acrostic I?'

His robot attendant made a sound like heavy breathing for five seconds, and then pronounced Acrostic I to be one of two planets circling a yellow sun on the periphery of Smith's Burst, which is a small intragalactic nebula many light years from any form of civilization.

Alastair's eye fell sadly on the word 'Resident', which so neatly knocked away the props from under his pleasant life as Protagon of Sconn. All relish fled immediately from his existence. He stood up dripping.

128

'It's been an honour to know you, Protagon,' the robot said as it blew hot dry air over him.

Space travel in those days was definitely not what it is now: then, it might take you sixteen weeks to do as many light years. Their ships, mere tubs which seldom could carry more than one hundred souls, had correspondingly to take more food, fuel, facilities and equipment for the long voyage. Even a planetary governor was allowed no excess baggage. Alastair stepped aboard the SS *Garfinkle* with two trunks (supplied by the company) and no secretaries; all that he loved he had to leave behind.

On the long and tedious voyage into exile, most of which he passed with Obliveen pills, Alastair outgrew his homesickness. True, he still recalled with regret Sconn Territory, and, it must be admitted, the little spicery on Ganymede; he still thought with affection of his friends; he still dwelt lovingly, although without much faith, on the farewell words of the Virgin Rosalynd: 'Adieu, sweet Alastair, I will be true'; but he resolved to make the very best of Acrostic I. It may be that The Plan was already forming in his mind: aware of his own uselessness, he knew it would only be by exerting that talent to the utmost that he would make anything of his banishment. Perhaps it was during these vacant hours he coined the word supercity.

At last they entered the regions of Smith's Burst, and the *Garfinkle* put Alastair down on his planet before hurrying off to more magnificent and exploited areas.

Acrostic I was not the best of all possible worlds. Its atmosphere was thin, and sickening to breathe until one became acclimatized. Although it was larger than Earth, it possessed almost no metals or heavier elements, so that its gravity was just enough below normal to produce a lightheaded effect. Its orbit held it too close for comfort to Acrostic (the sun) and the days were very hot; because its axial revolution was slow and the atmospheric blanket was thin, the nights were very cold.

Storms, snow, frost, heat-waves, drought and floods moved with monotonous irregularity across the battered face of Acrostic I. Small wonder that the native Acrosticians, primitive, elephantine beings, numbered themselves

129

(for nobody else cared to do it for them) in hundreds merely.

The Earth colonists, when Alastair arrived to govern them, were a mere twenty thousand strong, all of them living within about eighty miles of Acrostic's only town, All Saints. This hopefully named shanty town was to be Alastair's home! He groaned as a *quaff*, the local variety of packhorse, bore him through the dusty streets to his residence. Vultures and tiny monkeys peered down from the rooftops at his lugubrious progress. The lack of metal showed itself all too plainly in a diversity of ways, from the lame architecture to the long beards; the lack of proper sanitation also made itself felt in the usual way. Large numbers of the colonists, literally under the weather, had given up their lands and drifted to town, where no occupation but immorality was open to them. Posters picturing makes of gun, displaying gigantic whisky bottles, advertising leg shows or inquiring whether the passer-by possessed Breath Appeal gave All Saints the air of a libellous parody on civilization. The Ultimate Lady had certainly settled her debts: Smith's Burst hath no fury like a woman scorned.

Alastair never despaired, nor took to drink. Instead, he took to *quaff* and travelled among the people, learning the true nature of the planetary situation; the people, suspicious at first, came to trust him as they realized he was not researching on their account. It took Alastair only a short while to find the truth about Acrostic I: it was a dead end: nobody left and nobody came.

Acrostic I was virtually unheard of on Earth. Nothing of its dull history or existence had seeped back home – except *one word*. Words get where goods cannot; they are frequently a planet's first export.

To you, Nathaniel, the verb 'to scutterbuck' is a staid and familiar old word meaning 'to kill time pleasantly'. In Alastair's time, however, the expression was for Earth something new, exotic, slangy. It had seeped back over the space routes, like a thousand other extra-terrestrial words, to become a temporary or integral part of our ever-expanding vocabulary. To Earth's masses, scutterbucking sounded something enjoyably exciting; as not infrequently happens, Earth's masses had the wrong end of the stick.

Alastair, being an amateur philologist, was intrigued by

this single thin connection between home and the ball to which he had been politely exiled. He *quaffed* out with a human interpreter to the nearest native settlement to investigate the strict meaning of the word and found that scutterbucking (or, more correctly, skutterbucking) is an Acrostician form of hibernation, undergone when the weather is particularly foul. Voluntary rather than seasonal, the condition of scutterbucking is accompanied by grotesque withering of the grey Acrostician flesh and blissful indifference to externals, a considerable asset on a place like Acrostic I.

Very shortly, *Galactic Life*, Earth's leading telemag, produced a feature called 'Come Where Scutterbucking Comes From!' It was illustrated with flashes of the dwarf, three-breasted Acrostic Monkeys, which apart from their one outstanding peculiarity are all but human in appearance; careful choice of background concealed the true height of these creatures (nine inches in the largest specimen, Nathaniel). As the telefeature, while failing to mention Acrostic's odd climate, let slip that the monkeys were the planet's highest form of life, it was only a matter of time before a thin trickle of male tourists began to plod anxiously round the streets of All Saints, seeking what everyone means by 'local colour'.

As a frontier planet, Acrostic I had been 'wide open'; anyone who wished might come and go on it. Alastair proceeded to change all that. Customs sheds were erected by the space port, an elaborate tariffs system was introduced, a barn-like hotel-hospital was built, wherein newcomers could spend an enforced and expensive period of isolation and acclimatization. The lucrative business of currency regulation was established, together with passport, visa and identification systems, all of which cost money – all of which went to the Resident Governor.

But the tourist trade was not the only nor the strongest string to Alastair's bow, although it brought him enough money to carry out the rest of his ideas.

He began making official reports home. New Pork, which was at that time the hub of World Administration, was gratified. Generally it was an impossible task to induce reports (which also meant returns) from anywhere but the major worlds; since all communications travelled via ship, the smaller galactic fry could always claim 'Lost in Transit' to any unpleasant memorandum, a claim which might take years to refute conclusively.

New Pork responded with true bureaucratic fervour to Alastair's tentative advances. Department upon department dispatched sheaves of every imaginable type of form and questionnaire, and filed with glee the mocked-up statistics or nil returns which Alastair sent back.

What percentages of female colonist underwent marriage at the following age groups . . .? What was the average yield per acre of the following types of wheat . . .? What species of Earth cattle flourished best under Acrostic conditions . . .? What *were* conditions on Acrostic in terms of average annual rainfall, monthly rainfall, annual sunshine, monthly sunshine, isobar, isotherms . . .? Etc.

It seemed as if the vast ledgers of Earth would absorb for ever the flow of information.

The spaceships, which had never called more than twice in a decade, began to make monthly visits to All Saints. They brought with them, besides paper, wealth; they took back with them, besides paper, rumour of a growing city. All Saints was taking on a faint tinge of sophistication: there were fewer adverts for makes of guns and more for breath appeal.

Tourists returning to Earth soon revealed the disillusioning truth about the poverty of the local fauna, and said something about the climate of Acrostic. But the flow of visitors, rather than dwindling, redoubled. This is strange merely if we know nothing of human nature; no tourist ever admits to having been taken in, and so – while admitting the monkeys and the weather – they made great play with the scenery and local customs. Very soon it was not fashionable to admit you had never visited that little paradise in Smith's Burst.

Meanwhile, New Pork continued to absorb Alastair's reports.

But suddenly the flow of statistics homewards stopped. The outward flow of questions immediately doubled. What had happened to the Acrostic Administration? Had rebellion broken out? Had there been a plague? And if so, what percentages of the following age groups (male and female) had perished?

The Acrostic Administration lay back comfortably in his wicker chair and enjoyed a rest. It was his first day of scutterbucking since he had arrived, many moons ago. I neglected to tell you, my Nathaniel, that Acrostic I had a moon, a useless little thing called Rose which only shone in the day-time. Alastair was reading something which gave him more pleasure than anything he had read since his arrival. It was written by one of All Saints' first tourists, who had been fleeced of every cent he possessed on his first day down, flung in gaol for debt until his return ship had left, and was now a respected member of the community. He had just sent Alastair a poem, 'Daylight, Rose Bright'. It was not a brilliant poem, but it was the first one ever written on Acrostic I. They were going up in the universe.

After a suitably long interval had elapsed, and Earthly agitation had reached maximum, Alastair sent World Government a brief note. His entire administration had collapsed from overwork: they must send him an XIVIC Master Computer. Upon receipt of a guarantee that one would be installed in full working order as soon as possible, he would do his best to resume routine.

The guarantee duly arrived. Now he had them!

Even on the surface, his was a great victory. Think for yourself, Nathaniel, if possible. These Fourteen-one-Hundreds, as the computers were called, were gigantic machines even by our standards. They were so complex and important that it was possible to use them as instruments of colonial policy: for they remained always possessions of Earth, serviced by Earthmen, so that once a colony world grew big enough to require one (i.e. also big enough to be a potential threat) it would have installed upon it a small, autonomous unit of Earth. Never before had a Fourteen-One-Hundred been installed on a planet with less than a billion voters, yet here was Acrostic I with no more than fifty thousand population all told. Additional relish was added to Alastair's jubilation by the facsimile signature at the bottom of the guarantee: Ultimate Lady Vera Manchester IXA. He predicted a fall right down the matriarchy for that lady very soon.

A pair of government ships came and stood nose upwards outside All Saints. Machinery and men were disgorged. Night and day, storm and fine, the work of erecting the Master Computer went on. When the ships were emptied they hurried off home to fetch the next instalment of Fourteen-One-Hundred parts. Money began to flow freely in the town, as it will anywhere with government capital in the vicinity. For the first time, the colonist farmers were almost content with the prices their produce fetched. Alastair, a kindly fellow at heart, was happy to see his self-salvation scheme also benefiting others.

Earth was well and irredeemably committed on the project before the sad news filtered back to them. Fourteen-One-Hundreds would never work: there was no hydro-electric power on Acrostic I!

To the indignant messages that asked why Alastair's Administration had not informed World Government of this, he made the truthful answer that (a) they had not asked him, and (b) the situation could have been deduced from given information. Such small electric plants as there were in All Saints were powered by wooden windmills; an uncertain business, of course – but what was one to do on a planet like Acrostic I, without metal?

A host of brooding experts was unleashed by the next space-ship; they brooded because they had been ordered to discover what one was to do for power on a planet like Acrostic I, or else . . .

They soon found that, as Alastair had long been aware, the elements ruled the planet. Sun, wind, frost and rain had eroded and erased any mountains that Acrostic might once have possessed, leaving only a sandy surfaced billiard ball of a world. Such few streams as there were ran lazily and shallowly. The fringes of the sea offered hundreds of miles of stagnant swamp land. There could be no hydro-electric power.

The brooding experts divided into two camps. One indented to Earth for mining and drilling equipment, and then disappeared into the wilds to survey for coal or oil; the other submitted to Earth a plan for a submarine plant to draw power from the tides, and then disappeared into the taverns and stews of All Saints. In being strictly accurate, I should

134

add that there was a small third faction, who washed their hands of the whole affair and returned home in disgust.

It happened that the ship which arrived to take them back brought a letter from the Virgin Rosalynd. I hope you have not forgotten the Virgin Rosalynd, Nathaniel, for Alastair had not forgotten her; she had proved to be a model of devotion our modern women might well copy.

Her personal news was that she was well, still in love with her clever, clever governor and had just been appointed a Pen-Ultimate Lady. Her general news was that Acrostic was well in the public eye: its miniature monkeys were now Earth's favourite pets, it formed the subject of a popular song: 'If I was As Powerless As Little Acrostic' ('I'd still toss Dick, Tom and Harry aside to make you my bride'), and was also the subject of a Public Inquiry.

It was the Public Inquiry rather than the popular song or the monkeys which set the seal on Alastair's success. The population doubled almost overnight as Independent Body after Independent Body moved in to Look Into Things. They were followed by press reporters, tele and film men and other such adjuncts of the comfortable life which had not previously been seen on Acrostic. A more frivolous element, who found it *fun* to live in such a place, also appeared. They were followed by exploiters and confidence men, the 'You live Illness-free on a Metal-free world' type. Then came the legislators. Then the entertainers.

It was quite a crowd!

Two years passed before the Public Inquiry published its results. Before they appeared, World Government – in a bid for popularity – decided that the nice thing to do was to plunge into the matter bald-headed and give Acrostic I a nice nuclear plant. Machinery started rolling again. So Fourteen-One-Hundred was finally put to work, by which time there was plenty for it to work on. Acrostic was a thoroughly going concern, thanks to Alastair's super-citations.

But that came later. First came the Report. It convicted World Government of squandering so many million pound-squareds of public monies without properly and conscientiously entering into due investigation of the existing circumstances and of, moreover, as hereinafter and heretofore stated within the meaning of so on and so on. It meant, in brief, that Someone had Blundered.

Alastair took his triumph modestly; he had grown up since arriving at All Saints. Indeed, it was almost in him to feel regret when he learned that the Ultimate Lady Vera had been summarily deposed, for she was the Someone who had Blundered. And when the long-waited invitation to return to Sconn Territory actually arrived, he debated endlessly about accepting it. He wrote to the Pen-Ultimate Lady Rosalynd: would she join him on Acrostic?

She replied that as she had just been elected Ultimate Lady herself, she was unable to leave Earth: would he not join her there?

So – he did. A man of more character would have stayed with his success, one feels. People are very odd, Nathaniel, present company not entirely excepted.

There is a Tide

How infinitely soothing to the heart it was to be home. I began that evening with nothing but peace in me: and the evening itself jellied down over Africa with a mild mother's touch: so that even now I must refuse myself the luxury of claiming any premonition of the disaster for which the scene was already set.

My half-brother, K-Jubal (we had the same father), was in a talkative mood. As we sat at the table on the veranda of his house, his was the major part of the conversation: and this was unusual, for I am a poet.

'... because the new dam is now complete,' he was saying, 'and I shall take my days more easily. I am going to write my life story, Rog. G-Williams on the *World Weekly* has been pressing me for it for some time; it'll be serialized, and then turned into audiobook form. I should make a lot of money, eh?'

He smiled as he asked this; in my company he always enjoyed playing the heavy materialist. Generally I encouraged him: this time I said: 'Jubal, no man in Congo States, no man in the world possibly, has done more for people than you. I am the idle singer of an idle day, but you – why, your good works lie about you.'

I swept my hand out over the still bright land.

Mokulgu is a rising town on the western fringes of Lake Tanganyika's northern end. Before Jubal and his engineers came here, it was a sleepy market town, and its natives lived in the indolent fashion of their countless forefathers. In ten years, that ancient pattern was awry; in fifteen, shattered completely. If you lived in Mokulgu now, you slept in a bed in a towering nest of flats, you ate food unfouled by flies and you moved to the sound of whistles and machinery. You had at your black fingertips, in fact, the benefits of what we persist in calling 'Western civilization'. If you were more hygienic and healthy – so ran the theory – you were happier.

But I begin to sound sceptical. That is my error. I happen

to have little love for my fellow men; the thought of the Massacre is always with me, even after all this time. I could not deny that the trend of things at Mokulgu and elsewhere, the constant urbanization, was almost unavoidable. But as a man with some sensibility, I regretted that human advance should always be over the corpse of Nature. That a counterblast was being prepared even then did not occur to me.

From where we sat over our southern wines, both lake and town were partially visible, the forests in the immediate area having been demolished long ago. The town was already blazing with light, the lake looked already dark, a thing preparing for night. And to our left, standing out with a clarity which suggested yet more rain to come, stretched the rolling jungles of the Congo tributaries.

For at least three hundred miles in that direction, man had not invaded: there lived the pygmies, flourishing without despoiling. That area, the Congo Source land, would be the next to go; Jubal, indeed, was the spearhead of the attack. But for my generation at least that vast tract of primitive beauty would stand, and I was selfishly glad of it. I always gained more pleasure from a tree than population increase statistics.

Jubal caught something of the expression on my face.

'The power we are releasing here will last for ever,' he said. 'It's already changing – improving – the entire economy of the area. At last, at long last, Africa is realizing her potentialities.'

His voice held almost a tremor, and I thought that this passion for Progress was the secret of his strength.

'You cling too much to the past, Rog,' he added.

'Why all this digging and tunnelling and wrenching up of riverbeds?' I asked. 'Would not atomics have been a cheaper and easier answer?'

'No,' he said decisively. 'This system puts to use idle water; once in operation, everything is entirely self-servicing. Besides, uranium is none too plentiful, water is. Venus has no radioactive materials, I believe?'

This sounded to me like an invitation to change the subject. I accepted it.

'They've found none yet,' I assented. 'But I can speak

with no authority. I went purely as a tourist – and a glorious trip it was.'

'It must be wonderful to be so many million miles nearer the sun,' he said. It was the sort of plain remark I had often heard him make. On others' lips it might have sounded platitudinous; in his quiet tones I caught a note of sublimity.

'I shall never get to Venus,' he said. 'There's too much work to be done here. You must have seen some marvels there, Rog!'

'Yes . . . Yet nothing so strange as an elephant.'

'And they'll have a breathable atmosphere in a decade, I hear?'

'So they say. They certainly are doing wonders . . . You know, Jubal, I shall have to go back then. You see, there's a feeling, er – something, a sort of expectancy. No, not quite that; it's hard to explain–' I don't converse well. I ramble and mumble when I have something real to say. I could say it to a woman, or I could write it on paper; but Jubal is a man of action, and when I did say it, I deliberately omitted emotional overtones and lost interest in what I said. 'It's like courting a woman in armour with the visor closed, on Venus now. You can see it, but you can't touch or smell or breathe it. Always an airtight dome or a space suit between you and actuality. But in ten years' time, you'll be able to run your bare fingers through the sand, feel the breezes on your cheek . . . Well, you know what I mean, er – sort of feel her undressed.'

He was thinking – I saw it in his eye: 'Rog's going to go all poetic on me.' He said: 'And you approve of that – the change over of atmospheres?'

'Yes.'

'Yet you don't approve of what we're doing here, which is just the same sort of thing?'

He had a point. 'You're upsetting a delicate balance here,' I said gingerly. 'A thousand ecological factors are swept by the board just so that you can grind these waters through your turbines. And the same thing's happened at Owen Falls over on Lake Victoria . . . But on Venus there's no such balance. It's just a clean page waiting for man to write what he will on it. Under that CO_2 blanket, there's been no spark of life: the mountains are bare of moss, the valleys lie

139

innocent of grass; in the geological strata, no fossils sleep; no amoebae move in the sea. But what you're doing here . . .'

'People!' he exclaimed. 'I've got *people* to consider. Babies need to be born, mouths must be fed. A man must live. Your sort of feelings are all very well – they make good *poems* – but I consider the *people*. I *love* the people. For them I work . . .'

He waved his hands, overcome by his own grandiose visions. If the passion for Progress was his strength, the fallacy inherent in the idea was his secret weakness. I began to grow warm.

'You get good conditions for these people, they procreate forthwith. Next generation, another benefactor will have to step forward and get good conditions for the children. That's Progress, eh?' I asked maliciously.

'I see you so rarely, Rog; don't let's quarrel,' he said meekly. 'I just do what I can. I'm only an engineer.'

That was how he always won an altercation. Before meekness I have no defence.

The sun had finished another day. With the sudden darkness came chill. Jubal pressed a button, and glass slid round the veranda, enclosing us. Like Venus, I thought; but here you could still smell that spicy, bosomy scent which is the breath of dear Africa herself. On Venus, the smells are imported.

We poured some more wine and talked of family matters. In a short while his wife, Sloe, joined us. I began to feel at home. The feeling was only partly psychological; my glands were now beginning to adjust fully to normal conditions after their long days in space travel.

J-Casta also appeared. Him I was less pleased to see. He was the boss type, the strong arm man: as Jubal's underling, he pandered wretchedly to him and bullied everyone else on the project. He (and there were many others like him, unfortunately) thought of the Massacre as man's greatest achievement. This evening, in the presence of his superiors, after a preliminary burst of showing off, he was quiet enough.

When they pressed me to, I talked of Venus. As I spoke, back rushed that humbling – but intoxicating – sense of awe

140

to think I had actually lived to stand in full possession of my many faculties on that startling planet. The same feeling had often possessed me on Mars. And (as justifiably) on Earth.

The vision chimed, and an amber light blinked drowsily off and on in Jubal's tank. Even then, no premonition of catastrophe; since then, I can never see that amber heartbeat without anxiety.

Jubal answered it, and a man's face swam up in the tank to greet him. They talked; I could catch no words, but the sudden tension was apparent. Sloe went over and put her arm round Jubal's shoulder.

'Something up,' J-Casta commented.

'Yes,' I said.

'That's Chief M-Shawn on the Vision – from Owenstown, over on Lake Victoria.'

Then Jubal flashed off and came slowly back to where we were sitting.

'That was M-Shawn,' he said. 'The level of Lake Victoria has just dropped three inches.' He lit a cheroot with clumsy fingers, his eyes staring in mystification far beyond the flame.

'Dam OK, boss?' J-Casta asked.

'Perfectly. They're going to phone us if they find anything . . .'

'Has this happened before?' I asked, not quite able to understand their worried looks.

'Of course not,' my half-brother said scornfully. 'Surely you must see the implications of it? Something highly unprecedented has occurred.'

'But surely a mere three inches of water . . .'

At that he laughed briefly. Even J-Casta permitted himself a snort.

'Lake Victoria is an inland sea,' Jubal said grimly. 'It's as big as Tasmania. Three inches all over that means many thousands of tons of water. Casta, I think we'll get down to Mokulgu; it won't do any harm to alert the first aid services, just in case they're needed. Got your tracer?'

'Yes, boss. I'm coming.'

Jubal patted Sloe's arm, nodded to me and left without relaxing his worried look. He and J-Casta shortly appeared outside. They bundled into a float, soared dangerously close to a giant walnut tree and vanished into the night.

Nervously, Sloe put down her cheroot and did not resume it. She fingered a dial and the windows opaqued.

'There's an ominous waiting quality out there I don't like,' she said, to explain our sudden privacy.

'Should I be feeling alarmed?' I asked.

She flashed me a smile. 'Quite honestly, yes. You don't live in our world, Rog, or you would guess at once what is happening at Lake Victoria. They've just finished raising the level again; for a long time they've been on about more pressure, and the recent heavy rains gave them their chance. It seems to have been the last straw.'

'And what does this three-inch drop mean? Is there a breach in the dam somewhere?'

'No. They'd have found that. I'm afraid it means the bed of the lake has collapsed somewhere. The water's pouring into subterranean reservoirs.'

The extreme seriousness of the matter was now obvious even to me. Lake Victoria is the source of the White Nile; if it ceased to feed the river, millions of people in Uganda and the Sudan would die of drought. And not only people: birds, beasts, fish, insects, plants.

We both grew restless. We took a turn outside in the cool night air, and then decided we too would go down to the town. All the way there a picture filled my head: the image of that great dark lake emptying like a wash-basin. Did it drain in sinister silence, or did it gargle as it went? Men of action forget to tell you vital details like that.

That night was an anticlimax, apart from the sight of the full moon sailing over Mount Kangosi. We joined Jubal and his henchman and hung about uneasily until midnight. As if an unknown god had been propitiated by an hour's sleep sacrificed, we then felt easier and retired to bed.

The news was bad next morning. Jubal was already back in town; Sloe and I breakfasted alone together. She told me they had been informed that Victoria had now dropped thirteen and a half inches; the rate of fall seemed to be increasing.

I flew into Mokulgu and found Jubal without difficulty. He was just embarking on one of the Dam Authority's survey floats with J-Casta.

'You'd better come, too, Rog,' he shouted. 'You'll probably enjoy the flight more than we shall.'

I did enjoy the flight, despite the circumstances. A disturbance on Lake Tanganyika's eastern fringes had been observed on an earlier survey, and we were going to investigate it.

'You're not afraid the bed will collapse here, too, are you?' I asked.

'It's not that,' Jubal said. 'The two hundred miles between us and Victoria is a faulty region, geologically speaking. I'll show you a map of the strata when we get back. It's more than likely that all that runaway subterranean water may be heading in our direction; that's what I'm afraid of. The possibility has been known for a long while.'

'And no precautions taken?'

'What could we do but cross our fingers? The possibility exists that the Moon will spiral to Earth, but we don't all live in shelters because of it.'

'Justifying yourself, Jubal?'

'Possibly,' he replied, looking away.

We flew through a heavy rain shower, which dappled the grey surface of the lake. Then we were over the reported disturbance. A dull brown stain, a blot on a bright new garment, spread over the water, from the steep eastern shore to about half a mile out.

'Put us down, pilot,' Jubal ordered.

We sank, and kissed the lake. Several hundred yards away rose the base of Mount Kangosi. I looked with admiration up the slope; great slabs of rock stood out from the verdure; crouching at the bottom of this colossus was a village, part of it forced by the steepness of the incline to stand out on piles into the lake.

'Leave everything to me, boss,' J-Casta said, grabbing a hand asdic from the port locker and climbing out on to the float. We followed. It seemed likely that the disturbance was due to a slight subsidence in the side of the lake basin. Such subsidences, Jubal said, were not uncommon, but in this case it might provide a link with Lake Victoria. If they could

143

pin-point the position of the new fault, frogmen would be sent down to investigate.

'We're going to have company,' Jubal remarked to me, waving a hand over the water.

A dozen or so dugouts lay between us and the shore. Each bore two or three shining-skinned fishermen. The two canoes nearest us had swung round and were now being paddled towards our float.

I watched them with more interest than I gave to the asdic sweep. Men like these sturdy fishermen had existed here for countless generations, unchanged: before white men had known of them, before Rome's legions had destroyed the vineyards of Carthage, before – who knows if not before the heady uprush of civilization elsewhere? – such men had fished quietly in this great lake. They seem not to have advanced at all, so rapidly does the world move; but perhaps when all other races have fallen away, burnt out and exhausted, these steady villages will come into a kingdom of their own. I would elect to live in that realm.

A man in the leading canoe stood up, raising his hand in greeting. I replied, glancing over his shoulder at the curtain of green behind him. Something caught my eye.

Above some yards of bare rock, a hundred feet up the slope, two magnificent Mvules – African teak trees – grew. A china blue bird dipped suddenly from one of the trees and sped far and fast away over the water, fighting to outpace its reflection. And the tree itself began to cant slowly from the vertical into a horizontal position.

Jubal had binoculars round his neck. My curiosity aroused, I reached to borrow them. Even as I did so, I saw a spring of water start from the base of the Mvules. A rock was dislodged. I saw it hurtle down into bush below, starting in turn a trail of earth and stones which fell down almost on to the thatched roofs of the village. The spring began to spurt more freely now. It gleamed in the sun: it looked beautiful but I was alarmed.

'Look!' I pointed.

Both Jubal and the fisherman followed the line of my outstretched arm. J-Casta continued to bend over his metal box.

Even as I pointed, the cliff shuddered. The other Mvule

144

went down. Like an envelope being torn, the rock split horizontally and a tongue of water burst from it. The split widened, the water became a wall, pouring out and down.

The sound of the splitting came clear and hard to our startled ears. Then came the roar of the water, bursting down the hillside. It washed everything before it. I saw trees, bushes and boulders hurried down in it. I saw the original fissure lengthen and lengthen like a cruel smile, cutting through the ground as fast as fire. Other cracks started, running uphill and across: every one of them began to spout water.

The fishermen stood up, shouting as their homes were swept away by the first fury of the flood.

And then the entire lower mountainside began to slip. With a cumulative roar, mud, water and rock rolled down into the lake. Where they had been, a solid torrent cascaded out, one mighty wall of angry water. The escaping flow from Lake Victoria had found its outlet!

Next moment, our calm surface was a furious sea. Jubal slipped and fell on to one knee. I grabbed him, and almost went overboard myself. A series of giant waves plunged outwards from the shore. The first one rocked us, the second one overturned our flimsy craft completely.

I came to the surface coughing and snorting. J-Casta rose at my side. We were just in time to see the float slip completely under: it sank in no time, carrying the pilot with it. I had not even seen his face, poor fellow.

Jubal came up by the fisherman, who had also overturned. But dugouts do not sink. We owe our lives to those hollowed tree trunks. They were righted, and Jubal and his henchman climbed into one, while I climbed into the other. The waves were still fierce, but had attained a sort of regularity which allowed us to cope with them.

The breakthrough was now a quarter of a mile long. Water poured from it with unabated force, a mighty waterfall where land had been before. We skirted it painfully, making a landing as near to it as we dared.

The rest of that day, under its blinding arch of sky, passed in various stages of confusion and fear.

It was two and a half hours before we were taken off the

strip of shore. We were not idle in that time, although every few minutes Jubal paused to curse the fact that he was stranded and powerless. Miraculous as it seems, there were some survivors from the obliterated village, women mostly; we helped to get them ashore and built fires for them.

Meanwhile, Dam Authority planes began to circle the area. We managed to attract the attention of one, which landed by our party. Jubal changed at once; now that he had a machine and men who, unlike the villagers, were in his command, he worked with a silent purpose allowing of no question.

Over the vision, he ordered the rest of the floats to attend to the villagers' needs. We sped back to Mokulgu.

On the way, Jubal spoke to Owenstown. They took his news almost without comment. They reported that Victoria was still sinking, although the rate had now steadied. A twenty-four-hour a day airlift was about to go into operation, dropping solid blocks of marble on to the lake bed. There, a fault about three miles square had been located; four frogmen had been lost, drowned.

'It's like tossing pennies into the ocean,' Jubal said.

I was thinking of the frogmen, sucked irresistibly down the vault. They would be swept through underground waterways, battered and pulped, to be spat out eventually into our lake.

Vision from Mokulgu, coming on just before we landed there, reported a breach in the lake banks, some twenty miles north of the town. At a word from Jubal, we switched plans and veered north at once to see just how extensive the damage was.

The break was at a tiny cluster of huts dignified by the name of Ulatuama. Several men, the crew of a Dam Authority patrol boat, were working furiously at a widening gap. The damage had been caused by the very waves which had swamped us, and I learnt that a small, disused lock had stood here, relic of an earlier irrigation scheme; so the weakness had been of man's making. Beyond the lock had been a dried-up channel some twenty yards wide; this was now a swollen, plunging river.

'Is this serious?' I asked Jubal. 'Isn't it a good way of getting rid of surplus water?'

146

He gave me a withering look. 'Where are we if we lose control?' he demanded. 'If this thing here runs away with us, the combined waters of Victoria and Tanganyika will flood down into the Congo.'

Even as he spoke, the bank to the south of the escaping waters crumbled; several yards were swept away, their place instantly taken by the current.

We flew back to Mokulgu. Jubal visioned the mayor and got permission to broadcast to the city. I did not hear him speak; reaction had set in, and I had to go and sit quietly at home with Sloe fussing daintily round me. Although you 'know' from a child that Earth is a planet, it is only when you drift towards it from space, seeing it hang round and finite ahead, that you can *realize* the fact. And so, although I had always 'known' man was puny, it was the sight of that vast collapsing slab of mountain which had driven the fact into my marrow.

To guess the sort of sentiments Jubal broadcast to the city was easy. He would talk of 'rallying round in this our time of crisis'. He would speak of the need for 'all hands uniting against our ancient enemy, Nature'. He would come over big on the tanks; he would be big, his fists clenched, his eyes ablaze. He was in touch with the people. And they would do what he said, for Jubal carried conviction. Perhaps I envied my half-brother.

Labour and supplies began to pour north to mend the damaged bank. Jubal, meanwhile, thought up a typically flamboyant scheme. *Tilly*, one of the lake steamers, was pressed into service and loaded full of rock and clay by steam shovel. With Jubal standing on the bridge, it was manoeuvred into the centre of the danger area and scuttled. Half in and half out of the rushing water, it now formed a base from which a new dam could be built to stem the flood. Watched by a cheering crowd, Jubal and crew skimmed to safety in a motor boat.

'We shall conquer if we have to dam the water with our bodies,' he cried. A thousand cheering throats told him how much they liked this idea.

The pitch of crisis which had then been engendered was maintained all through the next two days. For most of that time it rained, and men fought to erect their barrier on cling-

147

ing mud. Jubal's popularity – and consequently his influence – underwent a rapid diminution. The reason for this was two-fold. He quarrelled with J-Casta, whose suggestion to throw open the new dam to relieve pressure elsewhere was refused, and he ran into stiff opposition from Mokulgu Town Council.

This august body, composed of the avariciously successful and the successfully avaricious, was annoyed about *Tilly*. *Tilly* belonged to the local government, and Jubal had, in effect, stolen it. The men from the factories who had downed tools to fight the water were summoned back to work: the Dam Authority must tend its own affairs.

Jubal merely sneered at this dangerous pique and visioned Leopoldsville. In the briefest possible time, he had the army helping him.

It was at dawn on the morning of the third day that he visioned me to go down and see him. I said adieu to Sloe and took a float over to Ulatuama.

Jubal stood alone by the water's edge. The sun was still swathed in mist, and he looked cold and pinched. Behind him, dimly outlined figures moved to and fro, like allegorical figures on a frieze. He surveyed me curiously before speaking.

'The work's nearly done, Rog,' he said. He looked as if he needed sleep, but he added energetically, pointing across the lake: 'Then we tackle the main job of plugging that waterfall.'

I looked across the silent lake. The far shore was invisible, but out of the layers of mist rose Mount Kangosi. Even at this distance, in the early morning hush, came the faint roar of the new waterfall. And there was another sound, intermittent but persistent: beyond the mountain, they were bombing fault lines. That way they hoped to cause a collapse which would plug Victoria's escape routes. So far, they had had no success, but the bombing went on, making a battlefield of what had once been glorious country.

'Sorry I haven't seen anything of you and Sloe,' Jubal said. I disliked his tone.

'You've been busy. Sloe called you on the vision.'

'Oh that. Come on into my hut, Rog.'

We walked over to a temporary structure; the grass was

148

overloaded with dew. In Jubal's hut, J-Casta was dressing, smoking a cheroot as he dexterously pulled on a shirt. He gave me a surly greeting, whose antagonism I sensed was directed through me at Jubal.

As soon as the latter closed the door, he said: 'Rog, promise me something.'

'Tell me what.'

'If anything happens to me, I want you to marry Sloe. She's your sort.'

Concealing my irritation, I said: 'That's hardly a reasonable request.'

'You and she get on well together, don't you?'

'Certainly. But you see my outlook on life is . . . well, for one thing I like to stay *detached*. An observer, you know, observing. I just want to sample the landscapes and the food and the women of the solar system. I don't want to *marry*, just move on at the right time. Sloe's very nice but—'

My ghastly inability to express the pressure of inner feeling was upon me. In women I like flamboyance, wit and a high spirit, but I tire quickly of it and then have to seek its manifestation elsewhere. Besides, Sloe frankly had had her sensibilities blunted from living with Jubal. He now chose to misunderstand my hesitations.

'Are you standing there trying to tell me that you've already tired of whatever you've been doing behind my back?' he demanded. 'You – you—' He called me a dirty name; I forgot to make allowances for the strain he had been undergoing, and lost my temper.

'Oh, calm down,' I snapped. 'You're overtired and overwrought, and probably over-sexed too. I've not touched your little woman – I like to drink from pure streams. So you can put the entire notion out of your head.'

He rushed at me with his shoulders hunched and fists swinging. It was an embarrassing moment. I am against violence, and believe in the power of words, but I did the only possible thing; spring to one side and catch him a heavy blow over the heart.

Poor Jubal! No doubt, in his frustration against the forces of nature, he was using me only as a safety valve. But with shame, I will now confess what savage pleasure that blow gave me; I was filled with lust to strike him again. I can perceive dimly how atrocities such as the Massacre came about. As Jubal turned on me, I flung myself at him, breaking down his defences, piling blows into his chest. It was, I suppose, a form of self-expression.

J-Casta stopped it, breaking in between us and thrusting his ugly face into mine, his hand like a clamp round my wrist.

'Pack it up,' he said. 'I'd gladly do the job myself, but this is not the time.'

As he spoke, the hut trembled. We were hard pressed to keep our feet, staggering together like drunken men.

'Now what—' Jubal said, and flung open the door. I caught a rectangular view of trees and mist, men running, and the emergency dam sailing away on a smooth black slide of escaping water. The banks were collapsing!

Glimpsing the scene, Jubal instantly attempted to slam the door shut again. He was too late. The wave struck us, battering the cabin off its flimsy foundations. Jubal cried sharply as he was tossed against a wall. Next moment we were floundering in a hell of flying furniture and water.

Swept along on a giant sluice, the cabin turned over and over like a dice. That I was preserved was a merest accident. Through a maze of foam, I saw a heavy bunk crashing towards me, and managed to flounder aside in time. It missed me by a finger's width and broke straight through the boarding wall. I was swept helplessly after it.

When I surfaced, the cabin was out of sight and I was being borne along at a great rate; and the ugly scene in the cabin was something fruitless that happened a million years ago. Nearly wrenching my arm off in the process, I seized a tree which was still standing, and clung on. Once I had recovered my breath, I was able to climb out of the water entirely, wedge myself between two branches and regain my breath.

The scene was one of awesome desolation. I had what in less calamitous circumstances might have been called 'a good view' of it all.

A lake spread all round me, its surface moving smartly and with apparent purpose. Its forward line, already far away, was marked by a high yellow cascade. In its wake stretched a miscellany of objects, of which only the trees stood out clearly. Most of the trees were eucalyptus: this area had probably been reclaimed marsh.

To the north, the old shore-line of the lake still stood. The ground was higher there and solid rock jutted stolidly into the flood.

To the south, the shore-line was being joyously chewed away. Mokulgu had about half an hour left before it was swamped and obliterated. I wondered how the Mokulgu Town Council were coping with the situation.

Overhead, the sun now shining clear, bars of pink, wispy cloud flecked the blue sky. The pink and the blue were of the exact vulgar tints found in two-colour prints of the early twentieth century A.D. – that is, a hundred years before the Massacre. I was almost happy to see this lack of taste in the sky matching the lack of stability elsewhere. I was almost happy: but I was weeping.

'They visioned me that one of the floats had picked you up – and not Jubal. Is there any hope for him, Rog, or is that a foolish question?'

'I can't give you a sensible answer. He was a strong swimmer. They may find him yet.'

I spoke to Sloe over the heads of a crowd of people. Mokulgu, surely enough, had been washed away. The survivors, homeless and bereaved, crowded on to high ground. Sloe had generously thrown open most of her house as a sort of rest-camp-cum-soup-kitchen. She superintended everything with a cool authority which suitably concealed her personal feelings. For that I was grateful: Sloe's feelings must be no affair of mine.

She smiled at me before turning to address someone behind her. Already the light was taking on the intensity of early evening. Above the babble of voices round me came the deep song of speeding water. It would continue for months yet: Africa was ruptured at her very heart, beyond man's mending.

Instead of flowing northward, fertilizing its old valley, Victoria crashed into our lake, adding its burden to the weight of water rolling west. While twenty-one million people perished of drought in Egypt, as many perished of flood and typhoid in the Congo.

151

I seemed to know what was coming as I stood in the crowded room, knowing Jubal dead, knowing the nation of Africa to be bleeding to death. We were dying of our own wounds.

The ten years to follow would be as terrible as the ten years of the Massacre, when every member of the white race had been slain.

Now we Negroes, in our turn, stood at the bar of history.

Pogsmith[1]

Dusty Miller and his wife were lucky. Not lucky to be on a year's holiday, because everyone higher than esp-inspectors qualified nowadays. Not lucky to be on Mercury, because although the new atmosphere breathed well enough it had not yet stabilized and typhoons were frequent. Not lucky to visit the Galactic Zoo, because its gates were open wide to all who could afford the entrance fee. But lucky because they were the one millionth and one millionth and one (or one million and oneth) human beings to go in.

The celebration of this numerical achievement entailed a lavish lunch, followed by a personally conducted tour round the zoo by the Director.

'I don't like him,' Daisy whispered.

'Shut up, he'll hear you,' Dusty snapped. He had reason for his belief. The Director possessed three of the largest ears Dusty had ever seen. But then the Director had been hatched on Puss II.

Nevertheless, the tour was highly stimulating. Dusty was delighted with every animal he saw. His wife was less happy, but she never enjoyed wearing space suits; by a quirkish, claustrophic effect, they gave her asthma. Unfortunately, they were highly necessary, since each block of the zoo naturally contained the atmosphere of the planet whose animals it housed – and nine-tenths of them were nothing less than death to human nostrils.

They had visited the Puss II block, whose inmates looked to Daisy and Dusty surprisingly like their distinguished escort, and had traversed the impressive Ogaeiou chain of buildings housing the Knitosaurs, gigantic crabs who

---

[1] Magazine editors have the innocuous habit of printing short puffs before each story. When this story appeared in *Authentic*, it was preceded by this witty (and accurate) caption: 'Pogsmith was a planet and a superbeast. The former had a negative escape velocity, the latter a positively escapist ferocity.'

weaved their own shells from a natural-nylon seaweed, when they came to a large domed erection.

'This,' the Director claimed impressively, 'is our latest addition to the zoo. Within, we shall find the only extant life form of the newly discovered planet Pogsmith.'

'Wasn't that the place there was all that fuss about?' Daisy asked.

'There is always a fuss about a newly discovered planet,' the Director said severely. 'Territorial rights, etc. . . .'

'Shall we go in?' Dusty asked hastily. He had known for years that his wife was dull and provincial; he just happened to love her that way. While for the Director he held every respect – but a growing repulsion.

'First,' replied the great man, 'depress the yellow switch you will feel just in front of the central ridge of your helmets.' He showed them by example. 'That will protect us from the thought waves which this creature sends out. It sets in action a dead field about the brain.'

He looked pointedly at Daisy, as if to imply that she was already safeguarded by such means. When they had complied, they entered.

The ground plan was the usual one. A spiralling observation ramp circled an enormous glassite dome which contained the alien species and fragments of its customary surroundings. At the beginning of the ramp was a fortified gate into the dome and a large panel of information, such as details of topography, atmosphere, planetary year, etc.

The lighting was dim.

'Low angstrom range,' the Director commented.

'I can't see them,' Dusty said, peering into the bowl of gloom.

'It,' said the Director. 'We only managed to catch one.'

'What is the name of the species?'

'Er – Pogsmith.'

'Oh . . . After the planet? I thought they only named dominant species after the planet?'

'This is the only, consequently the dominant, species, Mr Miller.'

'I see. Then how do you know they are not – people, rather than animals?'

'Why, they *behave* like animals.'

'I don't see that that's any – never mind; where is this creature, Mr Director? I can see nothing in there but an old bucket.'

'That, at the moment, is Pogsmith.'

Taking hold of a wheel set in an upright in the glassite, the Director spun it, setting in motion an automatic prodder. It reached out and tipped the bucket gently over. The bucket turned smoothly into a red nose, from which a hand extended in the direction of the Director.

The latter coughed, turned away, and said: 'Until the creature condescends to turn into its usual shape, you might be interested to hear about the first and only expedition to the strange and remote planet of Pogsmith.'

'Well, thanks very much,' Daisy said, 'but I think perhaps we'd better be—'

'It so happens,' the Director said, 'I was on the exploratory ship as zoologist at the time. You are singularly fortunate to hear this first-hand account.

'Pogsmith the planet was so named after Pogsmith, our radio operator – a sort of memorial to the poor fellow. The only thing they had in common were peculiar features. The operator had one eye and a ginger beard, and the planet – well . . .' He rotated his claws in the famous Puss gesture of amazement.

'Pogsmith is the only planet in a system of three giant suns, a red, a yellow and a blue one. It is smaller than Mercury and, containing no heavy metals, has an extremely low density. Yet during a period of its orbit it comes almost within Roche's Limit of two of the suns. The wonder is that this fragile little world did not disintegrate eons ago! It only seems to survive this perilous part of its course by speeding up its axial revolution tremendously.

'This we noted as we glided in for a landing. The amazing thing was that the planet held an atmosphere, a pungent mixture of neon and argon which we found stayed electrostatically attracted to the surface, due to the continual absorption through it of random and charged gamma particles which combined—' Noting the blank expression on Dusty's face, the Director cleared both his throats and changed his tack.

'There were no seas, but the ground was broken and

mountainous. We found a plain near the equator and feathered down. The ship immediately rose again. The captain swore, touched the fore jets and set our tail firmly in the dust once more. The ship was immediately flung back into the air. We could not stay down! So we floated and chewed our nails. On other planets, the difficulty is always getting off them; yet here the situation was paradoxically reversed.

'Everyone was completely baffled, until I came forward with the obvious solution. The planet's mass was so low and its axial rotation so fast that centrifugal forces had overcome gravity at the equator! Following my careful instructions, the captain moved to the north pole, and there we could land in the usual manner. An additional advantage was the lower temperature – only 160°. At the equator it had been about 245°.

'I only tell you this to make the point that any life on such a world was bound to be eccentric.'

'Oh quite, Director. Daisy dear, are you all right?' Dusty Miller bent anxiously over his wife, who was fluttering her eyes.

'Yes, fine. Don't interrupt, dear. You were saying?'

'We climbed out, the five of us – in space suits, of course. It was eerie to a degree. The sky was nearly black, owing to the tenuous atmosphere, although there were a few very low grey clouds. The blue sun moved from about five to twenty degrees above the horizon, revolving so rapidly round the sky that it looked like an azure spiral. Every now and then, the red sun would appear, climb to zenith and sink again. Unfortunately, we were too far north to see the third sun; I remember feeling vaguely aggrieved about it at the time.

'What a spectacle, though! We stood amazed. Both visible suns were at last fourteen times as big as a full moon on Earth and their shifting, blending shadow spun a kaleidoscope of stupendous colour. We cried our delight aloud, lifting up hands that had become unpredictable rainbows.

'Pogsmith had no eye for beauty. He had, as I said, only one eye, and this was on the main chance. He disappeared over that low hill which is always near any spaceship about to encounter danger in all the science-fiction stories I have read. We heard his startled shout, and ran to see what was

156

wrong. A hundred yards ahead of him was a torpedo. It was scampering towards him. It had legs. These changed to wheels, and the wheels to flappers.

'Abruptly it stopped. It changed again – into something very like a terrestrial pig. That, we have found since, is its natural form. But under the fluctuating conditions that exist on its world it has developed protective and projective mimicry to an extraordinary degree.

"Come on," Pogsmith bellowed. "Let's capture it!"

'I was naturally in favour of the idea. But Pogsmith acted first.

'He flung himself on the creature. It was an unwise thing to do, and I should have behaved differently. Even as he moved, the amazing animal altered its form again. It grew boots, a ginger beard, a space suit. It turned, in fact, into an absolute double of Pogsmith.

'They fought desperately together. We closed in upon them and pulled them apart – no easy matter for only four of us.

'Then came a problem. Which of them was Pogsmith? Neither showed any inclination to turn into anything further. The pig, with a good deal of common sense, realized he was safe in his disguise.

'Both cursed when we prodded them. Both vowed he was the only genuine and original Pogsmith. Both begged to be released.

'So, at my suggestion, we released them, the idea being that the fake would immediately attempt to escape. But no, both stood tamely there and suggested a return to the ship. Evidently the pig's curiosity had been roused.

'We only resolved the deadlock by a brilliant idea of mine. Obviously the creature could only simulate outward appearances; we had but to take blood slides to tell one Pogsmith from the other.

'They both came meekily to the air lock. But there a strange thing happened. We stopped. We looked again at the twins. The Captain spoke first.

"Silly of us," he said. "I know which the real Pogsmith is – it's this one," and he clapped his hand on the nearer of the two.

'We all agreed vehemently with him. At the time it was

suddenly more than obvious which was which. We pushed away the one we decided was the fake and hurried into the ship, shutting the lock behind us.

' "Phew!" one of the crew said. "Lucky we suddenly saw sense. Let's get away from here!"

'And so we did. We were off and away at once, leaving the planet and its suns far behind. The incident had destroyed a lot of our self-confidence; for one thing, no doubt each of us had the thought: "Supposing more of the creature had come up and joined in the fun? Should we ever have sorted ourselves out?"

'Pogsmith, always taciturn, was more silent than ever. We did not like to remind him of his unpleasant experience, but finally I asked: "Are you feeling yourself again, Pogsmith?"

'For reply, he winked his one eye at me and slowly – turned into a pig!

'We saw it all then. We had been tricked by some form of mass-hypnotism into leaving the real radio op. behind. By then we were three days' spaceborne, and poor old Pogsmith had air enough for, at a maximum, thirty-six hours. What could we do? As a memorial to our late friend, we christened the planet Pogsmith, and kept heading for home.

'The crew were not only furious with the creature, they were frightened of it, and its power. They voted to scoot it out of the airlock at once. But I spoke up in the cause of science, and explained what a valuable zoological discovery we had made. After much argument, the masquerader's life was saved, and we brought it here, to the zoo.

There was a short silence in the dome.

'A very extraordinary tale indeed!' Dusty Miller exclaimed.

'The truth is frequently extraordinary,' the Director said, with emphasis.

'Do you reckon he's pulling our legs?' Daisy whispered to her husband.

'I don't know.'

They turned and stared solemnly into the arena. Pogsmith had resumed its natural form. It was decidedly porcine, although its face bore an expression of almost classical serenity seldom noticeable on pig countenances. Seeing it was being observed, it commenced to change shape.

'Actually, it is rather parrot-like,' the Director said contemptuously. 'It never composes its own shape, almost always copies something it has seen. Look you notice it is doing me now . . .'

Mrs Miller let out a loud shriek.

'When has it seen you naked?' she asked.

'Madam, I assure you I'm not—'

'Never mind how good the likeness is,' Dusty said sternly. 'I did not bring my wife here to be insulted by that obscene creature or anyone else! I suggest we leave this instant.'

'Very well then,' snapped the Director angrily, 'although I am in no way responsible for that thing's behaviour.'

'Do let's get out,' Daisy said, her face still crimson. 'Take my arm, Marmaduke.'

'You go on, dear, with the Director. I won't be a minute – I just want to read this information panel again.'

He prodded her surreptitiously in the ribs to make sure he was obeyed. As soon as they were out of sight, he tried the inner door. It was merely a portion of the arena wall, indistinguishable from within, but easily movable from without by the turn of a wheel.

'We'll soon see whether it wasn't a pack of nonsense he was telling us,' Dusty muttered to himself. He never liked to believe anything until he had personally tested its veracity. The next moment he was inside the dome.

The naked Director withered and shrunk into Pogsmith's natural shape. It turned and faced Dusty inquisitively, snorting quietly.

'All right, old boy, there, there now, just want to have a proper look at you,' Dusty said soothingly, making a coaxing noise and extending one hand. For a moment he was alarmed at his temerity. Was the thing carnivorous or not? He halted. They surveyed each other from five yards' range.

'The lighting isn't very good in here,' Dusty said apologetically. 'Let's see some of these stunts from close range.'

As if it understood – how efficient was that dead field round the brain? – the pig, with astonishing speed, grew a ginger beard and arms. It became Pogsmith. One eye glared at Dusty.

'This is a devil of a predicament,' it said. With animal savagery, it flung itself at Dusty, catching him a knock-out blow on the jaw, and bolted for the open door.

Feebly, he opened his eyes. An angry face glared down into his; it was the Director.

'Ah, Miller, conscious at last! Well, your visit to us is over. There's an auto-rocket here standing by to take you and your wife straight back to Earth.'

'Pogsmith?' groaned Dusty.

'You may very well ask! The unhappy creature must have been almost crazed by boredom from its confinement. It is now hiding among the zoo buildings, having so far eluded all our efforts to recapture it. You're lucky you weren't killed. Your infernal curiosity is going to cost us a pretty penny, I can tell you! You're a mischief-maker, sir, that's what – a mischief-maker!'

'You won't find Pogsmith by raving at me,' Dusty retorted irritably, brushing dust out of his clothes.

'Can't you see the poor man's had enough, Director,' Daisy asked, turning nevertheless to the poor man in question to whisper fiercely: 'A brilliant performance *you've* made of yourself, Marmaduke. Just you wait . . .'

Dusty rubbed an aching jaw and followed dejectedly along a metal ramp which led to a two-man shuttle. It was a small Mercury-Earth ship that would travel auto all the way: in five minutes he could be away from the scene of his foolishness – and there would be no eavesdroppers on whatever lecture was coming.

The Director followed them to the open hatch. There he caught Dusty's arm.

'No ill feelings,' he said.

Miller shook the Director's hand and his own head dazedly and passed into the ship. With a quiet click, the door closed behind him. He staggered through the airlock and sank on to an acceleration couch.

Daisy had hardly begun to unload her vocabulary before the growl of blast take-off drowned all other sounds. They hurled upwards, and in two breath-taking minutes stars and darkness showed outside and the bright crescent of Mercury floated below.

'Now . . .' said Daisy. 'Never in all my life—' She stopped, her mouth open, her eyes fixed glassily on a point behind Dusty's head. He turned.

The door of a small luggage store had opened. A figure as like the Director's as an egg is like an egg stood there glaring at them.

'How—' said Dusty.

'He's tricked us,' said the Director. 'He bound and gagged me . . . I've only just struggled free . . . He's – ooooh!'

He staggered back as Dusty attacked him. His foot slipped and he fell against the wall.

'Quick, Daisy, quick!' Dusty bellowed. 'Help me get him in the airlock. It's Pogsmith!'

She stood there wringing her hands helplessly. 'How do you know this is Pogsmith?' she asked.

'Of course it is,' snapped Dusty, glad to be again master of the situation. 'Isn't it obvious he'd try and escape like this? I'm not being fooled twice. Now lend a hand, will you?'

Still struggling and protesting, the Director was propelled into the airlock and shut in. Mopping his brow, Dusty pressed the manual switch that opened the outer door. There was a hiss of expiring air – and expiring Director.

At the Galactic Zoo the incident was soon forgotten. The Director quickly recovered his old prestige. But he was never the same man again – he had a tendency, in private, to grow red whiskers and one triumphant eye.

Outside

They never went out of the house.

The man whose name was Harley used to get up first. Sometimes he would take a stroll through the building in his sleeping suit – the temperature remained always mild, day after day. Then he would rouse Calvin, the handsome, broad man who looked as if he could command a dozen talents and never actually used one. He made as much company as Harley needed.

Dapple, the girl with killing grey eyes and black hair, was a light sleeper. The sound of the two men talking would wake her. She would get up and go to rouse May; together they would go down and prepare a meal. While they were doing that, the other two members of the household, Jagger and Pief, would be rousing.

That was how every 'day' began: not with the inkling of anything like dawn, but just when the six of them had slept themselves back into wakefulness. They never exerted themselves during the day, but somehow when they climbed back into their beds they slept soundly enough.

The only excitement of the day occurred when they first opened the store. The store was a small room between the kitchen and the blue room. In the far wall was set a wide shelf, and upon this shelf their existence depended. Here, all their supplies 'arrived'. They would lock the door of the bare room last thing, and when they returned in the morning their needs – food, linen, a new washing machine – would be awaiting them on the shelf. That was just an accepted feature of their existence: they never questioned it among themselves.

On this morning, Dapple and May were ready with the meal before the four men came down. Dapple even had to go to the foot of the wide stairs and call before Pief appeared; so that the opening of the store had to be postponed till after they had eaten, for although the opening had in no way become a ceremony, the women were nervous of going in alone. It was one of those things . . .

'I hope to get some tobacco,' Harley said as he unlocked the door. 'I'm nearly out of it.'

They walked in and looked at the shelf. It was all but empty.

'No food,' observed May, hands on her aproned waist. 'We shall be on short rations today.'

It was not the first time this had happened. Once – how long ago now? – they kept little track of time – no food had appeared for three days and the shelf had remained empty. They had accepted the shortage placidly.

'We shall eat you before we starve, May,' Pief said, and they laughed briefly to acknowledge the joke, although Pief had cracked it last time too. Pief was an unobtrusive little man: not the sort one would notice in a crowd. His small jokes were his most precious possession.

Two packets only lay on the ledge. One was Harley's tobacco, one was a pack of cards. Harley pocketed the one with a grunt and displayed the other, slipping the pack from its wrapping and fanning it towards the others.

'Anyone play?' he asked.

'Poker,' Jagger said.

'Canasta.'

'Gin rummy.'

'We'll play later,' Calvin said. 'It'll pass the time in the evening.' The cards would be a challenge to them; they would have to sit together to play round a table, facing each other.

Nothing was in operation to separate them, but there seemed no strong force to keep them together, once the tiny business of opening the store was over. Jagger worked the vacuum cleanser down the hall, past the front door that did not open, and rode it up the stairs to clean the upper landings; not that the place was dirty, but cleaning was something you did anyway in the morning. The women sat with Pief desultorily discussing how to manage the rationing, but after that they lost contact with each other and drifted away on their own. Calvin and Harley had already strolled off in different directions.

163

The house was a rambling affair. It had few windows, and such as there were did not open, were unbreakable and admitted no light. Darkness lay everywhere; illumination from an invisible source followed one's entry into a room – the black had to be entered before it faded. Every room was furnished, but with odd pieces that bore little relation to each other, as if there was no purpose for the room. Rooms equipped for purposeless beings have that air about them.

No plan was discernible on first or second floor or in the long, empty attics. Only familiarity could reduce the maze-like quality of room and corridor. At least there was ample time for familiarity.

Harley spent a long while walking about, hands in pockets. At one point he met Dapple; she was drooping gracefully over a sketch-book, amateurishly copying a picture that hung on one of the walls – a picture of the room in which she sat. They exchanged a few words, then Harley moved on.

Something lurked in the edge of his mind like a spider in the corner of its web. He stepped into what they called the piano room and then he realized what was worrying him. Almost furtively, he glanced round as the darkness slipped away, and then looked at the big piano. Some strange things had arrived on the shelf from time to time and had been distributed over the house: one of them stood on top of the piano now.

It was a model, heavy and about two feet high, squat, almost round, with a sharp nose and four buttressed vanes. Harley knew what it was. It was a ground-to-space ship, a model of the burly ferries that lumbered up to the space-ships proper.

That had caused them more unsettlement than when the piano itself had appeared in the store. Keeping his eyes on the model, Harley seated himself at the piano stool and sat tensely, trying to draw *something* from the rear of his mind . . . something connected with spaceships.

Whatever it was, it was unpleasant, and it dodged backwards whenever he thought he had laid a mental finger on it. So it always eluded him. If only he could discuss it with someone, it might be teased out of its hiding place. Unpleasant: menacing, yet with a promise entangled in the menace.

If he could get at it, meet it boldly face to face, he could do ... something definite. And until he had faced it, he could not even say what the something definite was he wanted to do.

A footfall behind him. Without turning, Harley deftly pushed up the piano lid and ran a finger along the keys. Only then did he look back carelessly over his shoulder. Calvin stood there, hands in pockets, looking solid and comfortable.

'Saw the light in here,' he said easily. 'I thought I'd drop in as I was passing.'

'I was thinking I would play the piano awhile,' Harley answered with a smile. The thing was not discussable, even with a near acquaintance like Calvin because ... because of the nature of the thing ... because one had to behave like a normal, unworried human being. That at least was sound and clear and gave him comfort: behave like a normal human being.

Reassured, he pulled a gentle tumble of music from the keyboard. He played well. They all played well, Dapple, May, Pief ... as soon as they had assembled the piano, they had all played well. Was that – natural? Harley shot a glance at Calvin. The stocky man leaned against the instrument, back to that disconcerting model, not a care in the world. Nothing showed on his face but an expression of bland amiability. They were all amiable, never quarrelling together.

The six of them gathered for a scanty lunch, their talk was trite and cheerful, and then the afternoon followed on the same pattern as the morning, as all the other mornings: secure, comfortable, aimless. Only to Harley did the pattern seem slightly out of focus; he now had a clue to the problem. It was small enough, but in the dead calm of their days it was large enough.

May had dropped the clue. When she helped herself to jelly, Jagger laughingly accused her of taking more than her fair share. Dapple, who always defended May, said: 'She's taken less than you, Jagger.'

'No,' May corrected, 'I think I *have* more than anyone else. I took it for an interior motive.'

It was the kind of pun anyone made at times. But Harley carried it away to consider. He paced round one of the silent rooms. Interior, ulterior motives ... Did the others here feel the disquiet he felt? Had they a reason for concealing that disquiet? And another question:

Where was 'here'?

He shut that one down sharply.

Deal with one thing at a time. Grope your way gently to the abyss. Categorize your knowledge.

One: Earth was getting slightly the worst of a cold war with Nitity.

Two: the Nititians possessed the alarming ability of being able to assume the identical appearance of their enemies.

Three: by this means they could permeate human society.

Four: Earth was unable to view the Nititian civilization from inside.

Inside ... a wave of claustrophobia swept over Harley as he realized that these cardinal facts he knew bore no relation to this little world inside. They came, by what means he did not know, from outside, the vast abstraction that none of them had ever seen. He had a mental picture of a starry void in which men and monsters swam or battled, and then swiftly erased it. Such ideas did not conform with the quiet behaviour of his companions. If they never spoke about outside, did they think about it?

Uneasily, Harley moved about the room; the parquet floor echoed the indecision of his footsteps. He had walked into the billiard room. Now he prodded the balls across the green cloth with one finger, preyed on by conflicting intentions. The red spheres touched and rolled apart. That was how the two halves of his mind worked. Irreconcilables: he should stay here and conform; he should – not stay here (remembering no time when he was not here, Harley could frame the second idea no more clearly than that). Another point of pain was that 'here' and 'not here' seemed to be not two halves of a homogeneous whole, but two dissonances.

The ivory slid wearily into a pocket. He decided. He would not sleep in his room tonight.

They came from the various parts of the house to share a bed-time drink. By tacit consent the cards had been post-

166

poned until some other time: there was, after all, so much other time.

They talked about the slight nothings that comprised their day, the model of one of the rooms that Calvin was building and May furnishing, the faulty light in the upper corridor which came on too slowly. They were subdued. It was time once more to sleep, and in that sleep who knew what dreams might come? But they *would* sleep. Harley knew – wondering if the others also knew – that with the darkness which descended as they climbed into bed would come an undeniable command to sleep.

He stood tensely just inside his bedroom door, intensely aware of the unorthodoxy of his behaviour. His head hammered painfully and he pressed a cold hand against his temple. He heard the others go one by one to their separate rooms. Pief called good night to him; Harley replied. Silence fell.

Now!

As he stepped nervously into the passage, the light came on. Yes, it was slow – reluctant. His heart pumped. He was committed. He did not know what he was going to do or what was going to happen, but he was committed. The compulsion to sleep had been avoided. Now he had to hide, and wait.

It is not easy to hide when a light signal follows wherever you go. But by entering a recess which led to a disused room, opening the door slightly and crouching in the doorway, Harley found the faulty landing light dimmed off and left him in the dark.

He was neither happy nor comfortable. His brain seethed in a conflict he hardly understood. He was alarmed to think he had broken the rules and frightened of the creaking darkness about him. But the suspense did not last for long.

The corridor light came back on. Jagger was leaving his bedroom, taking no precaution to be silent. The door swung loudly shut behind him. Harley caught a glimpse of his face before he turned and made for the stairs: he looked noncommittal but serene – like a man going off duty. He went downstairs in bouncy, jaunty fashion.

Jagger should have been in bed asleep. A law of nature had been defied.

167

Unhesitatingly, Harley followed. He had been prepared for something and something had happened, but his flesh crawled with fright. The light-headed notion came to him that he might disintegrate with fear. All the same, he kept doggedly down the stairs, feet noiseless on the heavy carpet.

Jagger had rounded a corner. He was whistling quietly as he went. Harley heard him unlock a door. That would be the store – no other doors were locked. The whistling faded.

The store was open. No sound came from within. Cautiously, Harley peered inside. The far wall had swung open about a central pivot, revealing a passage beyond. For minutes Harley could not move, staring fixedly at this breach.

Finally, and with a sense of suffocation, he entered the store. Jagger had gone through – there. Harley also went through. Somewhere he did not know, somewhere whose existence he had not guessed . . . Somewhere that wasn't the house . . . The passage was short and had two doors, one at the end rather like a cage door (Harley did not recognize a lift when he saw one), one in the side, narrow and with a window.

This window was transparent. Harley looked through it and then fell back choking. Dizziness swept in and shook him by the throat.

Stars shone outside.

With an effort, he mastered himself and made his way back upstairs, lurching against the banisters. They had all been living under a ghastly misapprehension . . .

He barged into Calvin's room and the light lit. A faint, sweet smell was in the air, and Calvin lay on his broad back, fast asleep.

'Calvin! Wake up!' Harley shouted.

The sleeper never moved. Harley was suddenly aware of his own loneliness and the eerie feel of the great house about him. Bending over the bed, he shook Calvin violently by the shoulders and slapped his face.

Calvin groaned and opened one eye.

'Wake up, man,' Harley said. 'Something terrible's going on here.'

The other propped himself on one elbow, communicated fear rousing him thoroughly.

'Jagger's *left the house*,' Harley told him. 'There's a way outside. We're – we've got to find out what we are.' His voice rose to an hysterical pitch. He was shaking Calvin again. 'We must find out what's wrong here. Either we are victims of some ghastly experiment – or we're all monsters!'

And as he spoke, before his staring eyes, beneath his clutching hands, Calvin began to wrinkle up and fold and blur, his eyes running together and his great torso contracting. Something else – something lively and alive – was forming in his place.

Harley only stopped yelling when, having plunged downstairs, the sight of the stars through the small window steadied him. He had to get out, wherever 'out' was.

He pulled the small door open and stood in fresh night air.

Harley's eye was not accustomed to judging distances. It took him some while to realize the nature of his surroundings, to realize that mountains stood distantly against the starlit sky, and that he himself stood on a platform twelve feet above the ground. Some distance away, lights gleamed, throwing bright rectangles on to an expanse of tarmac.

There was a steel ladder at the edge of the platform. Biting his lip, Harley approached it and climbed clumsily down. He was shaking violently with cold and fear. When his feet touched solid ground, he began to run. Once he looked back: the house perched on its platform like a frog hunched on top of a rat trap.

He stopped abruptly then, in almost dark. Abhorrence jerked up inside him like retching. The high, crackling stars and the pale serration of the mountains began to spin, and he clenched his fists to hold on to consciousness. That house, whatever it was, was the embodiment of all the coldness in his mind. Harley said to himself: 'Whatever has been done to me, I've been cheated. Someone has robbed me of something so thoroughly I don't even know what it is. It's been a cheat, a cheat . . .' And he choked on the idea of those years that had been pilfered from him. No thought; thought scorched the synapses and ran like acid through the brain. Action only! His leg muscles jerked into movement again.

Buildings loomed about him. He simply ran for the nearest light and burst into the nearest door. Then he pulled up sharp, panting and blinking the harsh illumination out of his eyes.

The walls of the room were covered with graphs and charts. In the centre of the room was a wide desk with vision-screen and loudspeaker on it. It was a business-like room with overloaded ashtrays and a state of ordered untidiness. A thin man sat alertly at the desk; he had a thin mouth.

Four other men stood in the room, all were armed, none seemed surprised to see him. The man at the desk wore a neat suit; the others were in uniform.

Harley leant on the door-jamb and sobbed. He could find no words to say.

'It has taken you four years to get out of there,' the thin man said. He had a thin voice.

'Come and look at this,' he said, indicating the screen before him. With an effort, Harley complied; his legs worked like rickety crutches.

On the screen, clear and real, was Calvin's bedroom. The outer wall gaped, and through it two uniformed men were dragging a strange creature, a wiry, mechanical-looking being that had once been called Calvin.

'Calvin was a Nititian,' Harley observed dully. He was conscious of a sort of stupid surprise at his own observation.

The thin man nodded approvingly.

'Enemy infiltrations constituted quite a threat,' he said. 'Nowhere on Earth was safe from them: they can kill a man, dispose of him and turn into exact replicas of him. Makes things difficult . . . We lost a lot of state secrets that way. But Nititian ships have to land here to disembark the Non-Men and to pick them up again after their work is done. That is the weak link in their chain.

'We interrupted one such ship-load and bagged them singly after they had assumed humanoid form. We subjected them to artificial amnesia and put small groups of them into different environments for study. This is the Army Institute for Investigation of Non-Men, by the way. We've learnt a lot. . . quite enough to combat the menace . . . Your group, of course, was one such.'

Harley asked in a gritty voice: 'Why did you put me in with them?'

The thin man rattled a ruler between his teeth before answering.

'Each group has to have a human observer in their very midst, despite all the scanning devices that watch from outside. You see, a Nititian uses a deal of energy maintaining a human form; once in that shape, he is kept in it by self-hypnosis which only breaks down in times of stress, the amount of stress bearable varying from one individual to another. A human on the spot can sense such stresses . . . It's a tiring job for him; we get doubles always to work day on, day off—'

'But I've always been there—'

'Of your group,' the thin man cut in, 'the human was Jagger, or two men alternating as Jagger. You caught one of them going off duty.'

'That doesn't make sense,' Harley shouted. 'You're trying to say that I—'

He choked on the words. They were no longer pronounceable. He felt his outer form flowing away like sand as from the other side of the desk revolver barrels were levelled at him.

'Your stress level is remarkably high,' continued the thin man, turning his gaze away from the spectacle. 'But where you fail is where you all fail. Like Earth's insects which imitate vegetables, your cleverness cripples you. You can only be carbon copies. Because Jagger did nothing in the house, all the rest of you instinctively followed suit. You didn't get bored – you didn't even try to make passes at Dapple – as personable a Non-Man as I ever saw. Even the model spaceship jerked no appreciable reaction out of you.'

Brushing his suit down, he rose before the skeletal being which now cowered in a corner.

'The inhumanity inside will always give you away,' he said evenly. 'However human you are outside.'

Panel Game

It was Christmas. Snow fell by courtesy of Home-Count Climatic.

Rick Sheridan came off shift early, flying his helic deftly through the white clouds, and keeping by long custom between the altitude levels prescribed for his particular consumer-class. As far as he might be said to have a character, his character was cheerful. He exhibited this cheerfulness now by whistling.

The sound filled the little cockpit, competing with the bope music issuing from the 3-inch screen telly strapped on his wrist.

Christmas! It was proverbially the time of festivity and maximum consumption. It was a period when everyone would be happy – except, possibly, he warned himself, his wife, Neata. Her moodiness had become trying of late. The mere thought of it knocked his whistle off key.

For the difficult business of landing, Rick switched on to auto. This luxury had been fitted by Happy Hover Ltd only two months ago. With the faintest of sighs, the helic leafed down, below the clouds, below the aerial levels, below the rooftops, and squatted in the Sheridan back garden.

The garden was a large one, as gardens went, ten feet by sixteen, and covered by neo-concrete. Rick jumped out and stretched himself. Although he was all of twenty-eight, he suddenly felt young and healthy again. Appetite stirred sluttishly in his stomach.

'Oh for a bowl of tasty, toothable Cob Corners!' he cried exultantly, and bounded for the back door.

He was high enough up the consumer hierarchy to own a magnificent two-room dwelling. Walking through the Disposing room, he entered the Gazing room and called: 'Neata!'

She was sitting quietly at the Relaxtable, laboriously mending a little labour-saving device, her fair head bent in concentration. Her smile of welcome formed easily and naturally round her new teeth, and she jumped up, throwing her arms round him – carefully, so as not to crumple his teddy tie.

'Ricky, darling, you're early!' she exclaimed.

'I hit my quota ahead of schedule,' he explained proudly. 'Thanks to Howlett's.'

Their only child, Goya, jumped up and ran to greet her daddy. She managed to do it backwards, thus keeping her eyes fixed on the wall screens, where Sobold the Soap King was facing three dirty-looking criminals single-handed.

Rick's eyes glistened behind their contact lenses. He reflected how affectionate the child was for a three-year-old, but something in the little girl's actions must have displeased her mother, for Neata said irritably: 'Why don't you welcome your father properly?'

'Wanna see old Sobold slosh the slashers,' Goya said defiantly.

'You're old enough to guess what will happen,' Neata said crossly. 'He'll catch them and make them all wash in that creamy, dreamy lather that only Little Britches Soap provides.'

'Don't get angry with her,' Rick said. 'Remember, it's Christmas.'

He took Goya on his knee, and settled down with her to watch Sobold, his hunger forgotten. The wall-screens filled two walls. Before the end of next year, if he worked as well as he was working now, they might be able to afford a third screen. And one day . . . he blushed with excitement at the thought of being surrounded by an image in quadruplicate on all four walls.

A flicker of interference burst over the bright screens. Rick tutted with annoyance; the terrific technical accomplishment of telly was something upon which every civilized consumer prided himself, but it was nevertheless obvious that just lately there had been more misting than usual on the screens. Rick found himself recalling the rumours, dim and evasive, which he had heard while at work; rumours of a vile movement to overthrow the present happy régime, of determined men with new weapons at their command.

Dismissing the idea irritably, he turned full attention on

to the screens. Justice and cleanliness having overtaken Sobold's opponents, the next quarter of an hour was to be devoted to 'Mr Dial's Dairy,' a comic serial lampooning twentieth-century farm life, presented by the makers of Grinbaum's Meat Bars.

'Time for bed, Goya,' Neata declared, and despite the young lady's protests she was whisked into the Disposing room for an encounter with Little Britches, Ardentifrices and Juxon's ('Nunbetter') Drying powder. Rick seized this opportunity while he was alone to spend ten minutes looking into his Pornograph, but his attention was recalled by a jolly announcer in the Grinbaum uniform calling out: 'Well, customers, there we have to leave Mr Dial for now. Is his prize cow really going to calve? Will Sally Hobkin get that big kiss she deserves? Your guess is as good as mine, suckers. One thing *everybody* is sure about is the goodness, the sheer brothy, spothy goodness, of Grinbaum's Meat Bars. A whole carcass goes into each of those chewy little cubes.'

And then leaning, as it seemed, almost out of the screen, the announcer suddenly bellowed harshly: 'Have you bought *your* quota of Grinbaum's Meat Bars today, Sheridan?'

Cut. Screen blank. Ten seconds till next programme.

'He certainly puts that over well,' Rick gasped proudly, passing a hand over his brow. 'It always makes me jump.'

'It makes me jump too,' said Neata flatly, leading a night-dressed Goya into the room.

This device whereby consumers could be individually named was the latest, and possibly cleverest, accomplishment of telly. The announcer had actually named no names; instead, at the correct moment, a signal transmitted from the studio activated a circuit at the receiving end which, in every individual home, promptly bellowed out the surname of the head consumer of the family.

Neata pressed the Relaxtable, and a section of it sprang into a bed. Goya was put in, and given her cup of steaming, happy-dreaming Howlett's. She had hardly drunk the last mouthful before she sank down on the pillow, yawning.

'Sleep well!' Neata said gently, pressing the child's ear-plugs into place. She felt tired herself, she hardly knew why. It would be a relief when her turn came for Howlett's and Payne's Painless Plugs.

There was no switching the screens off and, now that telly provided a twenty-four hour service, the aids to sleep were a necessity.

'This is Green Star, B channel,' announced the screens. 'The Dewlap Chair Hour!!!'

'Must we watch this?' Neata asked, as three dancing, screaming nudes burst into view, legs waving, bosoms bouncing.

'We could try Green Star A.'

Green Star A had a play, which had already begun. They tried Green Star C, but that had a travel programme on, and Rick was bored by other countries – and a little afraid of them. They turned back to the Dewlap Hour, and gradually relaxed into semi-mindlesssness.

There were three coloured star systems, each with three channels, at their disposal, theoretically at least. But Green Star was the official consumer system for their consumer-class; obviously it would be wasteful for the Sheridans to watch White Star, which advertised commodities they could not afford, such as shower-purges, stratostruts, tellysolids and bingoproofs.

If they did watch White Star, there was, unfortunately, no guarantee that telly was not watching them. For since the installation of 'wave-bounce', some ten years ago, every wall screen was a reciprocal – which meant, in plain language, that every viewer could be viewed from telly. This inno-vation was the source of some of the very best programmes, for viewers could sit and watch themselves viewing telly.

Dewlap was showing one of the numerous and ever-popu-lar panel games. Three blindfold men and a blindfold woman were being passed patent custards, cake-mixes and detergents; they had to distinguish between the different commodities by taste alone. A compère in shirt sleeves awarded blows over the head for incorrect guesses.

Just tonight – perhaps because it was Christmas – the sight of Gilbert Lardner having his head tapped failed to enthral Rick. He began to walk about the Gazing room, quite an easy matter since, except for the Relaxtable in which Goya lay drugged, there was a complete absence of furniture.

Catching Neata's curious gaze upon him, Rick moved out into the garden. It was not fair to distract her from her viewing.

The snow still fell, still by courtesy of Home-Count Climatic. He did not feel the cool night air, snug in his Moxon's Mockwool. Absently, he ran his hand over the helic, its blunt vanes, its atomic motor, its telly suppressor, its wheels. All maintenance, of course, was done by the helic drome: there was nothing he could fiddle with. Indeed, there was nothing he could do at all.

Like a sensible fellow, like all his sensible neighbours – whom he had hardly so much as seen – he went back indoors and sat before the screens.

Five minutes later came the unprecedented knock at the door.

The shortage of arable land in England, acute in the twentieth century, became critical in the twenty-first. Mankind's way of reproducing himself being what it is, the more houses that were erected on the dwindling acres, the more houses were needed. These two problems, which were really but facets of one problem, were solved dramatically and unexpectedly. After telly's twenty-four-hour services were introduced, it was realized by those who had the interests of the nation at heart (a phrase denoting those who were paid from public taxes) that nine-tenths of the people needed neither windows nor friends: telly was all in all to them.

A house without windows can be built in any surroundings. It can be built in rows of hundreds or blocks of thousands. Nor need roads be a hindrance to this agglomeration: an airborne population needs no roads.

A house without friends is freed from ostentation. There is no longer any urge to keep up with the Joneses, or whoever may come in. One needs, in fact, only two rooms: a room in which to watch the screens, and a room in which to store the Meat Bars and other items which the screens hypnotize one into buying.

Super-telly changed the face of England overnight.

The Sheridan house, like a great many others, was in the midst of a nest of houses stretching for a mile or more in all directions; it could be reached only by something small enough to alight in the garden.

So for many reasons the knock on the door was very much a surprise.

'Whoever can it *be*?' asked Rick uneasily.

'I don't know,' Neata said. She too had heard rumours of a subversive movement; a momentary – and not unpleasing – vision attended her of two masked men coming in and smashing the wall screens. But of course masked men would not bother to knock.

'Perhaps it's somebody from Grinbaum's Meat Bars,' suggested Rick, 'I forgot to buy any today.'

'Don't be so silly, Rick,' his wife said impatiently. 'You know their factory must be purely automatic. Go and *see* who it is.'

That was something he had not thought of. You had to hand it to women . . . He got up and went reluctantly to open the door, smoothing his hair and his tie on the way.

A solid-looking individual stood in the drifting snow. His helic was parked against Rick's. He wore some sort of a cloak over his Mock-wool: obviously, he was of a higher consumer-class than the Sheridans.

'Er . . .' said Rick.

'May I come in?' asked the stranger in the sort of voice always hailed on the screens as resonant. 'I'm an escaped criminal.'

'Er . . .'

'I'm not dangerous. Don't be alarmed.'

'The little girl's in bed,' Rick said, clutching at the first excuse which entered his head.

'Have no fear,' said the stranger, still resonantly; 'kidnapping is not one of the numerous offences on my crime sheet.'

He swept magnificently past Rick, through the dark Disposing room and into the Gazer. Neata jumped up as he entered. He bowed low and pulled the cloak from his shoulders with an eloquent gesture which scattered snow over the room.

'Madam, forgive my intrusion,' he said, the organ note more noticeable than ever. 'I throw myself upon your mercy.'

'Ooh, you talk like someone on a panel game,' Neata gasped.

'I thank you for that from the bottom of my heart,' said the stranger, and announced himself as Black Jack Gabriel.

Rick hardly heard. He was taking in the thick-set figure in its smart attire, and the curiously impressive streak of white hair on the leonine head (the fellow must be thirty if he was a day). He also took in the meaningful way Neata and Black Jack were looking at each other.

'I'm Neata Sheridan, and this is my husband, Rick,' Neata was saying.

'A delightful name,' said Black Jack, bowing at Rick and grinning ingratiatingly.

'It's only short for Rickmansworth,' said Neata, a little acidly.

Black Jack, standing facing but entirely ignoring the screens, began to speak. He was a born elocutionist, and soon even Rick ceased to blush – a nervous habit which manifested itself on the rare occasions when he was face to face with a real human being.

Black Jack had a dramatic tale to tell of his capture by armed police, who had chased him across roofs thirty stories above ground level. For the last nine years he had been imprisoned in Holloway, condemned to hard labour, knitting hemp mittens for the cameramen of Outside Telly.

Suddenly, only a few hours ago, an opportunity for escape had presented itself. Black Jack had broken into the Governor's suite, exchanged clothes, and flown off in the Governor's helic.

'And here I am,' he said. 'I just landed at random – and how lucky I was to find you two.'

Despite some opposition from an outbreak of bope music from the screen, Rick had been listening with great attention.

'If it's not a rude question, Mr Black,' he said, 'what did you do wrong?'

'That's rather a long story,' Black Jack said modestly, knitting his eyebrows but positively smiling at Neata. 'You

178

see, England used to be rather a strange place. In those days – you must have seen so much entertainment you would not remember – there was a government. There were also several industries, and something known as "free enterprise" flourishing. The government used to "nationalize" (as they called it) any industry which looked like getting too big and prosperous.

'Well, one of these industries was called Television – telly is the modern term. It was getting so big, the government took it over, but it was *so* big, it took over the government. A case of the tail wagging the dog, you see.

'Soon, everything was telly. And perpetual entertainment did a lot of good. Now half the people in the country work – directly or indirectly – for telly. It did away with unemployment, over-employment, strikes, neuroses, wars, housing problems, crime and football pools. Perpetual entertainment was here to stay.'

'You tell it so well,' Neata said. She was virtually cuddling against him. 'But what did you do to earn your long prison sentence?'

'I was the last Prime Minister,' Black Jack said. 'I voted against perpetual entertainment.'

Neata gasped.

So did Rick. Drawing himself up, he said: 'Then we don't want any of your sort in our house. I must ask you to leave before the H. Brogan's Watches' show comes on.'

'Oh, don't make him go,' pleaded Neata. She suddenly realized that here was the calibre of man she had been waiting for. He might well be leader of the rumoured subversive movement: he might cause interference on every wall screen in the country: but she could forgive – no, applaud! – everything, if he would just roll his eyes again.

'I said "Go",' demanded Rick.

'I had no intention of staying,' said Black Jack coolly. 'I'm on my way to Bali or Spain or India or somewhere without perpetual entertainment.'

'Then what did you come here for in the first place?' Rick asked.

'Merely to borrow some food to sustain me on my journey. The governor's helic happened not to be provisioned for a long flight. Surely you'll do that for me?'

179

'Of course we will – if you must go,' said Neata.

'Why should we?' asked Rick. 'I'll be a Dutchman if I lift a finger to help a criminal.' But catching sight of his wife's clenched fists and suddenly blazing eyes, he muttered miserably; 'OK, call me Hans,' and made off into the Disposing room.

Ardently, the self-confessed Prime Minister turned to Neata. 'How can I ever thank you for your assistance, madam,' he breathed. 'It will be useless for you to forget me, for I shall never forget you!'

'Nor I you,' she said. 'I think – oh . . . I think you're wonderful, and – and I *hate* the telly.'

With swimming eyes, she peered up at him. He was pressing her hand: *he* was pressing *her* hand. It was the most wonderful moment of her life; her heart told her she was closer to the Meaning of Existence than she had ever been. Now he was leaning towards her – and Rick was back in the room again.

Hardly daring to leave them alone, he had snatched up a bag of dried prunes, two cartons of Silvery Soggmash, a cake, a sackful of Dehydrated Olde English Fishe and Chyps ('There's no food like an old food') and a tin of Grinbaums which had been previously overlooked.

'Here you are,' he said ungraciously. 'Now go.'

Black Jack was meekness itself, now his object had been gained. He seemed, indeed, pleased to be off, Neata thought dejectedly; but doubtless such police as could be spared from viewing would be on his trail, and he could not afford to delay.

Rick followed the intruder out into the snow, which was still falling by courtesy of H-CC. Black Jack flung the provisions into the boot of his helic and jumped gracefully into the driver's seat. He raised a hand in ironical salute and called: 'Happy Christmas!' The helic lifted.

'Good-bye!' Neata called romantically and then, more romantically still: '*Bon Voyage!*'

But already the machine was lost in the whirling white flakes.

'Come on in,' Rick grunted.

They exchanged no words indoors. Morosely, Rick glared at the wall screens. Somehow, now, the savour was gone.

180

Even the H. Brogan's Watches' Show had lost its appeal. He got up and paced about restlessly, fiddling with his teddy tie.

'Oh heck,' he said. 'Let's try White Star. I don't suppose any supervisors are watching us. We need a change, that's what.'

He flicked the controls over to White Star A, and gasped in astonishment. Neata gasped too, a little more gustily.

A sumptuous lounge showed on the screens. An immaculate announcer and three immaculate guests were leaning back in their chairs to watch a figure enter a door and approach the camera.

The figure, in its swagger cloak, with the distinguished streak of white in its hair, was unmistakable. It bowed to the unseen audience.

Nervously, a little over-heartily, the announcer was saying: 'Well, consumers, here comes the scallywag of the Bryson Brainbath Hour, safe back in the studio.' And turning to the newcomer he said: 'Well, Gervaise McByron – alias Black Jack Gabriel – your forfeit in this special Christmas edition of our popular panel game, "Fifty Queries", in which you got lowest score, was to go out and talk your way into a green consumer-class home, returning with a souvenir of your visit. You've certainly carried out instructions to the letter!'

Popular White telly-star McByron smiled lavishly, said: 'I did my best!' and deposited some prunes, some Soggmash, a cake, Fishe and Chyps and a tin of Grinbaums at the announcer's feet.

'Your patter was terribly convincing,' said the announcer uneasily. 'I just hope none of our viewers believed a word you said about – er, Big Mother Telly. I almost believed you myself, ha, ha!'

'You'll get suspended for this, McByron,' opined a decorative lady who had been included on the panel for the sake of her undulating façade. 'You went too far. Far too far.'

'We watched every moment of your performance in the Sheridan shack via wave-bounce reciprocal,' said the announcer. 'I just hope none of our viewers believed a word—'

'Tell me, McByron,' cut in the decorative woman coldly, 'what did you really think of Mrs Sheridan?'

'If you want a frank answer,' began McByron bluntly, 'compared with you, Lady Patricia So-and-So Burton, she was an absolute—'

'And so ends this special Christmas edition of "Fifty Queries",' cried the announcer frantically, jumping up and waving his hands. 'It was brought to you by courtesy of Bryson's Brainbaths. Don't forget: a mind that thinks is a mind that stinks. Good night, consumers, everywhere.'

Cut. Screen blank. Ten seconds to next programme.

Slowly, Rick turned to face his wife.

'There!' he said. 'Disgraced! That – that trickster! We were just a spot of amusement on a snob-class panel show. *Now* are you ashamed?'

'Don't say anything, please, Rick,' Neata said distantly. There was something so commanding in her tone that her husband turned away and abjectly switched back to Green Star.

Neata walked pensively out of the room. She still clutched the wicked little device which McByron, alias Black Jack, had pressed into her hand. Then, it had been startlingly cold; now, her palm had made it hot. She knew what it was, she knew what she had to do with it.

'Deadly . . .' she whispered to herself. 'Deadly . . . The end of civilization as we know it.'

The metal was a challenge in her grasp.

Ah, but McByron was clever! She was dizzy at his impudence. Although evidently a leading tellystar, he was nevertheless a saboteur, a member – perhaps the leader! – of the subversives. And he had dared to pass on this weapon and to deliver his inspiring message of doubt in front of thousands of viewers.

'What a man!'

Neata was out in the snow now. She looked with strained face at the little device. It had to be fitted on to Rick's helic. Poor Rick –but he would never know! The thought that she was helping in a mighty, silent revolution lent her determination.

Quickly, she bent down and fitted the anti-telly suppressor into Rick's helic.

Dumb Show

Mrs Snowden was slowly being worn down. She had reached the stage now where she carried about with her a square of card on which the word DON'T was written in large letters. It was kept tucked inside her cardigan, ready to be produced at a moment's notice and flashed before Pauline's eyes.

The ill-matched pair, the grubby girl of three and the shabby-elegant lady of fifty-eight, came up to the side door of their house, Pauline capering over the flagstones, Mrs Snowden walking slowly with her eyes on the bare border. Spring was reluctantly here, but the tepid earth hardly acknowledged it; even the daffodils had failed to put in an appearance this year.

'Can't understand it at all,' Mrs Snowden told herself. 'Nothing ever happens to daffodils.' And then she went on to compile a list of things that nevertheless might have happened: frost – it had been a hard winter; soil-starvation – no manure since the outbreak of hostilities, seven years ago; ants; mice; cats; the sounds – that seemed most likely. Sound did anything, these days.

Pauline rapped primly on the little brass knocker and vanished into the hall. Mrs Snowden paused in the porch, stopping to look back at the houses on the other side of her high brick wall. When this house had been built, it had stood in open fields; now drab little semi-detacheds surrounded it on three sides. She paused and hated them. Catching herself at it, she tried instead to admire the late afternoon light falling on the huddled roofs; the sunshine fell in languid, horizontal strokes – but it had no meaning for her, except as a sign that it was nearly time to blackout again.

She went heavily into the house, closing the door. Inside, night had already commenced.

Her granddaughter marched round the drawing-room, banging a tin lid against her head. That way, she could hear the noise it made. Mrs Snowden reached for the DON'T card, then let her hand drop; the action was becoming

183

automatic, and she must guard against it. She went to the gramwire-tv cabinet, of which only the last compartment was now of use, and switched on. Conditions at home were a little better since the recapture of Iceland, and there were now broadcasts for an hour and a half every evening.

Circuits warmed, a picture burned in the half-globe. A man and woman danced solemnly, without music. To Mrs Snowden it looked as meaningless as turning a book of blank pages, but Pauline stopped her march and came to stare. She smiled at the dancing couple; her lips moved; she was talking to them.

DON'T, screamed Mrs Snowden's sudden, dumb card.

Pauline made a face and answered back. She jumped away as her grandmother reached forward, leaping, prancing over the chairs, shouting defiance.

In fury, Mrs Snowden skimmed the card across the room, crying angrily, hating to be reminded of her infirmity, waving her narrow hands. She collapsed on to a music stool – music, that dear, extinct thing! – and wept. Her own anger in her own head had sounded a million cotton-wool miles away, emphasizing the isolation. At this point she always crumpled.

The little girl came to her delicately, treading and staring with impertinence, knowing she had the victory. She pulled a sweet face and twizzled on her heel. Lack of hearing did not worry her; the silence she had known in the womb had never left her. Her indifference seemed a mockery.

'You little beast!' Mrs Snowden said. 'You cruel, ignorant, little beast!'

Pauline replied, the little babblings which would never turn into words, the little noises no human ear could hear. Then she walked quietly over to the windows, pointed out at the sickening day, and began to draw the curtains. Controlling herself with an effort, Mrs Snowden stood up. Thank goodness the child had some sense; they must blackout. First she retrieved her DON'T card from behind the ancient twentieth-century settee, and then they went together through the house, tugging the folds of black velvet across the glass.

Now Pauline was skipping again. How she did it on the

184

low calories was a matter for wonder. Perhaps, thought Mrs Snowden, it was a blessing to be responsible for the child; so, she kept contact with life. She even caught an echo of gaiety herself, so that they hurried from room to room like bearers of good news, pulling blackness over them, then sweeping on the sonic lights. Up the stairs, pausing at the landing window, racing into the bedrooms, till new citadels were created from all the shabby darknesses. Pauline collapsed laughing on her bed. Seizing her, tickling now and again, Mrs Snowden undressed her and tucked her between the fraying sheets.

She kissed the girl good night, put out the light, closed the door, and then went slowly round, putting out all the other lights, downstairs, putting all the lights out there.

Directly she had gone, Pauline climbed out of bed, stamped into the bathroom, opened the little medicine cupboard, took out the bottle with the label 'Sleeping Pills'. Unscrewing the top, she swallowed a pill, pulling a pig's eyes face at herself in the looking-glass as she did so. Then she put the bottle back on its shelf and slammed the little door, hugging to herself this noisy secret.

None of these things had names for her. Having no names, they had only misty meanings. The very edges of them were blurred, for all objects were grouped together in only two vast categories: those-that-concerned-her and those-that-did-not-concern-her.

She trailed loudly back to her bed in the silence there was no breaking, making pig's eyes all the way to ward off the darkness. Once in bed, she began to think; it was because of these pictures she stole her grandmother's pills: they fought the pictures and turned them eventually into an all-night nothing.

Predominant was the aching picture. A warmth, a face, a comforting – it was at once the vaguest yet most vivid picture; someone soft who carried and cared for her; someone who now never came; someone who now provoked only the water scalding from her eyes.

Elbowing that picture away came the boring picture. This tall, old-smelling person who had suddenly become everything after the other had gone; her stiff fingers, bad over buttons; her slowness about the stove; her meaningless

185

marks on cards; all the dull mystery of who she was and what she did.

The new picture. The room down the road where Pauline was taken every morning. It was full of small people, some like her, in frocks, some with short hair and fierce movements. And big people, walking between their seats, again with marks on cards, trying with despairing faces to make them comprehend incomprehensible things by gestures of the hand and fingers.

The push picture. Something needed, strange as sunlight, something lost, lost as laughter . . .

The pill worked like a time-bomb and Pauline was asleep where only the neurosis of puzzlement could insidiously follow.

Mrs Snowden switched the globe off and sank into a chair. They had been showing a silent film: the latest scientific advances had thrown entertainment back to where it had been in her grandfather's young days. For a moment she had watched the silent gestures, followed by a wall of dialogue:

'Jean: Then – you knew he was not my father, Denis?'

'Denis: From the first moment we met in Madrid.'

'Jean: And I swore none should ever know.'

Sighing, Mrs Snowden switched the poor stuff off, and sank down with a hand over her forehead. TV merely accentuated her isolation, everyone's isolation. She thought mockingly of the newspaper phrase describing this conflict, The Civilized War, and wished momentarily for one of the old, rough kind with doodlebugs and H-bombs; then, you could achieve a sort of Henry Moore-ish anonymity, crouching with massed others underground. Now, your individuality was forced on to you, till self-consciousness became a burden that sunk you in an ocean of loneliness.

Right at the beginning of this war, Mrs Snowden's husband had left for the duration. He was on secret work – where, she had no idea. Up till two years ago, she received a card from him each Christmas; then he had missed a year; then in the paper shortage, the sending of cards had been forbidden. So whether he lived or not she did not know; the question now raised curiously little excitement in her. Heart-sickness had ceased to be relevant.

Mrs Snowden had come to live here in her old home with her parents after she had been declared redundant at the university, when all but the practical Chairs closed down. In the lean winters, first her mother then her father died. Then her married daughter was killed in a sound raid; Pauline, a tiny babe, had come to live with her.

It was all impersonal, dry facts, she thought. You stated the facts to explain how the situation arose; but to explain the *situation*. . .

Nobody in the world could hear a sound. *That* was the only important fact.

She jumped up and flicked aside an edge of curtain. A rag of dirty daylight was still propped over the serried chimney-tops. The more those houses crowded, the more they isolated her. This should be a time for madness, she said aloud, misting the pane: something grand and horrid to break the chain of days. And her eyes swept the treble row of old textbooks over her bureau: Jackson's *Eighteen Nineties*, Montgomery's *Early Twentieth Century Science Fiction*, Slade's *Novelists of the Psychological Era*, Wilson's *Zola*, Nollybend's *Wilson* . . . a row of dodos, as defunct as the courses of Eng. Lit. they had once nourished.

'Dead!' she exclaimed. 'A culture in Coventry!' she whispered, and went to get something to eat.

'Tough old hag,' she told herself. 'You'll survive.'

The food was the usual vibro-culture, tasteless, filling, insubstantial. The hospitals of England held as many beri-beri cases as wounded. Sound ruled the whole deaf world. It wrecked the buildings, killed the soldiers, shattered the tympanums and ballooned synthesized proteins from mixtures of animo acids.

The Sound Revolution had come at the dawn of this new century, following thirty years of peace. Progress had taken a new direction. It had all been simple and complete; you just flushed the right electrostatic stress through the right quartz plates and – bingo! You could do anything! The most spectacular result was a global conflict.

The Powers warred under certain humane agreements: gas, fission and fusion weapons were forbidden. It was to be, indeed, a Civilized War. VM (vibratory motion) had the field to itself. It learnt to expand living vegetable cells a thousand-fold, so that a potato would last for two years' dinners; it learnt to pulverize brick and metal, so that cities could comfortably be turned to a thin dust; it learnt to twist the human ear into an echoing, useless coil of gristle. There seemed no limit to its adaptability.

Mrs Snowden ate her blown-up yeast with dignity, and thought of other things. She thought – for lately she had been straining after wider horizons – of the course of human history, its paradoxical sameness and variety, and then something made her look up to the tube over the mantelpiece.

The tube was a piece of standard equipment in every home. It was a crude ear, designed to announce when the local siren was giving a sound raid alarm.

She glanced indifferently at it. The lycopodium seed was stirring sluggishly in its tube; damp must be getting in, it was not patterning properly. She went on eating, gloomily wondering about the future generations: how much of the vital essence of tradition would be lost through this blanket of deafness?

Correct procedure would have been for her, at the stirring of the seed, to collect Pauline and stand out in the open. When the siren went, everyone else left their homes and stood patiently under the bare sky; then, if the sounds swept their buildings, they would be temporarily smothered by dust as the building vanished, but suffer no other harm. Mrs Snowden could no longer be bothered with this nonsense.

To her mind, it was undignified to stand in the chill air, meekly waiting. If enemy planes circled overhead, she would have had defiance to spur her out; but nowadays there was only the quiet sky, the eternal silence and the abrupt pulverization – or the anti-climax, when everyone filed sheepishly back to bed.

She took her plate into the kitchen. As she came back into the living-room, a reproduction of Mellor's 'Egyptian Girl' fell silently on to the floor, shattering frame and glass.

Mrs Snowden went and stared at it. Then, on impulse, she hurried over to the window and peered out. The encircling houses had gone.

Letting the curtain fall back into place, she rushed from the room and up the stairs. She was shaking Pauline before she gained control of herself, and then could not tell whether panic or exultation had sent her scurrying.

'The houses have gone! The houses have gone!'

Silence, in which the little girl woke sluggishly.

Mrs Snowden hustled her downstairs and out on to the front lawn, letting a bright swathe of light cut across the empty flower-beds. Somewhere, high and silent overhead, a monitor might be hovering, but she was too excited to care.

By a freak of chance, their house stood alone. Around them for miles stretched a new desert, undulant, still settling. The novelty, the *difference*, of it was something wonderful: not a catastrophe, a liberation.

Then they saw the giants.

Vague in the distance, they were nevertheless real enough, although incredible. They were tall – how tall? – ten, fifteen feet? More? With horror Mrs Snowden thought they were enemy troops. This was the latest application of the sound: it enlarged the human cell now, as easily as it enlarged vegetable cells. She had the brief idea she had read that human giants could not survive, or were impossible or something, and then the thought was gone, swept away in fear.

The giants were still growing. They were taller than a house now, thirty feet or more high. They began to mop and mow, like drunken dancers.

Unreality touched her. Pauline was crying.

A coolness swept her limbs. She trembled involuntarily. A personal alarm now, terror because something unknown was at her blood. She raised a hand to her eyes. It loomed away from her. Her arm extended. She was *growing*.

She knew then that the giants were no enemy troops; they were victims. You get everyone out of their houses. One type of VM levels the houses. Another inflates the people, blowing them up like grotesque rubber dummies. Simple. Scientific. Civilized.

Mrs Snowden swayed like a pole. She took a clumsy step to keep her balance. Dizzily, she peered at her blank bedroom window, staggering away to avoid falling into the house. No pain. The circuits were disrupted. Only numbness; numbness and maniac growth.

She could still crazily see the dancing giants. Now she understood why they danced. They were trying to adapt.

Before they could do so, their metabolism burnt out. They sprawled into the desert, giant dusty corpses, full of sound and silence.

She thought: It's the first excitement for years, amusedly, before her heart failed under its giant load.

She toppled; the DON'T card fluttered gaily from her bosom, spinning and filtering to the ground.

Pauline had already overtopped her grandmother. The young system was greedy for growth. She uttered a cry of wonder as her head rocked up to the dark sky. She saw her grandmother fall. She saw the tiny fan of sonic light from their tiny front door. She trod into the desert to keep her balance. She started to run. She saw the ground dwindle. She felt the warmth of the stars, the curvature of the earth.

In her brain, the delighted thoughts were wasps in a honey pot, bees in a hive, flies in a chapel, gnats in a factory, midges in a Sahara, sparks up an everlasting flue, a comet falling for ever in a noiseless void, a voice singing in a new universe.